DEVELOPMENT FOR FREE ASIA

DEVELOPMENT
FOR FREE ASIA

By

Maurice Zinkin

ISSUED UNDER THE AUSPICES OF THE
INSTITUTE OF PACIFIC RELATIONS

New Edition

GREENWOOD PRESS, PUBLISHERS
WESTPORT, CONNECTICUT

Library of Congress Cataloging in Publication Data

Zinkin, Maurice.
    Development for free Asia.

    "Issued under the auspices of the Institute of
Pacific Relations."
    Reprint of the new ed. published by Chatto & Windus,
London.
    Includes index.
    1. Asia--Social conditions. 2. Asia--Economic
conditions. I. Title.
HN666.Z55 1975   309.1'5   75-20982
ISBN 0-8371-8343-X

New Edition © Maurice Zinkin 1963

All rights reserved

First published 1956.

This edition originally published in 1963 by Chatto & Windus,
London

Reprinted with the permission of Chatto and Windus Ltd.

Reprinted in 1975 by Greenwood Press,
a division of Williamhouse-Regency Inc.

Library of Congress Catalog Card Number 75-20982

ISBN 0-8371-8343-X

Printed in the United States of America

PREFACE

THIS book has grown out of a paper originally written in 1953 for the Institute of Pacific Relations Conference at Kyoto, and suggested by Mr. William Holland. It would never have grown but for the encouragement of Mr. Peter Calvocoressi and the prodding of Mr. Gangadharan and my wife.

Since it has been written in such spare time as I could snatch from a very time-consuming job, it lays no claim to being learned. The ideas in it have grown from many discussions over many years, and there is hardly an ex-colleague in the Indian Civil Service, or a present colleague in Lever Brothers (India), Ltd., and the Reserve Bank Economists' Study Group to whom I do not owe something. Where one owes so much to so many, it is perhaps invidious to mention a few, but I feel a particular debt to Messrs. Azim Hussein, A. C. Bose, S. Boothalingam, P. C. Bhattacharya, M. J. Desai, L. K. Jha, K. B. Lall, H. V. R. Iengar, Nagendra Singh, M. V. Rangachari, Tarlok Singh, C. S. Venkatachar, N. M. Wagle, K. M. Panikkar, Mould and Rigby, and to Professors Raj, Sovani and Dandekar. I am further quite specially grateful to the small group on whom every single idea in this book has been tried: Messrs. A. D. Gorwala, H. M. Patel, V. K. Ramaswamy, L. Kumar, J. F. Sinclair, S. D. Deshmukh, P. L. Tandon and B. Ven tappiah, Prof. Gadgil and Mrs. L. Kumar.

I must also express my thanks to Mr. A. J. C. Hoskyns-Abrahall and to Sir V. T. Krishnamachari for having read and commented on the original paper in manuscript; to Mr. H. Saunders and Mr. U. L. Goswami, ICS, for much assistance; to Mr. A. S. Menon for many facts; to Mr. Frank Bower C.B.E., for advice on taxation problems; and to Dr. and Mrs. Toohey, Mr. and Mrs. Kumar Messrs S. D. Deshmukh, H. M. Patel and Wint, and Dr. I. G. Patel for comment on the final manuscript. A word, too, is due to Mrs. Sykes and Mr. Gangadharan for their patient typing.

I should perhaps here explain why most of the examples in the book have been taken from India. The main reason is that my experience has been overwhelmingly Indian. I have lived and worked in India for nearly the whole of the time since 1938 whereas my knowledge of the other countries of free Asia is con-

fined either to relatively short visits or to books. Visits and books
are, I hope, enough to give one a basis for valid generalizations;
but illustrations come best out of long personal experience.
There is also another reason. India is half of free Asia, and
whether India's Five-Year Plans and India's democracy succeed
or fail is crucial to the future of the whole. What is done in the
smaller countries is often interesting and usually important; but
what happens in India is vital.

Finally, I would like to pay tribute to Roger Heyworth to
whose memory this book is dedicated. Roger was more than a
friend; his alert mind, sharp wit, keen perception, vast knowledge and deep human understanding were an inspiration to all
who knew him. It is only natural that I should at once have
thought of him when I came to write this book, for our first
meeting in the spring of 1945 was entirely devoted to thinking
out weapons for India's fight against poverty. For Roger
Heyworth the East was not primarily a place in which to make
money, but a place where the Western techniques he knew
could be used to help peoples he had learned to love with all his
warm yet realistic heart.

CONTENTS

viii CONTENTS

Part One

GENERAL

———◦◦◦———

Chapter 1

CHANGE AND THE CONTENTED

THE great requirement for development is change; and Asia is beginning to realise it. Change is not easy. Asia has in the past been contented. Westerners and the Westernised have called this contentment pathetic. That does not make it less real, or the reasons for it less valid. Divine discontent in Asia is new, it still works very unevenly in the different layers of society, it brings with it the grave risk that the educated may become discontented enough to revolt before the peasants have become discontented enough to develop. But at least now it is there, working its way deeper and deeper into Asian society, creating the demand for a new life, for plans and reforms, steel mills and fertiliser. Thailand alone is still sunk deep enough in peasant happiness not to have to bother with economics.

Asia's contentment has in the past been responsible for much of its failure to develop. Those who are already satisfied for their own present and their children's future, have no reason to sacrifice today's enjoyment for tomorrow's advantage, and without that no economic advance is possible.

The Westerner tends to miss the point. He is accustomed to see only poverty and dirt in the East. He goes into a village and imagines that its people could go Communist tomorrow; yet the only foundation for his so imagining is that that is what he would do in their place. He does not realise that he is looking at a community, most of whose people still today have the deepest of all satisfactions; they have a place in a community; in the East unlike the West a man knows where he stands with his neighbours. He may not like them or they him; they still have to accept him and he them.

The Eastern peasant, where he has enough land, was, and is, right to be contented. He lives in a community which is largely self-governed. Village affairs are still very considerably left to the village council, or the village elders. He is master of his own time and his own labour. He can, if he is fair-minded and capable, attain to a position of authority and consideration amongst his neighbours, a position which may appear of no great importance to the district officials in the great world outside but usually is all that he or his family wants. In most areas he has above him neither squire nor parson; in many areas he does not have below him any large section of society so visibly poor—on his standards—that it burdens his conscience. His position is of course far from perfect. His officials are often corrupt, his moneylender usually extortionate, his landlord's agent (if he is a tenant) normally quite unconscionable; and, wherever there is war, in the present as in the past, he is looted by every side. But, nevertheless, he is the backbone of society; and he knows it.

That is why he is so highly resistant to change. Any class which is the backbone of society is bound to insist on a high degree of conformity if it is not to disintegrate into its constituent vertebrae. Any class which consists largely of small and equal owners will tend to look with some suspicion upon those who by their ability rise out of the common ranks, and with great approbation on those who reach age and respectability by following, with shrewdness but without doubts, in the traditional paths of their ancestors.

Until perhaps the middle of the nineteenth century everywhere, and today still in such places as Thailand, this old life gives complete satisfaction to its adherents. The Hindu division of a man's life into student, householder, service to society, and the attempt to obtain salvation, was one which covered every aspect of a man's nature. That it no longer gives universal satisfaction is due primarily to two factors, both of them quite recent. First, most of Asia has filled up. There is no longer room for the indefinite multiplication of peasant holdings. If the new generation is to be provided for, some method other than traditional peasant agriculture is required. Second, the industrial and scientific revolution which has occurred in the West in the last couple of hundred years has revealed to the whole world that the poverty, which has throughout man's history been accepted with reasonable cheerfulness as the inevitable lot of the many, need be accepted no longer. Such countries as the United States and Sweden and England provide examples of places where nearly everybody gets enough to eat, enough to wear, and a decent house to live in, where everybody can read and write and nobody need die for lack of the attention of a doctor. These are doubtless material benefits, less important perhaps than the spiritual discipline of Zen Buddhism or the mystical successes of so many Hindu saints. By no means everybody in the West is impressed by them, and there are many in the East who respond with a violent negative to what they consider to be Western materialism. But that is not the view of the majority. Most people in Asia are like most people in Europe and America. They like to have enough to eat; they prefer sulpha drugs to dying of dysentery; they even enjoy the cinema and the comics. As Western material standards are made more and more vivid to them by the steadily improving means of communication which are making the modern world one, they more and more demand that these benefits shall be made available to them too. They are not impatient; they are prepared to wait, prepared to accept that it will be many years before they reach the present standards or economic level of the more successful countries. But they do demand that something should be done; that they should be able to see some progress, some improvement, not just in their lifetimes but actually within the next few years.

Economic development has therefore become in almost all the countries of Asia the dominating question of the day. The leaders are determined to change; and now at last it looks as if the people may be willing to follow. Elections can be fought on five-year plans; villages are willing to help to pay for schools and maternity clinics; the peasant will accept the advice of Extension Service officers on seed and rotations and the breeding of cattle, in a way he previously did only in Japan; the need for savings has crept into political speeches; the popular press talks of productivity, and underemployment, and the need for technicians. Economics have arrived. The people would like to develop. They are not yet quite sure how; they are sometimes appalled by the difficulty of the road; they are occasionally tempted by Communism, which promises to push them along the road by force, and thus guarantees them that they will not be allowed to get discouraged by obstacles; they are always determined to place upon their politicians and bureaucrats a burden of leadership, of pulling and showing and directing them along the right way which the more fortunate politicians and bureaucrats of the West do not have to bear. However, the stirrings are there. Whether they get these by persuasion the Indian way, or by liquidation the Chinese way, or by firm direction the Japanese way, Asians now want to develop badly enough to be prepared to pay the price.

Chapter 2

THE PRICE OF DEVELOPMENT

THE price of development is high; a society which wishes to develop must be prepared to put development in the very forefront of its priorities, to want development harder than it wants anything else. The mechanics of development are difficult and very liable to go wrong; unless a country wants to increase its income very badly indeed, it will flinch at the difficulties; every time something goes wrong it will find solace in other, and older, satisfactions. One need not go so far as the Communists, with whom development takes precedence of the Ten Commandments. But the people of a country which wishes to develop must at least be willing to replace the generosity of ceremony and festival by skimping thrift, to exchange the pleasure of lying on a cot in the shade for back-breaking work, to buy savings bonds and share certificates instead of adorning their wives. Most difficult of all for many societies, contract must replace status, a measure of planning *laisser-faire*. The rich, the educated, the well-born must accept equality with the poor, the illiterate and those without grandfathers. All must reconcile themselves to the disappearance of the easy freedom of the law-and-order State; one cannot have a welfare State without the pettifogging interference of minor officials.

So high a price will not be accepted unless development becomes the central point of the people's ambitions as well as of State policy. Those who would rather go to the cinema than save the price of the seat, rather earn less in the place they know than be uncomfortable somewhere else, rather work hard at their hobbies than put something extra into their daily routine may day-dream about development; they cannot really want it.

In most underdeveloped countries, however, development cannot thus be made the centre of ambition without first overcoming a whole series of psychological blocks.

One of the main reasons why underdeveloped countries are underdeveloped is that their people have only recently made increasing their national income—getting rich—their major objective. They have therefore not yet learned all the mechanics, and some of the mechanics they do know they do not like because of hangovers from the past. It is not easy suddenly to work hard in societies which have always primarily valued the elegant

4

use of leisure, or to save in societies where a man's status is a function of the ostentation of his expenditure, or to invest productively in countries where the safest use of riches has always been to hoard them. Moreover, though nowadays people of the underdeveloped countries may be as eager to develop as their brethren in Europe or America, their real aim is frequently not development, but the consequences of development. They have found that, in the modern world, unless a country is rich its word will not carry any weight, its culture will be looked down upon, its people treated as inferior. Therefore, they want their countries to be rich. Unfortunately this attitude is, on the national scale, rather similar to that of the man who wants to make money as a means to gracious living. Experience suggests that such men do not take money seriously enough ever actually to make it. Similarly with nations. Those who want to be rich so that they can become powerful or so that their intelligentsia may be respected amongst the educated of the rest of the world find it difficult to settle down to the long haul of sacrifice and work and acceptance of unpleasant change that development demands. They are too easily diverted. They buy arms instead of building dams; their best brains become professors of literature instead of technologists; they choose showy schemes rather than profitable ones; their rich men, like Arab oil-kings, buy Cadillacs instead of irrigating their land.

This faint-heartedness is understandable, for really to give development first priority involves revolution upon revolution for the underdeveloped. Perhaps they may have to go so far as to absorb most of the institutions and attitudes of those Western societies which have become rich. Certainly the Communists seem to think so; the Western idea of free choice in marriage is as integral to the Chinese Revolution as Western-style heavy industry.

The cultures of the underdeveloped countries may well lose in this process something of their beauty, stability and piety; the qualities which lead to riches are not always pretty. They may produce fewer artists and saints and harmonious and adjusted personalities. The men who make a country's economic success are never saints and rarely harmonious. But that is the inevitable result of choosing a low-level objective. To become rich is less noble than the Hindu ideal of self-mastery and the renunciation of desire. But the underdeveloped countries have not renounced desire. They want to be rich. They can be rich; but only if they first change their values in all the ways that make getting rich possible.

In underdeveloped societies this may well mean turning society upside down. They are poor to a very considerable extent precisely because their values have not emphasised becoming rich. The areas, like the Amazon valley, which are poor by nature are the exception; Indonesia is not naturally poorer than Holland. Asia's difficulty is much more that its values give a low place to economics and change and making money, a high place to stability, saintliness and power. If it is more important to be in the winning snakeboat team at the Annual Regatta than to grow more rice to the acre, better regarded to be a Sub-Inspector of Police than the largest of shopkeepers, and a quicker way to Heaven to become a hermit than to give away one's self-made millions, then clearly the economic operation of society will be left to its least desirable or least dynamic members; and the undesirable and the backward can hardly be expected to do much developing.

Asia's failure to develop is not the result of some inherent inferiority in Asians, as so many Westerners used to believe. In fact, T'ang Chinese or Mauryan Indians were more prosperous, as well as more civilised, than their Western European contemporaries. Nor is the difference between Asian and Western values the result of any inherent extra materialism in Westerners, as so many Asians like to believe. The values of most of free Asia today are very similar to those of mediaeval Europe, and probably have very similar causes. Asia's reluctance to invest in anything less indestructible than land, or even to make a great effort in order to save, is largely the heritage of anarchy in the quite recent past—the eighteenth century in India, the twentieth in China. The importance of religion combined with the lack until recently of scientific knowledge applicable to Asian agriculture, produced an educational system with a quite one-sided emphasis on literary rather than scientific knowledge, on sitting at a desk rather than on using one's hands, on theology and the arts rather than on the wants of every day. Such an educational system can produce Chinese painting and Indian philosophy, just as the similar system of mediaeval Europe produced Salisbury Cathedral and St. Thomas Aquinas. It is not adapted to the production of fitters and chemical engineers. In addition, there is one difference between modern Asia and mediaeval Europe which is severely to Asia's disadvantage. In mediaeval Europe the free cities protected enterprise, gave an honoured position to the successful businessman, and obtained from their businessmen in return a strong social conscience. Asia has never had free cities, and its great States have always overtaxed, always given too much importance and too much power to the State servant. Its business-men in consequence all too often have the low standards of their too low position.

Europe has changed its values since the Middle Ages. It pro-duces fewer saints, perhaps also fewer artists, than in the Middle Ages; but the material well-being of its people, their control over their physical environment, is going up at a rate inconceivable to their mediaeval ancestors. What Europe has done Asia can do, has indeed already begun to do—in Japan much more than begun. But there will be a loss. When in India the income per head reaches that of the United States today, it may no longer produce saints like Vinoba Bhave. The world will be poorer as well as richer.

Part Two

ECONOMIC

———◦◦◦———

Chapter 3

INNOVATION AND THE RESPECT-ABILITY OF BUSINESS

NEARLY all economic development involves experiment and change or at least imitating somebody else's change or making use of somebody else's experiments. Countries become richer largely because people are always adopting new methods, learning new techniques, discovering new ways of achieving old ends, adapting their lives to new conditions. Nothing is more vital to development than a high propensity to innovate, a high level of willingness to accept and initiate change. The underdevelopment of Asia has to a considerable extent been due to its low propensity to innovate; the Asian peasant learnt how to grow his crops under the conditions of his village two thousand years ago. From then until this generation any experiment he might make was far more likely to end in crop failure and starvation than in riches. Naturally, therefore, Asia puts a heavy emphasis on custom and the ways of one's ancestors, naturally too the road to success has normally been through growing old in conformity.

It is important, therefore, for the development of Asia that the capacity to innovate, especially the capacity to absorb and apply technological knowledge, must be given a higher place than it has been hitherto. There must be built up a class of entrepreneurs, and managers, and successful farmers whose function it is to innovate, whose careers and fortunes depend on their doing so successfully. This is only possible if those who are successful are treated by society with that respect reserved at present for large landowners, great scholars, or senior servants of the State. In any society change is originally the work of the few, though the rest must be prepared to follow; and those few will not become entrepreneurs, or managers, or model farmers, unless to do so gives them the status they feel to be their due. People only apply their minds to inventing better mousetraps,

8

when, as De Tocqueville put it, the world beats a track to the door of those who succeed. In America this track was already being beaten 120 years ago, in De Tocqueville's day; in Asia it is not beaten yet; that is one of the reasons why America is now so rich and Asia still so poor.

In Asia indeed the process of making business respectable and exciting has little more than begun; and in 'business' we include farming for cash and a living, as distinct from farming for subsistence and as a way of life. The best boys tend to choose the Civil Service or the Army as they grow up; indeed, it is often difficult for them to do anything else, for such indigenous business as there is, is usually in the hands of family concerns belonging to some special class or caste who do not look outside their families for talent; and, when they do, usually do not treat properly the talent they find.

A change is, however, beginning, and in two ways. First, nationalisation opens to the whole community, and not only to the commercial classes, the opportunity to obtain posts in industry, and it gives to business something of the cachet of Government service. This is one of the main reasons for the attraction of Socialism for circles in Asia that are otherwise profoundly conservative. Second, and more important, is the effect of foreign investment. The American or British or Dutch firm comes from a country where to be engaged in trade has now been respectable for a very long time, made so by the tradition of the free city, by the Puritan emphasis on thrift and hard work as valuable in themselves, and, in England, by the discrimination against Nonconformists in State employment. These firms can therefore recruit whom they will in their own countries and have built up a thoroughly professional tradition. This tradition, much more than the pay, is at last attracting into business many of the pick of local youth, though the pay, too, is normally higher than anything most local firms are prepared to offer to anyone but a senior member of the family.

This influx of many of the brightest local young men into foreign firms is largely new. In the old days these firms usually preferred to employ their own nationals; it was so much easier; they needed less training, and could be imported to provide for an expansion of the business just when wanted. Nor were the best Asians usually particularly keen on going into foreign firms; they preferred the gradually expanding opportunities in Government service. Today the position has changed. Men imported from the home countries are terribly expensive; local nationalism is more and more insistent on the replacement of foreigners by

Z.D.F.A.

their own nationals—some countries make it very difficult to import even badly needed technicians; above all, good young men have at last become interested in business, partly because inflation has in most countries reduced the real pay of Government servants, partly because they now see that their countries require managers and entrepreneurs as well as soldiers and civil servants, partly because the biggest firms, the oil companies, for example, offer so professional a career that a boy can join them without feeling that he has jettisoned his standards for money. The big firms have, in short, become respectable, a young man well placed in one of them now counts as eligible for the most exacting father-in-law. Foreign business in Asia is therefore now getting a considerable number of very good men, some of whom have already become quite senior. These men are of an importance for the future of their societies out of all proportion to their still quite limited numbers, for they spend the whole of their working life in an environment where the values which have made for business success in other countries are part of the air they breathe. By the time they are forty, sometimes even by the time they are thirty, they have absorbed the attitudes to expansion and investment, profits and productivity, quality control and service to the consumer, which have made their firms successful in developed countries. Thus Asia acquires a leaven of Asian innovators and organisers that it can get equally easily in no other way. The managers of nationalised industries tend to become bureaucrats; they try to avoid losses more than to make profits, they are better at manufacturing than at marketing. The foreign manager is not usually sufficiently at home in the Asian society around him to be able to affect its outlook. If the educated classes who in Asia make policy are to acquire an understanding of the conditions business requires in order to be able to make its contribution, and of what characteristics distinguish a good business from a bad one, they must do so from fellow-Asians. And since these educated classes are of considerable size, there must be a good many of these fellow-Asians who understand business if their knowledge is to permeate the educated as a whole. That is why the gradual Asianisation of the cadres of the foreign firms operating in Asia is of such great importance. In some countries the process may be completed in a relatively few years, as it probably will be in India; or its completion may be a generation or more away, as it probably is on the Ceylonese plantations. Everywhere, Asianisation will speed development quite disproportionately, for in these new Asian managers Asia will be acquiring for the first time a core of leaders to whom it has become second nature to think in terms of expansion and the conditions necessary therefor.

As Asia changes, as it builds up its managers and entrepreneurs, the respect given to economic achievement is going up. Nevertheless outside Communist China, which has the usual Communist emphasis on fulfilling plans rather than loving neighbours, the admiration of Asia still goes to goodness rather than to success. This reduces the effort put into being successful without perhaps greatly increasing the amount of effort put into being good. There is in part an obvious historical explanation. A very large proportion of the trading classes of Asia do not have a good reputation as citizens. They charge monopoly rates of interest on the credit they give, they cheat their customers on price and quality, and they evade their taxes. One can exaggerate this unfavourable picture. The Gujerati business man in India is highly enterprising. The old Chinese Taipan's word was his bond, and many rural moneylenders show more sympathy to the peasants in a bad year than Government does. Nevertheless, the public stereotype of its commercial class is unfavourable; it associates them neither with hard work nor with honesty. This has disastrous economic results, for if business is to perform its function, businessmen must be believed to be good citizens, otherwise shareholders will not invest, Governments will interfere, workmen will believe they are exploited, and, above all, consumers will place no faith in advertising; and a great deal of innovation is dependent on the consumer's thinking that there is at least enough truth in what the advertisement says to make it worth his while to try a new product once. Businesses surrounded by general suspicion may still make a profit, but in the long run it will be a much smaller profit, and one made from continuing with old products and old methods rather than trying new ones. Such businesses cannot expect that Government will not interfere with them, or that they will be able to recruit the best men to be their managers, or that their labour will help in increasing productivity, or that their consumers will have enough faith in their brand names to give them a stable market. Such businesses can obviously contribute very little to development.

It is therefore a first essential for business to acquire for itself in Asia the reputation for being socially useful and commercially trustworthy which it has in the United States and in, at any rate a part, of Europe. The primary responsibility rests upon business itself. It must show itself honest, capable of taking a long view, willing to be a good employer and prepared to consider the country's interests as well as its own. The lead has to be taken by the big firms, which in many countries means to a very large extent by the foreign firms. Every company whose accounts are scrupulously kept, whose employees are properly treated and whose name on an article is a guarantee that it is value for money, contributes something to the creation of that favourable climate of opinion without which economic development is not possible. It is not enough for the big firms to be scrupulous. The little firms, too, have to play their part. When the customer can rely on the local shopkeeper not to cheat him with false weights or short measure, when the Government official can rely upon the applicant for a licence to fill up his application form truthfully, when the investor can trust the directors of the company into which he puts his money not to make money out of the company on the side, then business will have around it the attitude it needs in order to flourish. Not before.

The whole responsibility for the low view so many Asians take of business cannot be put on the businessman. Something must be blamed on Government. Everywhere in Asia there are plans and controls. The businessman in consequence is always having to explain what he wants to do to some official. This has a double disadvantage. Many businessmen are much better at knowing what to do than they are at putting their reasons down, and the official, inevitably, does not normally understand the intricacies of the particular business concerned. The official is frequently compelled by law to make the businessman's decision for him on where he should locate his plant, for instance, or on what is a reasonable rate of return on his capital, or on how rapidly he should take on local managers, or even on whether he should be permitted to invest in a particular direction at all. These are obviously decisions the official is not well qualified to make. The decisions, therefore, are for the businessman, quite unpredictable; he does not know on what basis they will be made, all that he knows is that his own basis of decision, profit, is one the average official disclaims. Inevitably, therefore, many businessmen, especially the smaller ones, spend their time trying to influence officials in various indirect ways. Inevitably, too, the businessman has to charge a risk premium in his price for the schemes the controllers frustrate, and the time which is wasted in explaining the obvious to planners who do not understand. But if as a result prices are high, or officials are seen winning too often with businessmen, it is business which loses repute.

Economic development requires more than that present businessmen should behave well enough to be respected. It requires that the artisan and the subsistence peasant should become businessmen, and should be admired for doing so. The subsistence peasant particularly, who is so large a percentage of all Asia's population, must become an economic man. He must base his operations on a proper calculation of profit and loss, and he must be able to obtain the respect of his village by successful calculation as easily as by observing the conventions of his ancestors. His agriculture, so satisfying over so many centuries as a way of life, must become his business, looked at with the same harsh realism, the same arithmetical coldness, as an accountant applies to his balance sheet.

If in Asia business becomes respected, and every peasant farm a business, Asian societies will not necessarily be happier than they are today. The qualities that make for the most rapid development are unfortunately in many cases somewhat self-regarding qualities. The small peasant or small business man may be able quickest to increase his production, and thus to increase the national income, by stinting his family and being less hospitable to his neighbours; neither will make him a very nice man, or a very pleasant neighbour. But every ambition of every society requires sacrifices; and getting rich quick—for which economic development is only a polysyllabic synonym—is no exception.

Chapter 4

INVESTMENT

ALMOST all the ways a community has of getting richer involve doing without now in order to be better off later. In other words, they involve investment. What one does without varies. It may be leisure, as when a village builds a road with voluntary labour; it may be consumption goods, things to wear or to eat, as when production is directed to making machinery rather than cloth; it may be immediate earning capacity, as when a child is sent to school instead of being sent out to herd the goats, or a chemist is put on research instead of being employed in the works. Always, however, there is a sacrifice of present amenity for future production.

Development requires investment. In the Asian context, however, the term 'investment' requires some further definition. The fact that somebody has saved does not automatically mean that there will be investment. Hoarding is not investment. There is a sacrifice of present amenity, but no increase in future production. Buying jewellery is not investment. There is a sacrifice of present amenity, but the increase in women's pleasure which may ensue is not an increase in production; jewellery is like a refrigerator, a durable consumption good. Buying land, or existing stocks or shares, or a mortgage, even lending money is not in itself investment. There has been a sacrifice of present amenity by the purchaser or lender, but not by society as a whole. On the other hand there need be no saving in money for there to be an effective investment. When a primitive tribesman cuts down jungle to make a millet field, or when a peasant digs himself a well, stops a gully, or builds himself a new hut, there is investment. The present amenities of leisure or immediate earning capacity have been sacrificed for future increase of production. When a clerk sends his son to college, or Government builds a polytechnic, or a peasant attends an adult literacy class, there is investment. Unless the new skills are left unemployed, the present sacrifice will in due course be rewarded by increased production.

These examples illustrate a very important side of Asia's problem. If Asia is to develop it must have investment, investment in things, investment in people. It must have railways and factory hands, power stations and atomic scientists, packing machines and peasants who can read instructions or a promissory note.

Before there can be this investment, somebody must do without his amenities, somebody must save, either actually in money or by giving up leisure. It is not, however, enough for there to be saving; the saving must be properly directed. Much of Asia's saving today goes, directly or through a loan by the saver, to someone less provident, to unproductive purposes, to hoarding and jewellery, ceremonies and festivals, display and the buying of existing assets, especially land. If all Asia had a living tradition as austere as Japan's, the amount available for investment would double even in India; in Ceylon or Thailand, it might considerably more than double. But if Asia wastes much of its savings, it also has potentialities for saving not available in more developed societies. The peasant works perhaps 200 or 250 days a year, and not all that he does is vital. There is free time which could be used for other purposes, for the improving of himself or his land. If he were to want to, if he were to understand their value, he could go to adult classes, or give his land the extra ploughings and weedings it so often needs, or build his village a road. That he usually does not do so is due more to ignorance and lack of organisation than to inertia or idleness.

The gap in Asia between the act of saving and the act of investment, between the investment opportunities and the knowledge or willingness to make use of them, has historical reasons. In the past most Asian investment was direct. The peasant cleared new land himself, or with the help of friends; a boy acquired skill by learning it from his elders. If the peasant had a surplus he spent it on enjoying himself, on marriages and festivals. There was usually nothing to invest it in; so he saved up for pleasure in the way a Westerner saves for a television set; and, even more than a Westerner with a television set, to get his pleasure at the right time, he would anticipate the saving and borrow; a child's marriage cannot always wait till father has money for the wedding. This worked very well in its time. The land was cleared and the weddings were enjoyed. It does not work now because, in most of Asia, there is no new land to clear, and what is required for investment is now so much more often money and the acquisition of skill than free time. One cannot build railways by each labourer making a bit of line for himself; or create mill-hands by each one learning from his father.

The problem is not that Asian societies have never invested, but that their forms of investment are mostly no longer suitable. In the past they have, in fact, invested very heavily, along certain limited lines. Over the past few hundred years, and over the past hundred years in particular, an enormous task of clearing jungle, draining swamps and generally bringing land under cultivation has been performed. In Burma, for example, land under rice went up from 354,000 acres in 1845 to 9,702,000 acres in 1935. In some areas this form of investment is still continuing. In Thailand the area under cultivation has gone up very considerably since 1945, and there is still plenty of room for expansion everywhere in Indonesia, except in Java. In the major areas of population, however, in India, Pakistan, Japan and Java, the room for such investment is now very limited indeed. Either there is no waste land to be put under cultivation, as in many Bombay districts, or what there is requires methods and capital beyond the peasant's capacity. In West Pakistan, for example, the extension of cultivation is only possible after major irrigation works have been built. In parts of Central India much land is under a weed called Kans, whose eradication requires special tractors. The capital that the peasant is able to give, his own time and that of his bullocks, is no longer enough. Machinery and technicians are needed, for which money, and not merely time, has to be provided.

There has been a similar development with skill. The Asian peasant and handicraftsman are by no means clodhoppers. Japanese rice farming or the manufacture of Banaras brocades requires as delicate a combination of techniques as anything in the West, and both longer training and harder work than most Western employments demand. But these techniques no longer always work in a changing world. The Banaras brocade gets undercut by something cheap and machine-made. Japanese farming requires the use of night-soil, which people have now discovered spreads disease.

Above all, these are techniques with little capacity for either adaptation or expansion. The peasant and the handicraftsman know one answer; when conditions change, they can rarely find another. The Indian peasant will still grow millet and use a pair of bullocks when his holding has got down to a single acre; he has never tried or heard of the gardening methods that enable a Japanese farmer to do quite well even from an acre. The handloom weaver who has always made a nine-yard sari loses his market if the fashion changes to five. The old methods all assume a static society. Expansion comes from repeating the same recipe on a larger scale; more land is brought under the same form of cultivation, or a bigger population means more women needing more five-yard saris. For these investments Asian societies have always been prepared; they have always found the bullocks or the looms which they required. What they find difficult is to build fertiliser factories so that land already under cultivation may be more intensively farmed, or hydro-electric dams so that the weaver may get a power-loom. These require organisation, and skill, and a mobilisation of money and physical resources, of a quite different sort from anything required in the past. Even the great Khmer monuments of Angkor, or the irrigation works of South India, are not comparable, for they, like the clearing of jungle, involved mainly the organisation of existing skills and free peasant time.

Today, if the existing population is to be given a higher income and the increase in population is to be provided for, investment has to take new forms. New skills have to be created at every level, from that of the managing director to that of the yard weighman, while capital has to be got together in money, in large quantities, and in the hands of people who know how to invest though it may not be they who saved.

The need for skill perhaps needs little emphasising in a world where the most advanced countries are perpetually worried that they may not be producing enough engineers and scientists. It is perhaps not so obvious to the Westerner, or the urban Asian, how far this need for skill goes. He may realise that it takes years to make a bridge engineer; he does not always realise that it is also a major training task to turn a peasant or an artisan into a ticket collector, or a fitter, or just the man who taps the railway carriage wheels to see if they have a defect.

The clearest example of this is mechanical skill. Machinery is one of the modern world's main ways of getting larger production for the same amount of human effort. Any society which wishes to develop economically must become skilled in the use of machinery. This is, of course, one of those great truths which, once it is stated, is so obvious as to make one wonder why it was necessary to state it at all. It is, nonetheless, a truth whose consequences are quite revolutionary.

Asian societies are basically unmechanical, not because of any inherent defect in their people but because of their social structure and their traditionally very limited use of anything which requires either steel or precision. A motor-bus engine or a lathe requires a whole new world of ideas from a man accustomed to a bullock-cart and a wooden plough. If a bullock-cart wheel is allowed to go out of true, the bullocks have to work a bit harder, and that is all. If an omnibus wheel goes out of true, the bus may well fall off an embankment. If a bullock-cart is left unoiled it will squeak, and that is all. If a lathe is left unmaintained, it goes out of order, with the loss of what may be a very large sum of money to its owner.

These are obvious examples, but the changes in behaviour required go beyond the obvious. In the village a man who wishes to lie in bed half-an-hour longer in the morning can, unless he is a labourer, make up by working half-an-hour longer at night, and most Asian villagers are not labourers. In a factory if a man goes half-an-hour late, his machine lies idle for half-an-hour, and the half-an-hour cannot be made up at the end of the shift. In the village there is always a great deal of leisure time for holidays and weddings. There are times when there is nothing to do in the fields, other times when it does not matter whether one does what has to be done on Tuesday or on Wednesday. For a man accustomed to such freedom, the discipline of a factory or mine must be irksome. So workers take time off for family ceremonies or to go to their villages for the harvest; absenteeism is high and the leave allowed has to be long, very often twice or three times what the workman gets in Europe. And both the absenteeism and the long leave mean either that wages must be low, which in turn means that demand for anything but essentials is also low, or that costs must be high, which makes industry uncompetitive. Either way expansion is made more difficult.

Therefore, from the apparently quite simple need to have people who can look after machines one is led on to the major requirement of a Western-style urban working-class, people who are as proud of a well-kept machine as they once were of properly looked after bullocks, and whose attitudes to punctuality and discipline, productivity and more skill, are those of the factory and not of the farm. Asia has to have what Europe and America have, though there too, not in adequate measure, workers who identify themselves with the factory or mine in which they work, and who realise that their wages depend upon its efficiency. Partly this is a matter of good education and good personnel management, neither of which are cheap. Still more is it a matter of fixing the worker in the town, so that he regards himself as a citizen of the town, and not still as a man from village so-and-so come to work in the town temporarily to make some money. This requires more investment still, for it means the town must be a place in which he wants to live, and in which his wife and family can live. It must have water and sewage and parks; above all, it must have housing. Men who live three in a tenement room and keep their wives at home in the village will never become proper factory workers.

Facts such as these are at the heart of the paradox that Asia is poor, but for Asia to become rich costs more than for those who are already rich. There is not the social capital to draw on that countries like America and England have, neither the accumulated modern skills nor the individual housing, nor more concretely, the communications and the power.

In Asia, outside Japan, everything, or almost everything is to be built. Development means industrialisation, development means better farming methods; and both of these require investment before they can happen. A factory means buildings, and machinery, and specialised training for technicians. Fertiliser for peasants means a loan to carry them over the months from the time when they apply the fertiliser to the time when the increased crop comes in. Improved seed in place of the peasant's own means research stations, and seed-growing farms, and a distribution system. All of this requires money, investment. But before any of it can happen there has to be other, preliminary, still more massive, investment, in technical schools, in utilities, in ordinary literacy. The businessman cannot manufacture unless there is a water supply and a power supply, or unless there is a means of communication by which to bring in his raw materials and move his finished products. He cannot manufacture on a large scale unless he can get at his market. Villagers cut off for four months by the monsoon learn to do without his products, villagers who cannot read can neither learn the merits of his goods from advertising, nor how to use them from the instructions on the packet. Nor can the peasant farm in a modern way unless he can both get at the wider world, and be got at by it. A change from cereals to fruit or milk requires that the fruit and milk should be saleable; that means roads and refrigeration, grading stations and pasteurisation plants. A change from breeding cattle anyhow to breeding by artificial insemination from good bulls requires veterinary staff, and buildings, and proper feeding for the good bulls, and education in the importance of castrating the bad bulls.

All of this costs capital, and Asia is doubly short of capital, short because poor societies find it difficult to save, short too because the savings they do make are not properly mobilised. For a proper connection between savings and investment in a free society one requires the full range of the institutions of capitalism, from the bank to the insurance company, from the stock exchange to the businessman backing the bright young man with an idea, from the building society to the agricultural mortgage corporation and the co-operative society. In a Communist society, of course, the connection is made by force; the savings are made by compulsory loans and enormous turnover taxes, the investment is decided by the State which compels the savings; one of the attractions of Communism for Asians is that it does thus get over the gap their mostly pre-capitalist, or at most demi-semi capitalist societies find so hard to bridge. So much of free Asia's savings accumulate with moneylenders who lend them for consumption, with speculators who use them to buy gold, with clerks who spend their provident fund on a house, or with fathers and husbands who waste them on jewellery for their womenfolk, that sometimes it seems to them worthwhile to accept the liquidations of Communism so that their country may have steel works instead of weddings, atomic energy instead of jewellery.

At every turn, the free Asian societies except for Japan are hampered by the lack of proper credit institutions. The peasant can usually only borrow for an improvement at a ruinous rate of interest. The capital markets are so small that a million dollars is a very large amount to try and raise in any of them, and in some would be quite impossible except for a proposition which had an excellent record over many years. Even in India, much money has to be raised by debentures that should really be equity, and debenture flotations themselves are not easy. Many of the towns of Asia still have no banks; the recent nationalisation of India's biggest bank, the Imperial, had as one of its motives to push banking down to all those towns which act as local administrative headquarters, something which can only be done at a considerable loss. There are hardly any building societies, life insurance has not spread beyond the urban middle classes, and their poverty usually prevents their buying more than small policies. Co-operatives still only touch the fringe of the villager's needs; except in India, and even there their rapid recent expansion is the result of the injections of large amounts of what is in effect government money. The bright young man can rarely turn to anyone but a relative, though he might get something from a State bank or Finance Corporation. In short, investment in Asia is practicable only for the State, which can tax, create money, and borrow; for the small man who can make a small effort from his own resources; and for the firm, especially the big firm, which can plough back profits. It is a list which excludes most people and most enterprises; its narrowness is one of the main causes of the slowness of Asia's development.

The dilemma of Asia is thus stark. It needs enormous investment, yet its savings are inadequate, and not always mobilisable. So inadequate has investment—mobilisation of savings—been that in the fifty years to 1950 perhaps only Malaya and Ceylon, with their large plantation sectors, and Japan, with its increasing capitalism, have done more than keep up with the increase in population; much of Java, and parts of India and Pakistan may not have done that. Clearly, if there is to be any rapid increase in production, and thus in welfare, then very much larger quantities of capital are required than present savings provide, at least as at present used. There must be more savings; and they must be invested productively, not comsumed or hoarded. Savings certificates bought because a man no longer buys gold help just as much as savings certificates bought because he is not spending his latest rise.

Chapter 5

SAVINGS

INVESTMENT requires savings. The problem of under-developed countries is that their very underdevelopment makes it almost impossible for them to save enough. Saving is much harder for the poor than for the rich. Admittedly, poverty or riches by themselves do not entirely determine the rate of savings. That depends also upon the traditional standard of living, otherwise obviously the United States would save 60 or 70 per cent of its income and countries like India and China would save nothing at all. The relatively high rate of savings prevailing in Japan before the war, particularly, was a result of the traditional austerity of Japanese life. The fact that a community is poor, therefore, does not mean that it cannot save at all, but it does mean that its savings are likely to be small and obtained by the sacrifice of necessities and not merely luxuries. Provision for old age and a rainy day which is so basic to the saving of the West, is very difficult in countries where for many people rainy days happen every day and where the provision for old age has traditionally been to produce a fine crop of children.

No doubt in the past savings in the Western sense were not vital for most Asian communities. In societies of peasants, small shop-keepers and artisans it is a perfectly reasonable assumption that when a man gets old his children will keep him in return for his handing over to them his land or his tools or his shop, and in societies where most people either have land or a hereditary skill in the manufacture of products they sell to known customers, it is quite reasonable to tide over a bad year by borrowing from a moneylender. Moreover, the traditional agriculture and crafts-manship of Asia do not require any large capital other than labour and hereditary skill. For many centuries land could be obtained for the effort of clearing or embanking it, and the cost of a new handloom or carpenter's tools was never more than a few dollars. The only incentive to saving was the need to provide for the ceremonies which accompany deaths, births and wed-dings; and, enjoyable though the ceremonies are, they are not productive investments.

Modern investment requirements, therefore, involve a change in the ways of producing and using capital in Asia much greater than anything which has happened in Europe; for, in Europe, even in the Middle Ages, such trades as textiles, wines and timber required very considerable working capital, and the free cities provided a place where men could accumulate undisturbed by the arbitrary exactions of some local despot, and where successful accumulation meant a respected position in the community and the hope of local office. That is why it was these cities which provided the capital which financed the development of the modern world, from the voyages of exploration to the first factories; that is why, too, it was these cities which developed the Puritan virtues of thrift and concern for one's business reputation, on which have been built so much of the West's industrial and commercial growth. It is not an accident that so many of the biggest businesses in Britain and the United States were built up by Nonconformists. There is in Asian history no equivalent of Bruges or Venice or London, of the Cadburys or the Chamberlains. Nowhere in Asia has the capitalist ever been safe against the tax gatherer for long; nowhere in Asia in the past could the merchant hope one day to be Mayor of his city.

When they come to build up savings, therefore, Asian communities have to change the whole trend of their history, the whole way of thought of their people. In Asia there is no such propensity to save as in the West, and it is this lack which is one of the main temptations to the ruthless shortcut of Communism, with its compulsory saving by forced labour, confiscation and planning targets that must be met. In a Western society, left to itself and with reasonable taxation, the savings required for economic development are produced automatically by the self-deprivations of many hundreds of thousands of people. In the extreme cases of the United States and Canada these savings are produced, even at the present time of very high taxation, without any special effort by the Governments, and in Great Britain or France savings were adequate for 100 years until 1939. The failures in the inter-war period were of proper investment, not of saving. It was effective demand, not people's willingness to restrict their consumption, which did not grow quickly enough. Western experience is therefore only partially relevant to what should be done in Asia, only a reminder that the best way of getting enough savings is for the people to want to save. The professional classes in Asia, for example, have always been thrifty. Their work and life induce in them attitudes of thrift, in much the same way as similar work and a similar life have in Europe.

To change attitudes of whole populations, however, especially when most of them are illiterate and live just above subsistence, is slow and difficult and requires many different approaches at once. Thus, in democratic countries like India savings campaigns with their repeated exhortations to thrift by men like Pandit Nehru, have some long-term effect on the public mind. Still more useful is propaganda against ostentatious spending. Most of the saving of these communities has traditionally gone into jewellery, because it was the safest store of value and because it could so easily be hidden from a raider, and into ceremonies, because, in a village, every man must live up to the standard set by tradition and his neighbours; therefore, anything which reduces the cost of weddings, or the number of bangles a woman is expected to wear, will increase savings by almost the full amount not so spent. To take a simple example, in the West when a daughter gets married she is very frequently given a house and furniture, or at least a trousseau of linen. The house represents a true addition to the nation's capital; the furniture and the trousseau are at least durable consumer goods. Amongst the rich she will also be given a settlement, and many people in the days before impossibly high taxation saved up so that the settlement could be given without impairing the family fortune. In Asia, by contrast, although very large amounts of money are spent on weddings, and a quite considerable percentage of the debts incurred are due to weddings, very little of it represents a creation either of capital or of durable consumer goods. The money goes either on a lavish feast or on such consumer goods as clothes, or on jewellery. Any legislation against large expenditure on ceremonies, any growth of public opinion which condemns such expenditure as vulgar ostentation, will do more to free the savings of Asia for investment than anything else possibly can.

An easier source of savings would be to mobilise the villager's unused time. On small peasant holdings there is never work enough for the whole year. On unirrigated farms in India the holder may have occupation only for three months. Some of the spare time is used on pilgrimages and ceremonies, some, even today, in such secondary occupations as carting and tree-felling. But much is idle time that could be used to economic advantage without any sacrifice at all. The Asian villager may, and does, value leisure more than such work-absorbed societies as the Scots, but he certainly does not want six months of it. In olden times some of this enforced leisure was used, either voluntarily or through forced labour, to provide work necessary to the community; village roads, for example, had to be built and maintained by the villagers. This system led to so much abuse and semi-slavery that it had to be abolished, but it could with advantage be revived now, at least in those countries where adult suffrage gives the villager protection, in that oppression would lose the Government votes. In India a beginning has already been made. In Uttar Pradesh, in one special week, two million dollars' worth of voluntary effort was put in; and most Indian States are now adopting a system by which Government will help only those who help themselves. If the villagers build the road, Government will pay for the technicians and the bridges. If the villagers build the school, Government will provide the timber. If the villagers subscribe to the loan, Government will construct the irrigation dam. If the peasant will dig the well, Government will give a loan for the cash expenditure. If the people will run a co-operative society, the Reserve Bank will help to finance it.[1] The approach is still only tentative; much effort and persuasion will be required before it can govern the whole of what Government does. But it is the right way. Asia is too poor still for the Welfare State to act as the all-bountiful provider to a passive people; the Welfare State can only work if the people themselves help, with their time as well as their money. Indeed, so much is this so that, in these communities where the cost of defence is everywhere a strain, there is a clear case for some form of conscription, which gives so much more defence for so much less money, and at the same time permits the inculcation of those habits of discipline, punctuality, regularity and organised teamwork which are so valuable a corrective to the sporadic rhythm of cereal agriculture.

However, even if all Asia's habits could be changed, private savings might still be inadequate. Even if nothing were to be spent on jewellery—and amongst the Indian middle class the nose-diamond and the gaudy bangle are definitely on their way out—there would still not be enough. Indian saving, for instance, might go up by a couple of per cent at the outside. Nor could all the mobilisation of voluntary labour which is conceivable add more than another 1 per cent or 2 per cent. The back of the problem would be broken, but the rate of saving would still not be as great as France's or Germany's. And the fact must be faced that it will be a very long time before nothing will be spent on jewellery; how much does the West waste on engagement rings?

Asia must, therefore, look beyond the private individual for the savings it needs; and the obvious sources are the institution, the business, and the budget.

[1] This is discussed at greater length in Chapter XVIII, Community Projects, and Chapter XVI, Co-operation and Credit.

The institution, notably the Insurance Company and the Co-operative Society but also the building society and the investment trust, is important both because it persuades the private individual to save, where left alone he probably would not save, and because it normally invests profitably the savings thus obtained. The business, and particularly the big business, is important because it represents the only considerable concentration of income from which savings can come without impossible hardship. Traditionally, in all developing countries, savings were made possible partly by gross inequalities of income. England in 1900 had the greatest unevenness of distribution of income in the whole world. The concentration of wide ranges of industry in Germany and Japan before the war in the hands of a quite limited number of families was the result of the fact that these families had been ploughing back profits for many years in societies where relatively few other people had been able to save, and that they had been able to get hold of a considerable proportion of what savings there were because many of the saving classes had no businesses of their own in which to invest. Today, large inequality of income is socially unacceptable, in Asia perhaps even more than in Europe, perhaps because in Asia so many large incomes come from land or house property and are much more often spent in conspicuous consumption than saved; and in Asia, moreover, the public's idea of a rich man begins at a very much lower income than it does in Europe or America. To have a Buick is within the range of many American workers; in Asia Buicks are a major symbol of riches, of that inequality of income which it is the function of taxation to cut down. The result is that in India, nearly two-thirds of the income taxes come from some 5,000 assessees; and many of these, inevitably, are big businesses.

Institutions and businesses, however, can only perform their function of gathering enough savings if they work in a proper atmosphere, and particularly within a suitable legal framework.[1] With the Insurance Company, for instance, there must be complete public confidence in its integrity. With the building society it must be reasonably possible for its clients to get land and materials to build. If land is difficult to buy because the title is bad—and in Ceylon, for example, even the development of land mortgage banks has been held up because it is difficult to show a really good title—or if cement or steel are under control, which always makes it very difficult for the little man to get a permit,

[1] Co-operative Societies are so important, and so special that they are discussed at length in separate chapters, Nos. XVI and XVII.

then obviously building societies will find it very difficult to develop. Above all, if the rate of interest is unduly low or there are
severe restrictions on the types of investment which Insurance
Companies can buy, whether by convention or by law, then
attracting savings will be difficult. The poorer the country, the
harsher the sacrifice involved in making any saving at all. Yet
the rate of interest on Government bonds in India or Pakistan or
Ceylon is (1962) about 2 per cent lower than in the U.K., and
only about $\frac{1}{2}$ per cent higher than in the U.S. These Governments still expect to borrow at $3\frac{1}{2}$ per cent and 4 per cent, although even in prosperous Belgium the Government pays $5\frac{1}{2}$ per
cent and the German States a little while ago paid as much as 9
per cent. At 4 per cent many people will buy a bicycle or a new
shirt where at 6 per cent or 8 per cent they would have bought
savings certificates, or a larger life policy. Moreover, the effect
of confining the institutions through which most middle-class
saving goes, and notably the Insurance Companies, so largely to
investment in Government securities—they usually have to have
half their assets in gilt edged—is to stunt industrial development. Nowhere in Asia are there the large numbers of people
with the habit of putting something in industrial equities which
one finds in England or the U.S. Industrial equities are very little
held outside the big towns, and even there are largely held either
by the very rich or by people who are speculators and not investors. With the increasing disappearance of the very rich, it
will in future not be possible for one man to put up two million
dollars to save a steel plant from liquidation, as the Maharaja of
Gwalior once did for Tatas, and the habits of the speculator
make ordinary shares so uncertain an investment that they tend
to keep the small saver out of the market altogether.

If, therefore, the money is to be found for sound enterprise,
and if there is to grow up a class of shareholders with enough
time and enterprise to control the vagaries and even the dishonesty of directors and managing agents, then it is necessary
for the large Insurance Companies and even the banks to place
more of their money in industrial equities, despite the risk that
this will involve some loss of liquidity for the banks, or some loss
of absolute security for the Insurance Companies. (After all, for
the saver himself no investment has been worse over these last
years of inflation than gilt-edged.) A great deal of the industrial
development of Germany and Japan, in both of which countries
there was the same difficulty of inadequate internal savings, was
financed by banks and insurance companies.

More important even than the institutions as a saver is the big business. In many countries nowadays corporate savings account for as much as half of total savings; in England, if one leaves out budget surpluses, they are very considerably more than half. In India they are, perhaps, one fifth. Moreover, apart from life insurance and savings certificates, this has been the only section of saving to show a very large capacity for increase over the last generation. In Asia, where so many people are independent proprietors that they do not find life insurance attractive and where most people are so poor that the $3\frac{1}{2}$ per cent of the savings certificate seems a very inadequate reward for not doing their consumption immediately, an increase in ploughed back business profits is much the most promising way of obtaining an increase in savings as a whole.[1]

The ways of obtaining such an increase are many. To begin with certain specific alterations in taxation are required. Thus, in many Asian countries the price level is several times higher than pre-war, yet depreciation allowances are still calculated on historical costs, with the result that most of the profits ploughed back are required to provide for the higher replacement cost of existing capital and are not available for expansion at all. Revaluation of assets on the French or Belgian model, with depreciation allowances calculated in future on the revalued prices, would free very large sums for new development. Again, in most Asian countries taxation levels are very high; if they could be brought down over-all so that dividends could be raised, there would be a much greater incentive for the saver to buy industrial shares. In India, for example, the price level is nearly 4 times pre-war, yet profits, largely as a result of price-control, were 10 years after the war still $2\frac{1}{2}$ times pre-war, and taxation is so severe that industrial share values for years remained only fractionally above pre-war. The saver may well feel that he would have done better to have spent his money in the first place and not to have saved it at all. If savers are to take risks on ordinary shares there must be in the long run and on the average be a steady rise in the real value of equities. The shareholder must get the benefit of his ploughing back.

Even if a reduction in corporation taxes as a whole is not possible, either because it would open a gaping deficit in the budget or because it would lead to a political reaction so severe that business confidence would be more damaged by the growth of leftist feeling than encouraged by the reduction in taxes, it should be possible greatly to reduce the taxes on undistributed profits.

[1] There are signs, however, that it might be possible to greatly increase peasant savings for the improvement of their own farming and for local works. See for a longer discussion, Chapters XVI and XVIII.

Undistributed profits are 100 per cent savings, and there is no
other form of reduction of taxes which can possibly yield so large
a reward in immediately increased investment. This is the only
case where none of the reduction can possibly go to consumption. Even from the social justice point of view it is much better
to permit fortunes to be built up by ploughing back, and then to
take away most of them in death duties, than to tax the savings
out of existence before the fortune, and the increase in the
national income which it involves can be built up at all. The
arguments against discrimination in favour of undistributed profits, which have been so powerfully put for a developed country by
the British Royal Commission on Taxation, hardly apply to Asia.

. It is not only in Asia itself that changes in taxation are required. A great deal of Asia's business is owned outside, mainly
in England or Holland or the U.S. So long as any reduction of
taxation in Asia itself only results in an increase of taxation in
the investing country, the Asian country loses revenue the
Government might have used for its own investment without
obtaining any increase in private investment. France does not
tax overseas income at all, and Great Britain has of late greatly
improved its system, by providing that overseas profits will not
be taxed so long as they can be segregated and earned in special
overseas corporations; moreover, Great Britain now allows a
company to keep, untaxed, the benefit of any special tax concessions an overseas country may give. The United States,
however, having given overseas investments certain advantages, is now talking of tightening up again.

Such concessions involve a sacrifice for the developed
countries which may be painful, not because of the revenue
which is lost, but because any successful encouragement to overseas investment is liable to threaten their balance of payments.
Great Britain would be better off if the money it has invested
overseas since the war had been put into the reserves, and the
United States present (1962) difficulties have been considerably
aggravated by its large foreign investments in recent years.
Since foreign investment is thus liable to be expensive for the
economy of the investing country, there might be a case for giving concessions only to investments in the underdeveloped
countries, or for giving larger concessions to such investments.

The underdeveloped countries themselves could give positive
taxation incentives. Pakistan already provides a whole series.
The income from new house property can be exempted from
taxes for a given number of years. The profits of a newly-estab-
lished industry can be given exemption from taxes up to a cer-

tain percentage of capital, or for a certain period. Extra depreciation in the first few years can be allowed on new machinery, or an investment allowance can be given over and above full depreciation. The money invested in approved industries by private individuals can be exempted from income tax up to a certain limit in the year of investment. These are the main possibilities and they all have one feature in common. In order to tempt people to save and invest, the Government sacrifices a certain amount of revenue in the present, but if the temptation succeeds and people invest profitably, then not only is the national income increased but Government itself gets very much larger revenues in the future.

The use of the budget as a regular means of creating savings is now virtually unknown in the developed countries except, significantly, for France. In Asia today it is a necessity. So much has to be done by the Governments, and their power of borrowing is so limited—the Government of India does well if it borrows from the public, as distinct from the banks, 150 million dollars in a year; the Government of Pakistan can probably not get more than 25 million. Therefore, the Governments must find some of their capital requirements by other means, either by higher taxes, so that capital expenditure can be financed from revenue, or by creating money.

The possibilities of higher taxes are strictly limited. The taxable capacity of the countries of Asia is so low that they have great difficulty in providing from revenue for such elementary duties of the State as defence and education. Pakistan has a population half as large as that of the whole United States, but its revenue is less than that of New York City. The level of taxation in much of Free Asia, especially in India and Pakistan, is already high, and can only be squeezed higher at considerable risk in loss of private savings, private initiative, and public content. India recently appointed a Taxation Enquiry Commission, whose report covered every conceivable possibility of getting more money, from making direct taxation finally crushing to increasing the land revenue; it is doubtful whether, if every one of their recommendations were accepted, the total extra revenue would add up to 1 per cent of the national income. In Asia budget surpluses for capital purposes cannot be achieved as an extra. They have to be in replacement of something. They mean that less can be spent on tanks and embassies, hospitals and stenographers. Every million that is taken out of revenue for capital involves the Cabinet in a painful conflict of priorities. Asian Finance Ministers, notably those of India and Pakistan, do not lack courage; but in the conflict of needs, all of which are crying, it is not to be expected that they will be able to pay from revenue for more than that part of their capital expenditure which brings no financial return, the schools where no fees are charged, or the irrigation which is purely protective.

There is left the creation of money, deficit finance. This has two very simple advantages. If money is created, the public has to buy it. And since the alternative is presented as an increase in taxes, political objections are normally few. It has an equally simple disadvantage. If too much money is created, inflation follows; and since many of the sources of revenue of Asian states are relatively fixed, land revenue, for example, or income-tax on salaries, in an inflation of any speed the State may end up with less real income than it began with; in China a stage was reached where the paper of the notes cost more than their value as money.

Balancing on this knife-edge requires considerable skill. It is not a policy for coalition governments or untrained finance departments, fond though both are of it. But in India, or Pakistan, or Ceylon, or Malaya, it has a very considerable place, a more considerable place than European experience would suggest. First, Asia is still extravagant of currency; it still makes little use of cheques. Therefore, when production increases, there is a corresponding, and by comparison with Europe, relatively large increase in the need for currency. Second, much of the Asian countryside is still at the subsistence or barter stage. The peasant grows his own food, and he pays for his shave or the washing of his clothes or the work of his labourers in grain. For the last hundred years development has been monetising the economy of the Asian village, and now the process is in most areas beginning to go quickly. As traditional connections break down, money replaces barter; as communications and knowledge of the market improve, and as yields increase, a higher and higher proportion of the crop is sold, while the peasant buys more and more of what he requires. All of this requires extra currency, and justifies deficit finance. Moreover, most Asian Governments, for political reasons, give their backward areas a somewhat disproportionate share of attention in their plans; since these areas are precisely those which at present use money least, the planned development which is today taking place over most of Asia is leading to a corresponding extra increase in the demand for currency. Finally, money creation in Asia could play much the same role as credit creation by the banks did in nineteenth-century Europe. It puts some of the resources of the community temporarily at the disposal of the entrepreneurial State.

Whether that leads to inflation depends on what the State does with them. If the State uses the money in a way which does not increase production, directly or indirectly, the money simply remains in circulation and prices go up correspondingly. If the State uses the money to increase production long-term, and if it does not get the money back, but only a return on it, then prices will go up; by how much will depend on how long it is before the extra production comes in, and whether the return is large or small. If the State uses the money to increase production short-term, and does so without diverting resources from other purposes, or by diverting them only to a small extent, and if the money is lent (or invested at very high rates of return) so that it comes back to the State quite quickly and could, theoretically, be cancelled, then prices will not go up, and could go down; for there will in the end be more production but no more than the original amount of money. It is here important that Asia has large underemployed resources of manpower, so that, especially in the countryside, it is possible to do much without diverting resources from other purposes; an extra weeding or a village road uses mostly idle time. This can be exaggerated; most works require co-operating resources which may be short; the village road itself needs culverts, and those who work on it, if they are paid, may then eat more; but, provided there is a proper emphasis on small rural programmes as against large industrial ones, it can be important.

These general theses may be illustrated by some concrete examples. If the State uses the resources to build barracks, clearly prices will go up. If it uses them to lend money at short-term for agricultural improvement, the extra production will come in and the money will be repaid to the State before prices have had time to go up, or at least to go up far; the end effect could therefore be deflationary and not inflationary. In between come cases like the building of a multi-purpose dam, where the money is tied up for a long period and prices will therefore go up before production comes in, and may or may not then go down again, and where, since the State is investing and not lending the money, there is no automatic cancellation of the created money through the repayment of the loan. This latter is the big risk of State-created money as against most nineteenth-century bank credit creation. The bank had to insist on the debt being paid off; if it left too much frozen as investments in industrial concerns it became illiquid and went bankrupt. The State does not go literally bankrupt; but inflation is a form of repudiation of its debts. If the States of Asia wish to create money, they should be sure to use it in a self-liquidating way, either in loans which have to be repaid or in new enterprises which have a very high rate of return. They can use safely on long-term low return enterprises only that part of their created money which is not a method of getting the temporary use of part of the community's resources, but corresponds to a real extra public demand for currency.

On these conditions, though on these conditions alone, it might be reasonable in the best-organised countries to create money on quite a considerable scale, perhaps of the order of 10 per cent of the circulation per year over a period of ten years or so. Neither the figure of 10 per cent or any other, however, can have much value except as an indication of the possible. How much money can be created depends so much on what the money is used for, how sensitive public opinion is to the idea of inflation, and how fast the economy is monetising, that prophecy is not possible; a good Asian Finance Minister today must be like a good nineteenth-century bank manager. He must take each proposition as it arises on its own merits and in the economic circumstances of the moment. The amount of money he can create is the amount he can put on the market without inflation; how much that is he can find out by experience, and in no other way.

Asia's need for savings is so overwhelming that to find means of increasing them is a pressing prescription of policy in every major Asian country. There is no single answer. The growth of big firms, reasonable taxation levels, incentives for the ploughing back of profits, budgetary surpluses, deficit finance, higher rates of interest, better savings institutions, the use of free labour, all have their place. More important than all else, however, is a change in public attitudes. If everyone in Asia placed thrift, and keeping out of debt, and laying up a nest-egg for the future, as high as do many of the professional classes; if everyone were as reluctant to spend an unnecessary penny as most of Asia's small traders, and had the horror of jewellery of an old-fashioned Scots Calvinist, the problem might still not quite be solved; it would at least be soluble.

Chapter 6

THE FUNCTION OF PROFITS

PROFITS are ill thought-of in Asia. To seek them is selfishness. To base plans upon them is making the haggling of the market more important than the necessities of the people. This hostility greatly impedes development. Profits are an expression of the difference between the real resources required to produce any particular thing and the real resources with which people are prepared to part in order to get it, both of course as translated into money terms. Therefore, as between alternative uses of the same resources, the one which gives the larger profit is also the one which will give the larger consumer satisfaction, the one which will, in other words, improve the standard of living more.

Therefore, the first guide of a planner in a poor country must be, by which use of his resources will he make the biggest profit. The profit may be used to reduce prices or increase wages or for the consumption of the entrepreneur, thus raising the standard of life directly; or it may be used to increase investment, thus raising it in the long run; or it may be used, via the taxation system, to provide education or defence, thus raising it indirectly. But in one way or another it must always make people better-off than they would otherwise be. Therefore, though rich countries can afford to invest without examining their profits too closely, if poor countries do likewise, they make life quite unnecessarily hard for themselves. The developed may occasionally be able to afford to use prestige or self-sufficiency or moral indignation as their test in place of profit; when the governing class of an under-developed country does so, they are titillating their own egos at the expense of their people.

These are reasonably self-evident propositions. Some explanation is required of why they are so often ignored. The reason would appear to be a confusion between the economic purpose of profit as a guide on the one hand and either the propriety of the profits which are in fact made, or the morality of those who make them, on the other. Some present profits are clearly improper, made possible only by a friction in the organisation of society, a monopoly, for example, or a tariff. Some other profits appear immoral because of the way income is distributed. If the rich can afford perfume and the poor cannot afford food, the perfume industry is likely to make more profit than the food industry. Finally, some of the people who make profits are ruthless, selfish and vulgar, and many believe that it is the profit motive which makes them bad, and that if they were working for society they would become good.

One does not, however, solve any of these problems by refusing to accept profit as a test. The poor do not get more food if the rich are stopped buying perfume. Many societies have despised profit as a motive; they have not, therefore, lacked for bad men. In all these cases, the moral unacceptability of the profits which are made are a symptom of a disease in the community; and diseases are not cured by attacking symptoms. One must attack the disease itself by prohibiting the monopoly, or reducing the inequality in the distribution of income, or converting the individual from his wickedness—or sending him to gaol.

An admirable example of the way in which the attempt to cure the symptoms instead of the disease can lead to wrong development decisions is the widespread belief that, in a poor country, necessities must always be made to come before luxuries. As a guide to the conduct of the individual himself, this is unexceptionable. A father who spends money on drink and leaves his children without milk is clearly a bad father. A rich man who gives no charity and buys his wife model frocks clearly commits sin. But as a guide to investment it is not nearly so good a rule. If what the public wants is football pools and not improving literature, then if the community's savings are spent on printing presses for good books, they will be wasted, for the good books will not be bought; and such proprietors of football pools as do exist will make fantastic profits, for they will have no competition. The economy of Great Britain between 1945 and 1950 provides many examples of precisely this phenomenon. It may be wrong for people to prefer things of no moral value to things of great moral value, but the statistics of drink and tobacco taxation in every nation show that nearly everybody does. Their habits can be changed by taxation, or preaching or subsidies. If father's drink is taxed so that his child can get free milk at school, or if the money the rich man might have spent on a mink coat is taken away from him in supertax so that a hospital can be built for the poor, then the pattern of consumption is effectively changed. But if all that is done is to refuse permission for new sweet factories and to lavish licences on new vitamin plants, then nothing will happen except that people will have to pay a great deal more for such sweets as they are still able to get. There is no guarantee that they will therefore be prepared to eat vitamins;

such a policy benefits no one but established sweet manufacturers —which explains why business so often makes its biggest profits under Socialist regimes.

The second constituent of the muddle about investment is the belief that a nation's prestige or safety requires certain forms of economic development. This is a particularly confusing muddle, because it is partly true and partly untrue. It is true to the extent that in a war any departure from autarchy must be weakening. England's need for imported food, India's dependence on imported aeroplanes, makes them more vulnerable than the United States or Russia, which both make aeroplanes and grow their own food. Those industries, therefore, which a nation has to undertake for its safety must have first priority, for there is no calculating the loss that may result from defeat in war. That does not mean, however, that every nation should try and do everything. The United States' production of synthetic rubber probably does more harm to American security, by weakening the economies of South-East Asia, than it does good by increasing American self-sufficiency, and England could only grow all that it eats by so reducing the standard of living and so diverting resources from other needs, that the will and capacity of its people to fight would be seriously impaired.

In Asia, which can so much less afford waste, Governments must consider with the greatest care the real costs of the schemes they foster. It may be that an automobile plant will considerably increase self-sufficiency, but if the number of automobiles required in any particular country is so small that they can only be produced locally at three or five or ten times the cost at which they could be imported, then probably the country would be stronger for putting these resources into something which would be economically more beneficial, a fertiliser plant perhaps, so that there would be more food, or new roads so that communications would improve. No general rule can be laid down; each case must be considered on its merits. But it can at least be said that in every instance where some industry asks for protection or for subsidy, the onus of proving that the benefits gained will more than offset the economic loss must be placed squarely upon that industry. At present in every country of the world, and Asian countries are no exception, a large number of industries are allowed to batten on the community without any commensurate return either in extra national safety or anything else.

The third confusion is the general belief that industry is more productive than agriculture and therefore countries should industrialise as fast as possible. It is, in general, historically true that over the last century industry has produced a larger income per head employed than agriculture, though there are some notable exceptions, such as Australia, New Zealand and the Argentine. But there is no immutable rule which requires that it should be so; the reason why it is so often so in practice is merely that, in most countries, there has been much more capital put into industry than into agriculture. With the great advance in agricultural science of the last generation, capital invested in agriculture, in research, for instance, or tube wells, may well give a bigger return quicker than any alternative industrial investment. Industry is very often not even as large a provider of employment as agriculture; irrigation, for example, which roughly doubles the amount of work to be done on each acre getting water, usually gives more employment than any other way of using the same amount of capital. The Indian irrigation schemes under the first Five-Year Plan were to give new employment to 2¼ million people, and fuller employment, perhaps an extra three months a year, to another 3 million.

There is only one satisfactory test for the use of resources, and that is to forget all *a priori* preferences, whether for industry or for agriculture, and to see which scheme gives the biggest return. That is as true for a Government as it is for an individual or a company.

Return, however, must be looked at overall. Thus the fact that local production is more expensive than imports may not be a final reason against developing it. The local production may be cheaper in the long run, though not in the short—the infant-industry argument. Or in countries with large underemployment, like India and Indonesia, it may save more by employing people who would otherwise have to be kept by the community than it costs; and here there is also the moral consideration that it is much healthier for the State if its citizens work than if they do nothing. The moral value of work as such may also be an argument in favour of cottage industry against factory industry, and in making one's calculations of their relative profitability, one must remember too that cottage industry may involve no social overheads whilst factory industry involves the community in very considerable expenditure. The craftsman stays in his house in the village, sends his child to the village school and uses an already existing well. The factory worker requires all the amenities of the town, housing, sewage, water supply and transport. When one calculates the relative returns one must make sure that one compares the total return and the total expenditure and not just the immediate return and the immediate expenditure on plant and buildings.

The infant-industry argument and the underemployment argument both have validity but both can be, and have been, pressed far too far. They both involve the risk that the economy will become so high-cost through the creation of uneconomic industries that exports will be severely hit. Then, with reduced exports, the economy would slow down for lack of imports, and more employment might be lost in the export industries than was gained in the industries created by protection; and throughout the consumer would be paying for the inefficiency or high costs of the protected industries.

The eventual consequences of the most defensible departures from the profit criterion are thus so unpredictable that the onus should always be on those who want to adopt some other criterion to prove their case. It should not be taken for granted that if an industry can show it is useful for the national defence, foreign competition must automatically be controlled by import quotas, or that if a work serves a socially useful purpose, it should automatically be given preference over another on which the returns will be higher but which fits less well into the planner's moral code. In short, there should be more *laisser-faire* and less interference of the sort which is motivated by every objective except that of giving the consumer the maximum satisfaction for the minimum use of resources.

A corollary of this is that there should be as little Government control of the development of private industry as possible. No Government official can possibly be as good a judge of whether a particular investment will make a profit as the man who is proposing to risk his own money. If a man is prepared to risk his money, or if he can persuade other people to risk theirs, then it is probable that in most cases the money will be fruitfully employed. There are exceptions. Some entrepreneurs are dishonest, others more plausible than capable. Others simply follow the trend until more capacity is provided than can be used. But in general the entrepreneur is quite a good judge. He knows how much money he can hope to raise; he can decide how much technical advice he needs, and he can make an estimate of what he is likely to be able to sell. If he goes wrong, he goes bankrupt and his business is sold to somebody else who can use its equipment better. There is no other test of the validity of planning as good as the astringency of bankruptcy.

Unfortunately, many Asian Governments are inclined to over-control. They are always trying to decide for the entrepreneur what he should do, where he should put his factory, what capital he should raise, whom he should employ, what he should make, and what he should charge; they are always propping up the unsuccessful, and penalising the successful by special taxes or special restrictions. Each measure separately can be defended. The consumer should not be overcharged; the investor should not be invited to subscribe to unsound issues; the unsuccessful may be pillars of society with many dependants; the successful may be destroying the living of other people. Many of the controls can also be defended taken together. The consumer and the investor must be protected against crooks, whether these crooks are people who evade their taxes or who give jobs to relations at the shareholders' expense or who steal other people's patents or who issue unduly glowing prospectuses. It is also necessary to prevent too many people using the same external economies. Everybody wants to go to the big towns because they have the railways, the ports, the skilled labour, the power and the amenities for managers' wives. But if everybody is allowed to go to the big towns the result will be that the State will have to spend enormous amounts in clearing slums, extending transport and dealing with all the problems that the coming together of millions of people always creates.

Nevertheless, the overall result, is an enormous slowing down of development, as the entrepreneur finds risk piled upon risk. To do anything he must make applications and hang around Government offices; the result is that many enterprises do not get started, because he does not have the time to make the application, or because the delays make them unprofitable (or simply give the entrepreneur time to get cold feet), or because the Government official does not understand the proposition and says 'no' to be on the safe side.

A good example is the strong tendency not to permit expansion in any industry where there is enough capacity. This is a decision the Government official is usually quite safe in taking. The existing manufacturers, who rarely welcome competition, will be on his side; the existing trade unions, afraid for their members' jobs, will be too. The politician, with a vague idea that in a country short of capital, capital should not be wasted, and that it is always wasted where new capacity is provided in an industry with enough capacity to satisfy the existing demand, will support him. Yet such answers must in the end give the economy hardening of the arteries. Indeed, the official has begun by asking the wrong question. Instead of 'Is this production really necessary?' he should have asked 'Will this production be cheaper than the old production? Will it produce the same satisfactions with fewer resources? Will it permit a reduction of price which will expand the market, give more employment and raise the standard of living?' And he should have a bias in favour of the answer 'Yes', for it is a foolish entrepreneur who enters an already over-supplied industry unless there is something he can do for the consumer that the existing suppliers do not do. The attempt to marry demand and capacity exactly creates the idea that existing producers have a freehold in their consumers and that to permit anybody to take any of them away would be to damage a deserving person with a family to keep. This is a view which appeals very easily to the charity of officials and politicians, especially as it is charity they can perform at the community's expense rather than at their own. What they ought, however, always to be remembering is that this deserving person may be technically incompetent, dishonest, idle, or out-of-date. The community must see he does not starve. It ought to retrain him for a job for which he is better fitted. It has no obligation perpetually to keep him at his accustomed standard of living.

The cost of slowing down change so that the individual will not be adversely affected can be afforded much less easily in poor countries than in rich ones; the United States can even afford its shipbuilding industry. But the temptation to protect the individual is at its strongest in poor communities, and especially in those of Asia, because ruin in a poor country is so much more serious than in a rich one. All over Asia to break a man's rice-bowl is the final offence. That the attitude is morally creditable does not stop its being economically disastrous, for it means that people who are already poor have to subsidise far more inefficiency and incompetence than the citizens of richer countries do. Tariffs in Asia run up to 80, 90 or 100 per cent, and in addition the Asian Governments increasingly use their foreign exchange controls to prohibit imports altogether where there is some local production, regardless quite often of either the quality or the price of that local production. Even within the country they are inclined to feel that there should be a place for everybody, that the small factory must be protected against the large factory, and the cottage producer must be protected against the small factory. The result is to pile inefficiency upon inefficiency. The large factory itself may be more expensive than imports, the small factory may be more expensive still, and the cottage producer may well be the most expensive of them all. A community which gives a place to everybody in this way can be neither competitive nor rich.

One example will illustrate the point. Every Government in Asia gives preference in its stores purchasing to local goods; some of them also give preference to cottage industry over mill production. Every time, this preference means paying a higher price or getting lower quality at the same price, it is in fact a diversion of money which could have been spent on development. How much the diversion amounts to cannot be stated because no figures are published on what these preferences cost, but it is certainly large; and the advantage is equally certainly never measured against the gain that could have come from investing the money.

None of these practices is peculiar to Asia. The world's economically most outrageous preference is the American Government's preference for home-produced goods under the 'Buy American' legislation, and the French and German Governments for many years permitted their cartels to protect inefficient producers quite as thoroughly as they are protected anywhere in Asia. These are rich countries which can perhaps permit themselves these indulgences, though one wonders sometimes whether, if France and Germany had had fewer cartels, they would not also have had fewer Marxists. But the countries of Asia have to make every penny tell if their standards are to go up, and the best way of doing that is still to let the entrepreneur decide for himself how he will spend his money, according to the old test of where he will make the most profit, and for Government to confine itself to giving him a free field and no favour. Every time the bite of competition hurts a man into cutting his costs or widening his market, some contribution is made towards that dynamism in the economy without which Asia cannot become rich.

The application of the profit principle to Government's own expenditure is somewhat more difficult. It is, however, of great importance, because everywhere in Asia a very large percentage of the capital expenditure is bound to be incurred by Government. It is, in general, Government which builds the railways and the roads, provides the electricity and the technological institutes, runs the telephone systems and the ordnance factories, and provides irrigation and improved seed. In most Asian countries Government's capital investment is half or more of the total investment in the modern sector of the economy, and the percentage is likely to increase rather than to diminish.

Government cannot in its schemes be guided purely by profits, because not everything which it does has a value which can be calculated in money terms. A decision on whether one should double a railway track or increase a grant to a University, build a new electrical transmission line or run an anti-malaria campaign, cannot be reached by a calculation of relative money profits; yet to get rid of malaria or to improve University education are not of less real economic advantage because the advantage is not exactly calculable. All that Government can do is to make a rough calculation of relative advantage, and even that will be overlaid by the general priorities the electorate lays down. The public may attach more importance to being healthy or learned than to being rich, and democratic Governments exist to carry out the wishes of their electorates. It is a purely Communist attitude that considers that economic development must be given first priority whether or not the citizens want it so, though it is everywhere true that a community which does not give some attention to riches is unlikely to be able to afford much health or learning either.

Many of Government's decisions must, therefore, in the end be political. That is indeed a reason why as large a sector of the economy as possible should be left to the private individual whose self-interest will drive him to try and create the maximum increase in the national income, unaffected by the long series of extraneous considerations which every Government must take into account.

Outside the social services, however, profit is crucial in Governmental planning also. In all Asian Governmental plans, a very large part of the expenditure goes not to the social services, where the return is difficult to work out, but to strict development, where the return can be estimated with quite reasonable accuracy; and, in strict development, there can be no excuse for not taking the project which gives the highest return. As between two irrigation projects, if one makes a profit of 20 per cent and another of only 4 per cent, one should always take the one which makes 20 per cent. As between an electricity project in an area where the load already exists and another in an area where the load will take a generation to develop, one should take the area where the load already exists. As between the extra railway track to relieve a railway line which is already overloaded, and a new railway into an undeveloped area which will take years to get enough traffic to pay, one should always take the extra track. As between a tube well which will yield 10 per cent in six months and a machine-tool factory which will also yield 10 per cent but only at the end of five years, one should always choose the tube well.

These are elementary principles, only made less elementary by the consideration that the calculation has in some cases to include not only the direct return to Government but also the indirect return to the people benefiting. It may be for example that when one includes the profit of the individual farmer, irrigation in a famine area that only pays 5 per cent may be more profitable in terms of the national income as a whole than irrigation in a desert which pays 10 per cent; and a new railway line that permits many unused resources to be brought immediately into use, may overall be more profitable than extra lines in already exploited areas, even though it shows a lower return to the railway administration. Making all allowances for these calculations, however, many plans in Asia as elsewhere seem to suffer from the fallacy that the late war has shown that finance is no longer important. There are all too many cases like the Hirakud Scheme in the first Indian Five-Year Plan which will only show a net return (i.e. a return above the rate of interest on the capital borrowed) in 1986.

The reasons are many. One is that one big scheme is much easier for a planner to manage than many small ones. Another is that social considerations tend to interfere with economic. A backward area is given schemes because it is backward, even though schemes in an already advanced area might show a much higher return. Another is political. A discontented area, or an area with a powerful Minister in the Cabinet, or an area particularly loyal to the Government in power, is always liable to get more than its fair share. Once a Government departs from the simple criterion of profit, there is no end to the criteria that can be put forward; and it finishes up by sanctioning schemes, none of which make much of a profit, and some of which may make a positive loss, yet all of which can be defended by the most high-sounding of arguments.

Economics is not concerned with the morality or immorality of the profit motive; nor is economics concerned with whether the satisfactions people are prepared to pay for are more or less valuable than those they are not prepared to pay for. All that economics can say is that the best method of giving society the maximum number of satisfactions for the minimum use of real resources is for everybody always to do that which yields the most profit. Profit, it must be repeated, is the measure of the difference between satisfactions (as measured in money) and use of resources (as measured in money). In a free market, if profit is maximum, the relation between effort put in and resources used up on the one hand, and satisfaction obtained on the other, is also at a maximum. This truth is particularly important for Asia, whose poverty means that satisfactions are rare and every resource except unskilled labour scarce. Asia can much less afford to use these scarce resources to give less than the maximum amount of satisfactions that could be squeezed out of them than can the United States or Western Europe.

All Asian planning, therefore, should make profit the centre of its attention. Yet so deep is the aversion to the idea of profit amongst many of the educated of Asia that none of the plans which have been prepared, not even the lengthy and detailed Indian First Five-Year Plan, discusses profit at all. This does not mean that in the preparing of these plans returns—profit—were not considered at all. It does mean that profit was not, as it should have been, the first consideration. The question the planners ask in Asia is not 'How can the national income (which, it must be remembered, is purely a measure of satisfactions in terms of money and takes no account of the relative moral value of those satisfactions) be increased the most at the least cost?' Instead they begin from a whole series of different premises and build upon them. They argue that wealth comes from industrialisation; so they create uneconomic industries and bolster them with protection. They accept that national safety requires a high degree of autarchy; so they build up defence industries and automobile industries which run expensively because their production is too small. They consider that the handicraftsman represents certain social values it is important to preserve; so they keep him in existence by subsidies. They worry about their balance of payments; so they lend money to shipping companies at uneconomically low rates of interest, or talk of synthetic petrol plants. They have the political pressures on their Ministers to consider; so they spread schemes evenly over the country and give special attention to backward areas. They share the intelligentsia's suspicion of the businessman and faith in the State; so they crib and cabin the businessman at every turn and extend the State's sphere constantly, though the State is short of entrepreneurial and managerial talent, and its size gives it a bias towards the long-term low-return scheme rather than the short-term high-return scheme.

The list of errors into which the ignoring of profit leads is long. Separately, they can each be justified by some non-economic consideration, from defence to human charity. Together they are keeping the people of Asia in poverty and squalor and ignorance for longer than is necessary. If the money spent in one five-year plan were all invested at the 20 per cent a businessman would regard as a reasonable return for many propositions, the next five-year plan could be financed from the profits of the first. Asian plans cannot quite be expected to reach that level. Some investments which are necessary, like communications and education, will not give so high a return however carefully one considers profit. What is, nevertheless, striking is that nowhere in Asian plans does it appear to be seriously taken into account that each plan should help pay for the next, that by choosing the most profitable schemes now the whole burden could be eased for the future. Asian planners appear to be prepared to tax, and borrow, and create money, for most of their investment for ever[1].

The reason is perhaps that in Asia, even more than in Europe, politicians are afraid that profits have a somewhat obscene sound, offensive to the purity of mind of their electorates. But nothing creates capital as quickly as profits, and the courageous politician might well find that his electorate would tolerate a good deal of such obscenity in return for the better life for their children it brings with it.

[1] The first sign of change is the Indian Third Five Year Plan is insistence that Government enterprise must make substantial profits to contribute to the Plan!

Chapter 7

THE PLACE OF THE FOREIGNER

THE changes which are necessary for Asian societies so that they may become rich are at once painful and all-embracing. The countries of Asia have to change their habits, their values, their social structures. In the past some of these changes have been imposed by colonial powers; in the present foreign friends may help Asia to achieve others. Most of the changing, however, Asia must do for itself. A change of values involves an inner conversion; changes of habits or of social structure are most effectively brought about by Asia's own leaders; these are tasks above all for the Asian politician. Asia must raise itself in the end by its own bootstraps.

The bootstraps of others are liable to break in the hand. Too much dependence on the foreigner leads to the feeling that development is easy, that its pains and sacrifices can be avoided, that change is not necessary; the oil company or the United States will provide. A people which leaves its developing to others becomes like a remittance-man. It does not work, it does not save, it does not invest, it does not learn new skills, it merely waits for the next allotment of aid—or oil royalty; its politicians, borne up on the flood of easy money, lead their people to no hard decisions, its upper classes add to their ancient privileges American habits of spending. There is still a net gain, something gets built with the foreigner's money; there is the railway which in Saudi Arabia joins the capital to the sea, or the schools and hospitals of Kuwait. But, unless the society changes itself; unless it grows within itself the capacity to take risks, to innovate, to invent, and to apply science to the improvement of everyday life; unless it changes its structure so as to give opportunity to the enterprise of all, and not only of a ruling clique; unless it learns to give the businessman the respect which in the past went only to the scholar and the holder of power, unless, in short, it makes itself economically effective, then, when the foreign money stops and the foreign entrepreneurs lose interest, the development will also stop. If uncle dies, and the remittance-man does not inherit his fortune, what does the remittance-man do next? If the oil runs out, and Saudi Arabia, or Iran, or Venezuela, have not previously become economically modern states, the position of their people will in the end be worse than it was at the beginning, they will have learnt the pleasures of wealth without having learnt how to create it.

Mr. Nehru is right when he insists to his people that the development of India depends on their efforts and their sacrifices, that it is not proper for them to rely on foreigners, or to beg from foreigners, or to change their policies in order to get aid from foreigners. Aid accepted with strings is liable to lead to a frustration and hate and loss of self-respect which will in the long run do more harm than the development the aid paid for did good. Nobody in the end willingly accepts not to be master in his own house; there comes a stage, as has happened in Indonesia, as is happening in Rhodesia, as may happen tomorrow in South Africa, when the determination to be master overcomes the desire to stay comfortable, and revolt imperils the very development which tutelage has produced.

There is no escape. If Asia wants to develop, it must carry the heat and burden of the day itself. Nevertheless the foreigner has a place. He can help in men, in knowledge, in sympathy, above all in money; the money to do the things Asians know need doing but cannot save enough to do themselves. The money can come as gifts, as loans, or as private investment. Each has its place. However it comes, it makes a great deal of difference to the speed of progress.

The thesis which seems to be behind the original American scheme of technical aid—Point Four—that the real need is free 'know-how', free technicians, is quite untrue. Asia does indeed need both know-how and technicians; but, on the whole, the most effective way of providing them is for Asia to have the money to pay for them, whether the payment is made by an Asian firm or Government hiring the skill it needs, or through the profits of a foreign private company whose managerial team is inseparable from its investment. The lone technical adviser, though useful sometimes for surveying ports or offering advice on the scope of a new industry, is not usually very effective unless he is an actual employee of the Asian Government concerned. Governments are like everybody else. If they do not pay for a man they do not make proper use of him. He does not get properly integrated into their organisation; he writes too many reports and does not do enough executive work; his advice, being free, is frequently not listened to; he may not even be very good —one does not look gift horses in the mouth.

The technique of the free technician is of advantage in two cases. The first is where it is politically embarrassing for a government to have to justify to its public the use of foreigners, especially when, as frequently happens, the salaries they have to be paid are much higher than those given to locals. The men are needed; even in India, technically the most advanced country except Japan, almost every major scheme in the Five-Year Plan requires the employment of some foreign technicians; but, if they are free, they can be justified more easily to a public which does not always easily understand that within, say, the general category of civil engineers, of which the country may have enough, there may be a special category of, say, high-dam engineers, of which there is a shortage. For these purposes, and to this extent, U.N. Technical Assistance, Point Four, and so on, are necessary; but it is a quite limited function.

The second way in which foreigners not paid for locally are of value is in education; and this time the value is very great indeed. Asian schools and universities are always short of money and of staff. Both they and Western universities and schools would benefit greatly from a much greater exchange of staff than ever occurs at present. The Western historian, for example, would benefit from seeing societies still operating in the way his own did in the past. The Western economist or sociologist would learn that many of his axioms are merely generalisations from the quite special experience of his own society. Grants directly from Western Governments to Asian Governments or universities for such exchanges would be inappropriate; but there is no reason why Western Governments should not finance such bodies as Head Masters' Associations, or Conferences of University Vice-Chancellors; only they are fitted to choose the men to go out, and to see that their careers do not suffer as a result of the interruption but, on the contrary, benefit from the wider experience it gives them; only they, too, can fit the Asian teacher or researcher into their own schools and universities.[1]

For sympathy and understanding Asia, like the rest of us, has endless need. Independence is new to most areas, democracy to all; to some neither has yet come. Inappropriate criticism and unwarranted pressure from outside undermine the stability without which no economic progress is possible. Those who do not recognise that the issues between India and Pakistan are deep and difficult, that it is no use attacking the arguments of the one with the premises of the other, help to divert into defence resources both need for development. Those who talk of the corruption, the incompetence, or the squalor of the East, without considering whether they are diminishing or whether the govern-

---

[1] This has been recognized by Great Britain's new Department of Technical Co-operation, and has long been acted on by France.

ments and peoples are doing something about them or not, provide powerful arguments for the Communists with their thesis that revolution and people's courts, and not reform and the rule of law, are the proper cures for such deep-seated evils. Those who disapprove of Mr. Nehru's independence of judgement might perhaps remember how like it is to pre-war American policy. The new governments in Asia must be handled with the gentleness of Her Majesty's Leader of the Opposition dealing with Her Majesty's Prime Minister, not the roughness of Senator McCarthy chasing the State Department.

The really important assistance Asia needs from the West, however, more important than either sympathy or men, is investment. The investment may be by a Western company, or it may be by an Asian Government using western money; it may be productive of cash dividends or of dividends in the health and knowledge of the people. Whatever its form, it is investment which is the need.

There is almost unlimited room for aid. The popular thesis, that the absorptive power of Asian economies is limited, is quite untrue. Admittedly, Asia can take in only small numbers of foreign technicians and relatively small amounts of dollar machinery at a time. Therefore, so long as aid is confined to paying for what comes from outside, it must be small.[1] But it should not be so limited. Requirements in education, for example, or health, or communications, are enormous, but they are not in the main requirements for imports. Countries like India or Pakistan could spend many millions on building schools and dispensaries, colleges and village roads, and still be able to find the staff and the materials within themselves. And, were the money so spent, the effect on economic progress would be great. An educated and healthy population at last brought into proper contact with the market could display economic initiative in a way which is quite impossible for the illiterate, the malaria-ridden, and the producer isolated from his market. New methods would be propagated much more quickly, intensive farming for milk and fruit and vegetables would be more widely possible and harvests would not be lost because of disease at harvest time. There would be a thousand ways in which the economy would benefit, and within a very few years.

The difficulty for Asian Governments is that they cannot get the money for all these needs by taxation; and the return, though large, is not immediate enough, and does not express itself

---

[1] Small can be a very relative term. India needs some £2000 million for its Third Five Year Plan, all for things coming from outside.

directly enough in larger tax revenues, to justify borrowing. Outside help would enable the governments to spend more of their own currency on bigger programmes, and then to counteract the inflationary effect by using the aid currency to import consumer goods. That way the absorptive capacity would be almost unlimited, almost as unlimited as the needs. Money spent on health, education, and roads, would moreover, have the advantage that it would come up against few of those bottle-necks of lack of skill which so often make industrialisation so difficult. There is no lack of students with the education to make primary teachers or of half-employed agricultural labourers able to make roads. The amount of money required would not even be very large. Two hundred million dollars spent on Indian village roads would provide connections with their market for forty or fifty thousand villages; the same sum would build primary schools in all the villages that still have not got them.

Aid is vital, for aid could make quickly possible that huge increase in the social services, which is required if Asians are to know enough and be healthy enough, and to move themselves and their goods freely enough, to be able one day to advance really quickly themselves. Almost equally important, however, are loans. All over Asia there are dozens of schemes, railways, irrigation works, telephone lines, even, as in India, steelworks, which would pay their 5 per cent or 6 per cent or perhaps 10 per cent, and would give new vitality to whole sections of the economy in addition, but which nobody has the money to do. Before 1914, the money could have been borrowed in the London or Paris capital markets, at 3 per cent or 4 per cent, on the general credit of the borrowing government. But since then there have been many repudiations, and England and France no longer have the money to lend, however much they may sometimes strain themselves for a member of the Commonwealth or of the French Union, out of reasons of sentiment. Borrowing from the World Bank is an only partially satisfactory substitute, since it lends for the foreign currency part of schemes while frequently what is required is the whole amount. Only the American capital market could play the rôle once played by London and Paris. Unfortunately, American investors in foreign bonds lost much of the money they lent in the '20s; there is no tradition in America, as there is in England, of holding sound overseas bonds as part of a balanced portfolio; above all, the law of most American States does not make foreign bonds an authorised investment for insurance companies.

The first necessity is a change in the law; the second is a

willingness amongst American investors to accept the not very large risk of buying the bonds of the more creditworthy Asian Governments, a willingness which cannot perhaps come until the U.S. and Canada themselves are less hungry for capital than in the present boom, and until American tariffs and customs regulations are sufficiently relaxed to enable Asian countries to earn, directly or by triangular trade, the interest on their borrowings. Until that happens, not only will the American investor hesitate to lend, but Asian governments like the Indian and the Ceylonese which have what is today the very rare distinction of never having defaulted on a debt, will hesitate to borrow. At present, the American Government frequently does the exact opposite of what is required. It has subsidised synthetic rubber, it has used a government monopoly of imports to drive down the price of tin, it has a tariff even on so non-competitive an import from Asia as jute goods—all actions which reduce severely Asia's capacity to earn dollars, and thus to pay for the machinery, the technicians, even the food, it needs for development. These may have been suitable policies for the 1930s. They are suitable no longer.

Most useful of all forms of foreign capital is that provided by the private investor. The amounts are, it is true, never likely to be really large. The biggest investment since the war has been by England in India; perhaps 60 million dollars per year has been put in, gross. Nothing comparable has occurred anywhere else in free Asia, except for oil. The investment in Pakistan has been small, in Ceylon and Indonesia there has been net disinvestment. India's 60 million dollars a year itself comes quite considerably from retained profits, and has been partly cancelled by disinvestment. The maximum private investment that might be possible for free Asia as a whole, and in the most favourable of atmospheres, would be the 1000 million dollars that Canada has on occasion absorbed per year. Today's practical possibilities are of course considerably lower than this not very high figure. Whatever was put in, however, would have a value out of all proportion to its size. If the enterprises were unsuccessful, the Asian country would keep the physical assets and have no contingent foreign exchange liability against them. If they were successful, and most would be, they would make a whole series of contributions to Asian development.

First, there is the actual production they create, the substitution of rubber or coffee for jungle, or the making of soap or hessian or clothes, tinned pineapple or petrol or caustic soda, where previously there were imports or nothing. This production brings about an immediate and obvious improvement of the standard of life. Then there are the indirect advantages. The big foreign firm brings with it all the attitudes which are required for economic development since the whole dynamic of its being is expansion. It judges alternative ways of using its money by the proper criterion of profitability, it ploughs back a large percentage of its earnings, it creates a cadre of local managers, it builds up a labour force of genuine industrial workers (not just villagers lost in the city), it pays its taxes—and the bigger the firm, the larger the taxes; and it gives the consumer the benefits of technical research, mass production, wide distribution and constant quality.

One might have thought that an institution so beneficent would have been universally popular. The behaviour of governments, Asian and Western, however, makes it clear, though odd, that it is not. Asian governments are apt to treat the foreign investor as a wild beast whom it is necessary to cage; without permission he is normally not allowed to invest at all, and even if he is allowed, he is checked by a whole series of leashes. He must take a proportion, perhaps a majority, of local capital, he must have a certain percentage of local employees, he must get permission to expand, or to locate his factory, or to rationalise his operations. That some of these restrictions also hit his local competitors is small consolation; they still destroy efficiency. Nor is his home government usually any more sympathetic. It may tax his overseas profits and prohibit his emigration, like the British Government in the 50's; or it may not allow him fully to set off overseas losses against home profits and may fail to support him adequately against unjust treatment, like the American Government. Foreign investment nevertheless continues. There are always some brave pioneers, and some firms who have no option; but if the foreign investor is once more to perform his wealth creating rôle on the scale of the days before 1914, he must be given back the freedom to decide and the freedom to accumulate which then was his.

For Asia to develop as it should, it needs all the investment it can get, whether from the savings of its own people or from outside loans, from Government aid or private enterprise. Too much time has already been lost in arguing about methods. What is needed is money, by whatever method.

If the money is to come, however, there must be two changes of attitude. First, the developed countries must recognise, far more than they have done hitherto, that to assist in the development of Asia is at once a moral duty and in their own interest: a moral duty because loving one's neighbour includes rescuing him from squalor and poverty; in their own interest because there can be no safety for freedom and democracy so long as two-thirds of the world live in a poverty which tempts them perpetually to every nostrum of escape, whether it be dictatorship, Communism or plain anarchy; in their own interests too because the quicker the underdeveloped countries develop, the bigger the market and the source of supply they will become; there may sometimes be short run problems of adjustment as when an underdeveloped country learns to make something it has previously imported or begins to use itself a raw material which it has previously exported. But in the long run people buy and sell more, abroad as well as at home, when they are rich than when they are poor. Second, the countries of Asia themselves must recognise that the foreigner can help, they must cease to see in every foreigner bearing gifts (or simply an investment on which he hopes to make a handsome profit) a Trojan horse come to infiltrate their new independence. Attitudes have already begun to change in these directions, on both sides, in India or Pakistan or Ceylon as in the United States or England. As the underdeveloped countries become more self-confident, they are less afraid that a foreign company, however big, may challenge their sovereignty. As the developed countries begin to realise the depth of the determination in the underdeveloped to catch up, their eagerness to help increases. Once the change is complete, the rest will follow. A Western country which considers assistance to the development of Asia as both its duty and its interest will hesitate neither to vote aid, nor to open its capital market to loans, nor to give tax exemptions to its nationals who invest in Asia. An Asian country which feels that foreign participation could make the process of development slightly less painful will welcome aid, borrow abroad whenever it can do so profitably, and make foreign capital and managers at home. Once there is the will, the details of the way will be easy enough to find.

Chapter 8

GOVERNMENT INITIATIVE

ASIAN Governments have to take more economic initiative
than Western Governments. The facts, not Socialist doctrine, make them do so. There are so many concrete tasks
the State must do because no private entrepreneur can or will,
either because he cannot find the money, or because he cannot
bear the initial losses, or because he cannot acquire the land
without an outcry he cannot face, or because he cannot collect
his dues. More important than these concrete tasks, however,
and less explicable in terms of any one difficulty or combination
of difficulties, is the initiative Asian states have to take because
development in Asia means change. The changes which have to
be brought about in Asia, moreover, do not arise naturally from
the growth of Asian society; they are a diversion, a transformation of the whole of society along lines which experience elsewhere has shown are necessary for economic development, but
which the communities of Asia can only achieve by conscious
effort, conscious leadership from above through the instrument
of the State. Asian peasants cannot themselves turn into modern
farmers, the State must show them how.

Laisser-faire is an admirable guide to economic action in a
society where people think economically, a society where people
have enough information to be able to decide where their interest lies, and enough eagerness for profit to be able to weigh
different possibilities for making money one against the other.
In Asia people like that are exceptions, often rather despised
exceptions.

It is true that amongst Asian businessmen one meets such
people with reasonable frequency. The big business acts in
reasonable accord with economic principle and is normally capable of balancing one investment against another to see which
will give the greatest long-term benefit. The small businessman
may have a very keen nose for money; unfortunately, it is usually
a very short-term nose. A profit tomorrow has an attraction for
him, as against a profit in twenty years' time, out of all proportion to the twenty-year rate of interest.

Big business, however, is still a small section of any Asian society, and small business by no means a big one. The majority of
Asian populations do not conduct their lives in accordance with

economics at all. They usually put their duty to God and their duty to their fellow villagers well before making a profit, and even where tradition and religion leave them free to go in for development, they very often do not have the knowledge to do so effectively. Economically speaking, therefore, they are doubly handicapped. They will not kill cows or eat pork, because of religion; they do not use enough fertiliser or weed killer because they do not have the knowledge of what they should use or how.

Moreover, in Asia, because it is poor, even if people both want to make money and know what to do in order to make it, they often cannot find the necessary initial investment. This is true for the individual villager, who is frequently unable to pay for sulphate of ammonia or a new well, however much he may realise they would be profitable. It is equally true for the village community as a whole, where very often no private individual or combination of private individuals can be found with resources large enough to do certain things. The villagers of a district may know perfectly well that the water to be obtained by damming a particular river could greatly increase their incomes; they may still not have the money to build the dam. The traders of a town may know that an asphalt road or branch railway would greatly increase their commerce; that does not mean that they can successfully form a company to build them.

A very large burden of economic initiative is therefore thrown on Asian Governments, which in the West can be left to private individuals to carry.

This burden takes two main forms. The first is the need to provide the utilities without which no modern economy can function. This is fairly obvious. These utilities in Asia are frequently too expensive for private individuals or corporations. The second is more complicated. The great mass of people in Asia now have a vague feeling that life could be easier and fuller than it is, but in most cases they do not have very much idea of what they themselves need to do in order to make it so. That knowledge is still mainly confined to the westernised middle class. Government is expected to mobilise it, to put it within the reach of the ordinary man.

The utilities which Government has to provide, and very often did provide even at the height of the nineteenth century, are in Asia very extensive. In the past it was virtually never possible to raise locally, except sometimes in Japan, more than a few million dollars for any project. For some large projects, some of the earlier Indian Railways for example, large amounts could be raised by foreign-owned companies, but in many cases in the past, and normally in the present, really large amounts can be raised only by Government. Nobody else has good enough credit. The World Bank, for example, when lending to a private borrower insists on a Government guarantee; amongst private companies probably none but the oil companies can now borrow in any western market for investment in Asia on the scale which is possible in the London market for so small but credit-worthy an Asian Government as Ceylon. The result of this famine of capital for utilities has been that most of Asia's ports and railways, which between them represent perhaps one-half of the total investment in the modern sector of Asia's economy, have always been built by Government. In addition, Government, as everywhere else, builds the roads, and in recent years, as hydro-electricity has become more and more important, a larger and larger proportion of the electricity works have been constructed by Government. In other words, in Asia virtually the whole substructure of a modern economy has been provided by the State, and unless the State takes these initiatives it is almost impossible for the private individual to build a factory or run a plantation. He would be able neither to move his goods, nor, in many cases, to get power for his machinery.

Even more important is State initiative in providing the major investments required for peasant agriculture. Over much of Asia the difference between a good crop and a bad one is whether or not the crop has had enough water. Irrigation is therefore vital, in a way it never is in Western Europe. Indeed, the peasant himself has made very large investments in irrigation. Large parts of Asia, the Ganges valley, for instance, are dotted with wells and waterlifts and small dams. But the peasant's resources are small. He can rarely afford a tube well, he can never afford a major dam, no matter how many of his fellows may co-operate with him. The result is that one of the main sources of the strength of the State in Eastern countries has always been the State control of the larger irrigation works. In countries like Iraq, when the State weakened, the irrigation works went out of order, and the whole community was affected as it never was by a weakening of central authority in, say, Scotland or Ireland. In Asia only the State has the resources to build the major dams, only the State can decide, and having decided, enforce its decision, how the water should be divided, and only the State can be sure of recovering the water rate sufficiently regularly and sufficiently cheaply to make its schemes profitable. So, whether one thinks of the Gal Oya scheme in Ceylon, or of the Sukkur Barrage in

Pakistan, or of the Bhakra-Nangal in India, one always finds that the really big schemes are State-run.

The burden of providing utilities is a heavy one for Asian States. Half the money in the plans Asian countries put forward for the first Colombo plan period was to be spent in power, communications, transport and irrigation.

The other task of Asian governments is more exacting than creating utilities. In Asia, the Governments have to change the minds and habits of their people, for without new knowledge and new attitudes economic progress must be desperately slow. There are western parallels, the United States Government's soil conservation programmes and extension services, or the French Government's alarm about alcoholism or the British Government's preaching of hard work and productivity, but they are limited and partial. In the West, it is the citizen who normally shows the way to Government, not government which educates the citizen. What is needed in Asia is more like what the Communist Governments have been doing, Russian Stakhanovism or the Chinese emancipation of women; that is one reason why Communism so often appeals, not in spite of, but positively because of, its terror. People feel that nothing less will shake the habits of centuries.

The whole social structure has to be changed, and in many ways; capitalism, individual enterprise, freedom, thrift, all these are in Asia today revolutions as enormous as they were in nineteenth-century Europe. Some of the changes needed are at first sight in no way economic, and many of them are not primarily inspired by economic motives. For example, the Indian Constitution bans untouchability. Such conduct as discriminates against untouchables, for example, by refusing them entry into a hotel or water from a public well, is a crime, and both the Centre and the States in India give certain advantages in education and employment to untouchables. The motive is the Gandhian feeling that the whole institution of untouchability is a perversion of Hinduism. The result is to enable untouchables once more to hold up their heads in society as equals; which in turn has a whole series of economic consequences. It is much easier for them now to go on strike for more wages, or to leave the village, or to become peasant farmers. It is now possible also for them to produce educated leaders of their own who can change the habits of the community much quicker than any outsider; and whether the habit is drunkenness, or improvidence, or lack of hygiene, changing it has economic as well as moral effects.

A whole series of such changes is required, changes which will

alter the very way the people think and the content of knowledge in their minds. And in all of this the governments must, in
Asia, take the lead. Admittedly, about the way people think
governments can perhaps do little directly; but government,
through the educational system and the nation building departments, very largely controls the sort of knowledge they have in
their minds; and as the content of the people's mind changes, so
will gradually the way they think.

The fundamental difficulty of Asia is ignorance, and particularly peasant ignorance. Even the lack of savings is partly the
result of the peasants' not knowing how profitably they could be
used. Illiteracy is part of the trouble; the peasant is managing a
little business, and he cannot run it well if he cannot keep
accounts or read a receipt or a market report or count change or
calculate whether one seed will give him a better return than
another. But the difficulty goes deeper than illiteracy; it affects
even the literate. The peasant has often just not heard of all the
discoveries which, largely in the last twenty years, have made it
possible for him to improve his life. So the State must tell him.

In the old-fashioned village if the young farmer picked up the
traditional lore of his ancestors, that was all he needed to know.
Except for a very few novelties like quinine and vaccination, the
outside world had very little to offer him. This position has
changed completely in the last generation. Now there are sulpha
drugs to cure his dysentery and paludrine for his malaria, anti-
biotics for a whole range of his diseases and DDT to kill the
insects which carry them before he gets ill at all. There are weed-
killers and pesticides to protect his crops, better seed and new
manures to give him bigger crops, artificial insemination and
rinderpest vaccines to provide him with better and healthier
cattle, contour bunding techniques to protect his land from erosion and tube-wells to give him water from deeper layers and
over a wider area. The list of discoveries is long and the individual peasant cannot hope to know of more than a few of them.
Nor, with communications and advertising media as bad as they
are over most of Asia, is it possible for most private firms to
popularise their discoveries with any speed or to penetrate really
deeply, though an occasional life-saver like penicillin spreads
with the rapidity of a forest fire. Only government has the universal representation and only government has the authority to
introduce all these innovations quickly. The Indian Community
Projects, for example, are an attempt to bring to the villager at
one time and through one agency all the chief ways of bettering
his lot modern science has made possible, and, though they have

only been going a short time, there are already many signs that success can be achieved by an approach which really sells to the villager the story of how he can make himself, his family, his crops and his cattle better and healthier by more work, improved methods and more modern remedies. The villager is not a fool nor is he, like so many European slum dwellers, the moronic bottom of society. In Asia the villager is three-quarters of the community, and there is in the Asian village as much intelligence and enterprise and willingness to learn as in any European residential suburb. The State has to bring the knowledge to him in assimilable form. He will do the rest.[1]

Nothing is more important for progress than changing the attitude of the villager. But he is not alone in his ignorance. Most of the rest of the community is equally unaware of most of the recent discoveries which now make a rapid advance for Asia possible for the first time. To them also the lead must largely be given by government. If machines are to perform their function of lightening human labour, government must provide technical schools and polytechnics and training workshops, or the machines will not have enough mechanics and fitters. If the big firms and the commercial departments of government are to expand the economy, colleges must be provided in which budding clerks and potential managers can obtain attitudes of discipline and regularity and knowledge of book-keeping and typewriting, management accounting or industrial chemistry.[2] If there is to be family planning to reduce the terrible waste of infant and maternal mortality, and to give development the chance to catch up with population, government will have to provide most of the clinics. If there is to be proper private enterprise even, government will have to protect the honest business man by seeing that taxes are not evaded, to protect the investor by regulating Stock Exchanges and enforcing a proper Companies Act—nothing damages investment more than the looting of shareholders by directors and managing agents—and to protect the worker by Factory Acts and proper conciliation procedures.

These are heavy burdens for any State to carry. No Western government has to face the prospect of transforming its whole society. In the West the people forced family planning on the governments. The accounts of the best companies are taken as the model for the Companies Acts. Private universities and grammar schools provided the model for the State's educational

---

[1] Community Projects are discussed in detail in chapter XVIII.
[2] See also chapter XIV.

efforts. Before the welfare State there were the friendly societies. And so on. The State's function is normally to generalise an idea or an institution which has already arisen spontaneously within the society. The State does not innovate. In Asia on the other hand the government must lead, or no one will. That the government is sometimes handicapped by inadequate servants and prejudiced politicians, that it is on occasion ineffective, is an argument for making it better; it cannot be an argument for doing nothing. The people want to become 'modern', and they do not themselves know how. If democratic governments do not show them, they will try something else. The *status quo* is no longer enough.

When there is so much to do, and when the State's means of doing it are so limited, it may seem odd that Asian States so often go beyond the necessities the facts force upon them into enterprises nothing but Socialist doctrine can justify. The State is short of money, of officials, of technicians, of politicians; yet it constantly goes beyond the functions it has to perform, because if it does not nobody will, into those which could be left to others. Even the small States run international airlines, though they are adequately served by the lines of others. Or road transport is nationalised, though private operators were already providing adequate services. Or electricity distribution in the big cities is taken over, only to go on afterwards in exactly the same way as it went on before. Or the State builds steelworks, though its private steelworks could have done all the expansion necessary had their prices not been held down to an uneconomic level.

The examples are legion. For each one by itself reasons can be given, though the reasons, it is to be noted, are not always economic. An international airline saves foreign exchange and gives prestige. A State road transport service may have better-kept buses, or better drawn-up timetables than private services. State electricity distribution may be able to borrow 1 per cent cheaper than private companies. State steelworks give the State a control of the most commanding of the economy's heights. The reasons are as multitudinous as the examples, and of an infinitely varying validity.

The common feature which runs through them all, however, is that each has been considered separately, and always with a bias towards Socialism, towards the solution which takes power away from the businessman and puts it in the hands of the bureaucrat, the politician, and the intelligentsia, who in Asia matter so much more. Because of this combination of pragmatism and bias, the questions which ought to be asked are very rarely even raised. Rarely is there any sign that anybody has said at any stage 'Could the money, the officials, the technicians, the Parliamentary and Ministerial time which this will cost be better used on some task nobody but the State can perform?'

Worse still is the waste of officials, experts, politicians and everybody's time on controls. The countries of Asia need exchange control on capital transfers; they may need import controls at times when the terms of trade turn sharply against them, or when they are importing unusually large quantities of capital equipment. There is probably no other control which performs any useful function, and there are many which positively hamper development. The reasons for control are many, and politically, in terms of doing what the electorate wants, they may be valid. Asian intelligentsias are frequently so suspicious of their businessmen that they are prepared to let them operate only if they can feel that through their instrument, the State, they can check and cross-check everything the businessman does. So one gets the innumerable demands for returns and statistics, the perpetual necessity for licences and permissions, the restrictions and the ministerial or bureaucratic suggestions under which business labours in almost all free Asia. It harms business. It also harms the State both because so much of the limited time of the State's best men is taken up in considering particular cases and because so many of the group pressures and conflicts of interest which abound in every society are thus concentrated upon the country's political headquarters. The result is not necessarily corruption, though in some Asian countries it produces corruption on a large scale; but the result is always and necessarily an immense diversion of effort from development into argument and supervision, a diversion which the States of Asia, with their limited number of men with the qualifications for development, cannot afford.

From the point of view of development it would be far better to have a general law than controls—for example, a tariff, as against an import control, or a general prohibition of new industries in particular places as against a control on the location of factories. The general law might cause an occasional hard case; but everybody would know where he was, all plans would be adjusted to the law, neither the businessman nor the official would waste time in argument. To vest discretion in an official is an easy way out when the politicians have not quite made up their mind what they want to do, but feel they must do something. It would, however, save everybody's time and prevent much frustration of effort, if the politicians would instead make up their mind in the first place what it is they want to permit and what to prohibit. The States of Asia have too much to do to fiddle away the time of their top officials and politicians in deciding whether 'X' should be allowed to import 100 bales of cloth or 'Y' to export 100 tons of groundnuts.

Part Three

POLITICAL

———◆❖◆———

Chapter 9

THE RÔLE OF THE POLITICIAN

IN Asia to develop means to change, and to change in directions governed more by the experience of the developed countries than by the spontaneous forces operating in Asian society itself. If India or Indonesia or Pakistan wish to become as rich as the United States or Switzerland, they cannot be left to grow, as the United States and Switzerland grew. They must be guided. Their people must be given a lead. Their politicians must make of development and the changes it requires the very centre of politics. That is why in Asia chronologically the first necessity for development is the right politicians. Others, economists, savers, entrepreneurs, officials, workers, all have their part to play; but they are only instrumentalists, the politician is at once composer and conductor in a concert which has the whole electorate for audience.

Politicians are vital even in industrially developed countries. The level of English taxation is cutting at the root of initiative. The balance of vested interests which constitutes so much of French politics has often threatened to make the French economy uncompetitive. The Democratic Party's suspicion of business probably delayed American recovery in the slump of the '30s. Governmental preoccupation with war preparations distorted the whole development of German industry.

They are doubly, quadruply vital in the underdeveloped countries of Asia.

In the advanced economies the politician can afford sometimes merely to follow his people. In the backward ones he must always lead. In the advanced economies the people have themselves made the material revolution which has happened in the last 150 years and they continue to show a high level of economic and scientific initiative. Ford built his business, Rutherford split the atom, without any politician helping. Indeed, in some of these countries the public have now acquired a certain sense

63

of self-preservation which prevents them from voting for politicians with no sense of how the economy works; it is hard, for example, to imagine an English Chancellor of the Exchequer with no conception of business at all.

But the damage done to Britain since the war, by its politicians and Treasury official's subordination of growth to sterling's international position is a warning of what can happen even to one of the leaders of nineteenth-century development. In economies more backward than the British, the politician's problem is more difficult still, his temptations greater, his role correspondingly more crucial. He has to lead, but he has also to represent, at least, if the country is democratic; and here it is the development of backward democracies with which we are primarily concerned. Doubtless, if one wants economic development regardless of all other values, there are other, undemocratic, ways of getting it. These make the politician's life easier, for they permit him to shoot his opponents. They do not make his role less vital, for he still chooses both the economic objectives and which opponents are to be shot. Here, however, it is assumed that an economic advance is not important enough to be worth purchasing by mass murder and the loss of freedom. This discussion will, therefore, be confined to the function of the democratic politician who cannot simply drive his people, but must also persuade them, who cannot make policy as he will, but must also get himself re-elected.

His difficulty is that in most of Asia it is precisely the wishes and the prejudices of the electorate which stand in the way of development. They *like* their society static, or their handicrafts protected, or their children uneducated, or their pigs uneaten, or their cows kept alive, or their reproduction uncontrolled. The list of the prejudices, beliefs and attitudes which stand in the way of development in one Asian country or another (and, indeed, in Western countries, too) is an endless one.

The fact that some belief, or prejudice, or attitude, stands in the way of an improvement in the standard of living is no proof that it is wrong. At the most it can only be an argument for re-examination. It is certainly no reason for committing sin, and may not even be a reason for social solecism, that one will be better off as a result. Far too much Western criticism of Asia rests on the unstated premise that whenever those societies have an attitude or belief which Western societies do not happen to have, and which also slows down or prevents development, then the attitude or belief must be changed, not because it is sinful or because it makes people unhappy, but simply because it makes them poorer. Yet this is a test few Westerners would accept for their own society. To take an extreme example, they would not accept euthanasia for old-age pensioners in order to reduce the burden of the aged on the working population, or compulsory sterilisation of the poor in order to reduce the cost of State education; nor has the fact that engagement rings are a quite unproductive expenditure of resources which would obviously be better invested in buying Savings Certificates had the slightest effect on the ordinary woman's determination to have one.

In dealing with other societies, one should pay them the compliment of assuming that they will not change their beliefs for reasons less strong than those for which the critic would change his own. This the politician knows, the economist far too frequently ignores. If a Hindu believes that killing cows is a sin so profound that it will cause him to be reborn in the next life as an animal, it is irrelevant to point out, as the economist so often does, that a cow which is too old for milking eats but gives no return; the argument is as much a waste of time as telling an English suburban housewife that she should have her dog put down because the meat he eats worsens Britain's balance of payments. If one wishes to change the Hindu attitude to cows, the only effective way is the politician's, to argue that the Vedas do not in fact require such respect for cows, and that it is a subsequent accretion which can permissibly be sloughed off again. Whether this is correct or not it is not for a non-Hindu to say; but it is obviously the best line of attack. Similarly with the Muslim aversion to eating pork. It is doubtless true that this interferes seriously with the efficiency of peasant farming; the pig is an ideal supplement to cereal-growing. But it is highly offensive to the people of the Muslim countries to assume that by proving that the pig is an admirable source of animal protein, and really quite clean, they will at once break what is to them the law of God. Their politicians know better. Either they attack the religion altogether, as the Communists do, or they leave the issue of pork aside. So again with Roman Catholics and birth control, or with the Israeli Government and sabbath observance. Theology cannot be answered by economics, only by better theology. The rules of the faith may be quietly ignored, or they may be re-interpreted, or it may be claimed that in new circumstances they no longer apply. What does not work, at least with decent people, is to tell them that they would be better off if only they would break a few of the commandments. It is the politician's strength that he knows, as the economist so often seems not to, that beliefs must be attacked with other beliefs. It is because the politician knows this in his bones—or else he is no politician—that he is so much more important than anybody else in economic development.

It is not only religious beliefs that he has to change, although they are very properly the most resistant. There are also the secular attitudes and prejudices, which are easier to alter, both because they have no divine sanction and because with them it is sometimes possible to be direct and make an appeal to material interest.

One may take two obvious examples. Many parts of Asia grow cereals and are hot. Work is much less attractive on a hot day than on a cold one, and on a very hot day, it is positively repellent, as we all know from personal experience. Cereal growing, also, though it requires intensive labour at certain times of the year, has at other times long gaps with nothing to do, in contrast to the mixed farming of Western Europe where there are always the animals to look after. Therefore in much of Asia there has developed a pattern of life, with much leisure, many festivals and ceremonies, and a considerable folk-culture. The interweaving of art and life in Bali, for example, is an attractive pattern, attractive enough to enchant most Westerners who come into contact with it. It is also a pattern which leaves a very small surplus over subsistence indeed.

If these societies want to be better-off, they must put more emphasis on work, less on leisure. There must be less factory absenteeism caused by long leave to go home for harvest or marriages. There must be more weeding and harrowing and less sitting on a cot under a tree, less talking in coffee houses and more study, less theory and more actual field work. All this will make life harder, and probably drabber; it may involve the sacrifice of old values. It might, for example, be necessary to accept efficiency as a test of whom one employs and whom one retrenches, where, traditionally, both in India and China, the feeling has always been in favour of sharing the work and retrenchment by juniority. But at the end of the hard work and the new values Asia would be much richer.

However great the increase in material welfare from such changes, there would be many imponderables to be set on the other side; and it is the politician's function to know both sides of the equation, where the economist knows only one. The economist can prove that if one ceases to have large parties for marriages and invests the money in irrigation instead, then in x years there is a probability of y that one will be z per cent better off. What he cannot say, since it is a matter of values and not of economics, is whether z per cent is enough to compensate for the impoverishment of one's social life; whether it is a good enough reason for not having one's friends to one's wedding now that one's children will in due course have more clothes to wear and more cigarettes to smoke. This is a balance each individual must make for himself; and leadership can come only from the politician, or perhaps sometimes the priest. It is, indeed, noticeable that when a lead is given in Asia on such a subject, it nearly always does come from the politicians. It is Mr. Nehru who tells his people to work hard, to save, to be less rigid about cows, to accept present sacrifice for the sake of future wealth. India's economists are, naturally enough, not inclined to such simple propositions. They are concerned with more technical problems, like the amount of inflation which may be expected from a given quantity of deficit financing. It is, moreover, also noticeable that when Mr. Nehru talks to his people on subjects apparently economic, his arguments very rarely are in fact economic. When he enjoins them to work hard, he talks not of production bonuses, but of the glory of India; when he adjures them to subscribe to a Government loan, he talks not of the rate of return, but of making India strong enough to stand against all the winds that blow. If Asians are to face the awful strain of pulling themselves up by their own bootstraps there must be some motive more powerful than money; self-respect perhaps, or the love of one's neighbour. To these depths of man's nature only the politician can appeal.

Because he has to appeal to man's deepest instincts, the politician's approach to economic development has to be less direct than the economist's, the official's or the businessman's. He knows that the main road has many, and well defended, barricades on it, so he gets off it and goes through the fields; it is longer and more zig-zag, but it is also surer in the long run. Thus, a father who believes that the virtue of his daughter will be destroyed if she becomes a stenographer is hardly likely to let her become one merely because he is told that an adequate supply of women stenographers is necessary if the national income is to rise by 2 per cent per annum. The straight economic appeal will not work. What has to be got at is the attitude to morals, not only of the father, but of society as a whole; of the potential fathers-in-law who might look down on the girl; of the boys who might refuse to marry her; of the men in the office who might not treat her with enough respect. What the politician has to do is to persuade the father that far from her virtue being lost his daughter will marry better; and fathers will not be persuaded for long unless their daughters do, in fact, marry better. Exhortation is not enough. There must be an actual change in society. Arguments about the economic working of society as a whole are simply not relevant. Fathers are not interested in overall figures, whether of personal income or of percentages of plan fulfilment. They are interested in their daughters; the only economic argument they have historically found convincing is their own need for the money their daughters may earn.

This may seem an extreme example. But for most people life is governed by what they think proper rather than by what, on a strict calculation, pays; the workman, for example, will normally do neither appreciably more nor appreciably less work than his mates think right; one of the major reasons for the difference between the productivity of the European and the American workman, both, after all, of the same stock, is the difference in the attitude of their mates to such questions as the acceptance of innovation or the speeding up of the pace of work.

In all Asian societies there are many such attitudes which are quite independent of economics. The Asian politician can, therefore, neither simply let well alone, nor simply draw up a plan and leave his civil service to carry it out. Before he can leave people alone, he has to lead them into creating an environment in which their desires, their weaknesses, and their forms of charity will be such that they will lead to saving, investment, a propensity for invention, the capacity for mobility and, above all, a willingness to change; for all but the very slowest of economic advances involve change, and change on a considerable, often revolutionary, scale. In Europe, the politician's task has been made easier both by the semi-independence of the mediaeval town, whose dependence on industry created in its governing class a very keen appreciation of the pre-requisites of economic development, and by Puritanism, whose emphasis on thrift, hard work and self-reliance, made generally admired precisely those virtues without which no community can become rich. The Asian politician has neither of these advantages. Asia's governing classes in the past mostly valued ostentation, not thrift; the looting of merchants in war, not the building up of business in peace; the freedom from work which came from noble birth, not the hard effort on which crops and handicrafts depend. To the great Hindu lawgiver, Manu, even agriculture was degrading, and only now is the upper-caste landowner of Northern India, the Rajput or the Brahmin, beginning to put his hand to the plough.

That is why in so many underdeveloped countries, politicians and electors alike have so often plumped for a plan. They feel that they cannot rely on the people's own initiative, that the public's whole attitude must be changed first. They feel that can only be done if what is required is written down, put in concentrated form, and then drummed into the public as their patriotic duty.

A plan however does not do the job by itself, automatically. It must be practicable. The Chinese Nationalist Government once produced a very pretty railway plan which included a railway across the top of Tibet and the high Himalayas; nobody, of course, had made either a traffic survey or a cost estimate. So, too, priorities by themselves are not enough, they must be acceptable to the public which has to pay for them and which is expected to benefit from them. If the public wants another benefit at a different price, then the politician, even if his own proposals are economically more sensible, is likely to be able to get them through only at the cost of more social friction than they are worth. Economically, English food subsidies should have been taken off much earlier than they were, but the practical result might quite easily have been strikes and social unrest to an extent that would have done far more damage than the removal of the subsidies would have done good. So the politicians were right to leave them on.

It is this constant gap between what is economically most profitable and what is politically most sensible which makes the politician's rôle at once so vital and so difficult. So many of the reactions of his electorate to the measures he knows to be economically advantageous have nothing to do with economics, that he has perpetually to be prepared to reach an economic destination by a non-economic route.

The Communist answer to this dilemma is simple. They cut the Gordian knot. The minority of the Western-minded seize power and dragoon the rest of the society into Westernising whether they like it or not. This Westernisation is, of course, limited to material needs. Chinese Communists like to see their girl students in blouses and jeans, they do not care whether they appreciate Beethoven and Michelangelo or not. They insist that their people must now acquire the attitudes to work, to saving, to innovation and to efficiency of a nineteenth-century businessman; but they have a positive objection to most of the Ten Commandments. So while the nineteenth-century businessman could only dismiss his employees for such offences as unpunctuality or spoiling work, the Communist Manager can usually arrange to have them sent to forced labour as saboteurs. The Communist, to take our previous example, does not need to persuade fathers that their daughters' virtue will be safe if they become stenographers. All they have to do is to conscript the daughter, possibly incidentally explaining to her that her father's objection makes him an enemy of the people and that her proletarian duty is to inform on him to the secret police. It is this capacity of Communist regimes to enforce the intellectual's will on the people by force which constitutes so much of its appeal to so many Asian intellectuals.

In a democratic country this easy way-out of force does not exist. The politician has to persuade, and, while persuading, he has to go on getting re-elected. Yet, the very directions in which he has to persuade makes getting re-elected more and more difficult. He has, for instance, to ask for sacrifices; and then the public is liable to blame him because they have had to go without. His new enterprises inevitably involve some waste; and the public may well remember the waste and forget the enterprise. He has to demand constant change in old and settled ways of life, and those whom he intellectually convinces of the need for these changes may yet remain emotionally unconvinced; their subconscious may still hanker after a past in which no such strain was put on them. The obvious scapegoat for their hankering is the politician. That is why, although there may be countries where one can make prime ministers of persons of whom half the population has never heard (Mr. Truman was not exactly well-known when he became President; M. Laniel was positively obscure when he became Prime Minister), in Asia, if something is to be achieved quickly—and speed is admittedly of the essence—the politicians must be men whom both the masses and the classes know and trust. A Nehru or a U Nu can put through a Five-Year Plan. A King Farouk cannot.

The process by which the politician achieves his end of economic development is complicated and obscure. Certainly he does not argue to his electors as a manager argues to his Board of Directors, he does not say that on this scheme the return could be so much per cent, and on that scheme so much per cent. Nor will he tell his people that if they wear cotton instead of silk for ten years, then with the difference it will be possible to build so many electric power stations. He is perfectly well aware that those who have to do without the silk may not be those who will benefit from the power stations. So he has to adopt other techniques as well as plain economic argument. He may resort to compulsion. He taxes silk and gets the tax accepted by appealing not to the self-interest but to the patriotism and the charity of his rich He may use incentives, for example, tax reliefs on new industries, or guaranteed prices for higher production. But the politician knows that their effect is limited. Higher interest rates increase saving; but one does not persuade a man to buy savings certificates instead of a silver anklet for his wife's birthday merely by increasing the yield from 3 per cent to 4 per cent. It is much more effective to reduce the son's willingness to keep the father in his old age if he has *not* bought savings certificates! The politician has to be prepared to use every weapon in the armoury, from tears to the flag, if the public are to be pushed and pulled into doing all the tiresome things which are the pre-conditions of development.

An excellent example of what happens is the first Indian Five-Year Plan. This plan was primarily a programme of Government capital expenditure, including a proper set of interdepartmental and inter-State priorities. It could have been simply a Government working document, but then the objective of enlisting public interest and of obtaining from the public the willing sacrifice needed to make the planned expenditure possible, could not have been achieved. If the public was to accept the extra taxes the Indian Government was imposing, to take the risks involved in its deficit financing, and to accept the controls and the relatively low priority for welfare, all of which the Plan involved, then they had to be made to feel that there was more to it than so many million acres of irrigation or so many new factories. They had to *believe*, and not just intellectually to accept, that something was being done for the glory of their country and the future of their children. That explains the long introduction to the published plan, with its insistence on democracy and its presensation of the importance of a better standard of life in terms which go far beyond materialism into the place of India in the world and the duty of the rich to the poor.[1] It also explains the way in which Government presented the plan to the public. Ministers talked about the need for a great national effort, they never said anything about turnover and returns. The tone is that of a revivalist, not a shareholders', meeting. The Government of India judged, rightly, that the only way to get through a plan on the scale of theirs in a society in which material development as such does not yet have the appeal to the imagination that it has had in the United States for 100 years, was to play on the feeling that India's poverty is a natural disgrace, in the shame of which each citizen has his share.

It is a necessary approach, but it produces an inevitable

[1] This first part of the Indian published plan is the best thing ever written on democratic planning.

dilemma. In order to induce people to make sacrifices beyond those they would make on their own judgement of their material needs, they have to be constantly reminded not merely that they are poor, but that to be as poor as they are is an intolerable state, to escape from which any sacrifice is justified. The Indian politician is thus driven to a position where in order to create content in the future he must create discontent in the present; and elections are held in the present. In order to scotch Communism in the long run, he must increase its chance of winning at the next election.

Nor does the dilemma of the Indian, or indeed of any democratic Asian politician, stop there. The Communist has a party line and a revealed analysis; until the next zig-zag in the line or a new commentary on what Marx or Lenin really meant— Stalin is now less in fashion—his policy is clear, and, because it is so very Victorian, reasonably consistent. Industrialisation and no nonsense about handicrafts. Get rid of landlords and no nonsense about compensation. Westernisation and no nonsense about traditional clothes—an Indian or Pakistani Communist will wear trousers and a tie or a bush coat where an Indian Congressman feels he must wear churidar pyjamas and an achkhan, and a Pakistani Muslim Leaguer will wear an achkhan and a Jinnah cap. Equality for women and no nonsense about parental choice of marriage partners or the woman's place being the home. This uncompromising quality has hitherto prevented Communist party members from being more than a small minority of the population anywhere. But, for the making of revolutions and the running of totalitarian States, quite small minorities are enough, provided the majority is sufficiently passive.

The democratic politician can accept no such easy ways-out. He wants everybody to take part in politics. It is the great achievement of India's politicians that over half of their electorate votes; and their electorate consists of every adult man and woman, literate or illiterate, in the entire country. But the larger the actively interested electorate, the more conservative it is likely to be. This is a great source of political stability. But it can also be a considerable brake on the sort of change which is indeed to improve the standard of living. The Indian electorate accepts, and welcomes, new roads or railways or irrigation or insecticides. These are methods of improvement they know, or whose effects are easily demonstrable. They are prepared to give free labour to build village schools and village roads; they are prepared to adopt improved seed or the Japanese method of rice-growing if they have seen the results in increased yield on some neighbour's plot. They will accept such novelties as artificial insemination, even perhaps birth control. One may perhaps go so far as to say that they are amenable to any new idea which runs across no old one, and which can be shown to be to their advantage. Indeed, on such matters, whether it is better weeding or helping Government to build them a dispensary, they are more amenable to a democratic Government, than they would be to a totalitarian one. They prefer to be coaxed, not bullied.

The difficulty arises when the new idea does cut across an old one, if, for instance, in India, the politician were to wish to apply a monogamy law to Muslims, or to urge Catholics to birth control or Hindus to start a beef industry. These, of course, are strong cases. But there are hundreds of others. Indian Governments lose many millions of badly-needed revenue by enforcing prohibition, because so many people consider that stopping drink, which to most Indians is a sin, is more important than the schools or hospitals or roads which could be built with the revenue drink might provide. Other millions go to the support of the handloom and hand-spinning industry, whose products are usually considerably more expensive than mill products. Partly this is a tribute to the memory of Mahatma Gandhi. Partly it is because many people have a genuine preference for small scale industries which can be conducted by people in their own houses, in small towns and in villages; they do not like the 'dark Satanic mills' and the concentration of large numbers of workers in great cities which they bring with them. Partly it is because the public sympathises with the immobility, the difficulty in changing either home or job, of nearly all hand-weavers. What hardly anybody argues for is a policy by which either the customer would get as good cloth as the mill makes, or else the handloom industry would be allowed to die.

Yet another example is the difficulties the Indian politician has with the attitudes of Indian labour. The Indian worker is so poor, so often utterly uneducated, that he is eminently exploitable. In order to get enough to eat he is prepared to accept wages, housing, hours and factory conditions that would in richer countries be considered intolerable; it is less than a generation since it was not unknown for physical violence to be used on workmen. Therefore, the politician has to protect him by legislation limiting hours, preventing payment in truck, ensuring proper sanitation and reasonable protection for machinery and restricting arbitrary dismissal. But, because the worker is so weak, the legislation has to be rigid. Overtime is not permitted without the sanction of a Government inspector. There are elaborate rules about the recognition of trade unions. There is a compulsory adjudication procedure for disputes. There are large compulsory payments when a man is retrenched or laid off. Rationalisation may be prevented altogether if it will involve unemployment, or sometimes merely if labour objects strongly enough. Many of these rigidities may be necessary to prevent exploitation, but they all slow down development. In a country where capital is scarce and labour plentiful, they put a premium on using machines instead of men, for once a man is taken on, he may be impossible either to get rid of or to discipline, whilst difficulties over overtime make a proper flexibility in production more complicated. Attainment of flexibility is then made still more difficult by the deep-rooted labour preference for sharing the work rather than for each individual producing as much as possible in order to earn as much as possible.

It is a natural preference in a country where for centuries men have been more plentiful than capital; but it does not make for industrial efficiency; it adds considerably to the entrepreneur's costs—shared-out work usually means less output per machine—and therefore to his reluctance to invest. Economic development is slowed down for yet one more reason. So it is again when Government insists on measures of welfare that labour does not value at its true economic cost, elaborate pithead baths, say, or housing which has to be subsidised. Scarce capital, which might have been used for something more immediately productive, is used up, and there is no corresponding improvement in worker efficiency, because the worker, if he had been allowed to choose how the money was spent, would have given something else a higher priority.

Many employers, economists, and Government officials are well aware of how the tieing up of business in labour legislation puts a brake on all Indian development; the more enlightened ones however accept that much of the legislation is necessary, and would like changes only at a quite limited number of points. But only the politician can ensure that those limited changes are made, for only the politician can explain to the public and to labour alike that proper factory discipline, maximum outputs, reasonable flexibility in operation, and the power to retrench are all necessary if the entrepreneur is to take the risks of development in any but the few most profitable cases. It is because the politician has not yet done his job of explanation and persuasion as he should have done that Indian industry is so wrapped in an almost stifling cocoon of regulations, so hampered in every attempt to adapt to changing conditions by the profound belief of worker and public alike that the worker is entitled to a freehold in his job. To give unlimited security to those few already employed in factories is to ensure that there will be very few new factories to give employment to the many not yet so protected. But nothing can be done about it until the politician realises it.

The situations the Asian politician faces are difficult. The attitudes which have to be got rid of, like the Indian worker's desire to stick to his existing job, are so understandable, so easy to sympathise with. The requirements of development, like the need to give a relatively low priority to housing that has to be subsidised, are often so harsh; they may be accepted in totalitarian Russia, they are not so easy to put across to democracy's electorates who are looking for an easing of their traditional hard lot, not a further tightening of their already slim belts. The politician who wants development has to have some economic understanding; but that is secondary. What is primary is the need for a vision to put before the people, a picture of the present and future in which they can be swept up and by which they can be inspired.

It is not an accident that the greatest of all the plans of underdeveloped countries, the Indian Five-Year Plans, owe much of their inspiration, and most of the public's feeling that they are worth sacrificing for, to Pandit Nehru. Mr. Nehru is not a bureaucrat, and his statements of economic principle leave more than something to be desired. But he is the perfect politician. Through all he says and does pulses a passionate understanding that in India this is a time of transition, of change, of an old world crumbling and a new world about to be born. It is this passion, this understanding in its politicians which Asia must have, more than savings, more than foreign aid, more even than technicians, if it is ever to progress; for, if the passion and understanding are not there, the rest will turn to dust, the savings will be wasted, the foreign aid misappropriated, the technicians frustrated. For a society to develop, it must want to develop; for a society to want to develop its politicians must dream dreams of development. If the politicians are bad, the economic development will not happen, as there is the whole history of Latin America to prove.

Chapter 10

THE RÔLE OF THE BUREAUCRAT

BECAUSE the politician is so important in Asia, the bureaucrat is of the first importance too. The politician must have the vision of change and the gift of making the people see his vision as he sees it; but it is the bureaucrat who must bring the vision down to earth, who must formulate it in terms the administrative machine can carry out. And it is the bureaucrat again who, once the people have been made to see the light, must make the vision real in all the humdrumness of detail. In Asia, moreover, the bureaucrat has yet another importance. There has always in Asia, as in all peasant countries, been a great respect for the actual holders of power, a great willingness to accept them as leaders. Traditionally, these holders of power were not democratic politicians, but collectors and residents and governors of provinces. Some of the aura of the past still clings, so that it is often possible for the bureaucrat in Asia to fill the politician's rôle of leadership as well as his own. It is therefore crucial to development that the many problems vital to the creation of a good bureaucracy should be solved. The right men must be recruited. They must have the right standards. They must have the right relations with the politicians, a proper consideration for the public and an adequate sense of *esprit de corps* in their relations with their colleagues. In short, the whole of at least the upper bureaucracy of Asia needs to have standards and men like those which have made the Indian Civil Service as important as the leaders of the Congress Party for Indian development.

Some of the causes for the importance of the bureaucrat are common to developed and undeveloped countries alike, and are inherent in the very nature of bureaucracy. The bureaucrat both formulates and executes policy. The days when the politician could make satisfactory decisions by himself or with only non-official advisers have been gone for a century. In any country where he tries to do so power either becomes entirely arbitrary, as under Hitler in Germany, or subject to innumerable special and interested influences, as in Kuomintang China; neither makes for the happiness or the prosperity of the citizen. In the modern, complicated world no Government could work for very long on purely political decisions without the decisions becoming with time so inconsistent, so inadequately based on fact, that the

Government would cease to function because its citizens would no longer know exactly what was expected of them. In Asia, moreover, this importance of the bureaucrat is greatly increased both by the traditional respect of agricultural societies for the official, and by the extent to which the leadership in change is taken by the Government, and thus in practice by the official.

It is vital to Asian governments, therefore, that their bureaucracy should be, what the Indian Civil Service has always been called in India, the 'steel frame'. It must represent the accumulated experience of what can be done and what cannot, of what the public will stand for and what it will not, of what can be pushed down the throats of an unwilling minority with the force at Government's disposal and what cannot; Government hardly ever undertakes any measure of which all its subjects approve, and how violent the disapprovers become depends a great deal upon the capacity of the bureaucracy to make unwelcome shoes pinch as little as possible.

The bureaucracy not only brings the test of practicality to the politician's enthusiasms, but it also provides him with the precedents, it tells him what was done before with other people in like case. The bureaucratic passion for precedent is much sneered at; it is nevertheless essential. If people whose cases are similar are to be similarly treated what has been done in previous cases must be known, recorded and followed; and, unless Governments appear impartial between man and man, it will be much harder for them to obtain the people's willing acceptance of their measures. If the public is to be persuaded that Government's measures are taken for the good of the community as a whole, and not to satisfy the lust for power of some jack in office, or the special interest of those with money or pull, Government must not only treat those in like positions alike; it must be visibly seen to do so. Even in the old days nothing destroyed the king's authority more quickly than chopping the head off one noble and giving his daughter to another, for exactly the same sort of rebellion. On these terms every noble rebelled. Equally, nowadays, discrimination in quite minor matters can bring Government into serious disrepute. If, for example, Governments insist on stopping street betting, they must see that all street betting is stopped everywhere, and not do as so many authorities in fact do, leave to each policeman the discretion to decide in just what streets just what bets will be prohibited.

This may seem ridiculously obvious. But it is a lesson which has by no means yet been everywhere and always learnt, especially in economic controls. In the last fifteen years, there has been a strong tendency for Governments to reserve to themselves discretion to decide every case on its individual merits. Import quotas in many countries provide examples. The result is merely to repeat the lesson learnt in every legal system. Equity is desirable, but law is necessary. Judges may differ on the equity, officials can come to a hundred and one conclusions on the whereabouts of the public interest. The citizen must know where he is, he must be in a position to know beforehand how to conduct his affairs so as not to come into conflict with authority. He requires a rule, a law. If he wishes to put up a factory to make bicycle chains, and if that requires the import of special steel, he must be protected against any official having the power overnight to tell him that no more licences will be granted for that steel because he, the official, to whom the works do not belong, and who carries no risk of loss, has decided that it can be made with some different, and locally made, steel. Just as no real commercial law, no confidence in the validity of one's transactions, could grow up under the old Chinese rule by which the judge looked not to the contract, but to a fair compromise, so none except the slowest of economic development is possible in a community where to all the uncertainties to which an entrepreneur's life is naturally heir, there is added the major uncertainty of never knowing what public authority, in any one of its hundred manifestations, will or will not order, or allow, him to do.

There must be rules, or there is no bureaucracy, only a set of pocket dictators. It is for the electorate to decide in what direction it wishes its country to go; it is for the politician to give words to these desires and to turn them into a policy; it is for the bureaucrat to give the policy form.

It is not the bureaucrat's function to run counter to the politician over major policy. It is the politician who is responsible to the electorate, and the electorate and their instrument, the politician, are entitled to have their way even if they are wrong. The bureaucrat may point out risks which his experience has shown him will arise, but of which politicians and public are unaware; but that is all. If they will not listen, he must do as he is told. One of the difficulties of underdeveloped countries is that the bureaucrat does not always remember this distinction, and, when he forgets it, though the policy may be better, the Government may be undermined. Bureaucrats very often do know better than either ministers or electors, but if they insist too often on their better knowledge, the end is either ministries held by civil servants or a profound suspicion of the civil service amongst politicians and the public. One has seen both in Asia in recent years, and both make economic development in underdeveloped countries difficult. The sort of development under forced draft for which Asia longs requires unity of purpose between Government and public, and between the various elements which make up the Government. This unity can be obtained, temporarily, by totalitarianism. It can be obtained permanently in a properly functioning democracy. It cannot be obtained by a bureaucratic Government, however honest, capable and unselfseeking, as was finally proved in India between 1919 and 1939, unless the country is at a very primitive stage of its history indeed, so primitive that the public still believes Government House knows best, as in much of Africa before 1939, or perhaps in India in the 1870s and 1880s; but today there are no such places left.

The bureaucrat's place therefore is not to decide policy. His function is to formulate the policy when decided and then to carry it out. Development is threatened when the bureaucrat trenches on the spheres of the politician and the electors. It is threatened even more, and nowadays much more often, when the politicians and the electors trench on the legitimate sphere of the bureaucrat.

Much of the interference is the result of a failure by both electorate and politicians to realise just what is included in the bureaucrat's functions of formulation and execution.

The formulation of policy must include the whole process of giving it a shape in which it will fit into the machine with the minimum of friction and grinding teeth. The elector may vote that he is prepared to pay a sales tax; the politician may decide how much money it is to raise, on whom it is to fall, what sort of commodities it is to touch. The rules, the number of points at which the tax will be levied, the exemptions, the methods of payment, the organisation of the collecting department, transfers and promotions, are then best left to the bureaucrat.

A minister who is himself a good administrator can sometimes interfere with effect, but administration is a skill requiring both a particular kind of mind and, in the higher levels, long experience. Most politicians, and nearly all electors, have neither. The more they interfere, the more the machine groans. In our sales tax example, loopholes are left for evasion, incidence is uneven, officials are incompetent or afraid of dealers with influence. The result is that public resentment increases until there is a risk the voter will change his mind about having a sales tax at all.

Interference with the technical side of the bureaucracy by non-bureaucrats is thus one of the major risks to development, even in highly developed countries, and it is a particularly severe risk in underdeveloped countries, especially if they are newly free, and the bureaucracy and the politicians have previously been on opposite sides, as is true of most of ex-colonial Asia. The bureaucrat explains that a scheme is impracticable in the form the politician wants it, and the politician suspects his motives; or, sometimes, the bureaucrat dislikes the politician's ends, and does not quite apply all his mind to getting over the obstacles which may lie in their way—the most notorious example is the Weimar Republic, not an underdeveloped country at all.

The results are disastrous, for politician and bureaucrat cannot do without each other. If the bureaucrat is not listened to, if the scheme for a sales tax—or whatever it may be—is formulated against his advice and given to amateurs to execute, the tax will simply not be collectable, the scheme will simply not be carried out. Ever since independence, Governments in India have been trying to use social workers to perform part of the job of administering, and have on occasions taken their advice against that of their bureaucracy on the measures that were needed. The result has almost invariably been a failure, not because the social workers lack intelligence, or goodwill, or devotion to the public (sometimes they have more of all of these than the average bureaucrat) but because they do not have the bureaucrat's technical knowledge of the machine and of what it *can* make the public do, and what it *cannot*. One does not become a good judge merely by having a strong sense of justice, and social workers have the most dangerous of all faiths for an administrator; they believe in the innate goodness of man. They are inclined to think that it is enough to have a law for people to stop drinking; or to finance a co-operative society, for an aboriginal committee to be able to run it. They do not always realise that the justest tax is of no use if the rules are so loosely drawn as to leave innumerable opportunities for evasion, or if the collectors appointed are exemplary in their zeal for the community's uplift, but have so little legal knowledge that they can be tied in knots by every taxpayer's lawyer.

More disruptive still is any attempt by the politician to interfere in the details of administration—a besetting sin of politicians in developed as well as underdeveloped countries. Even in England the letters M.P.'s write on behalf of their constituents are not always well-judged, and the McCarthy-Army dispute is an admirable example of the sort of allegations of improper influence so often made in the U.S. But in England there is the protection of Tribunals of Enquiry, such as sat on Mr. Belcher; in the U.S., there is a particularly outspoken press. In Europe the damage done is greater, as is evident in the Stavisky scandal in France or the recent Montesi scandal in Italy. In underdeveloped countries the damage done is greater still, not because they are more corrupt—India, for example, is less corrupt than most European countries—but because they are poorer. A poor man is interested in smaller advantages than a rich man; a poor and illiterate man can be more easily intimidated or defrauded than a rich and well-informed one. It is unlikely that an American will try to get his Congressman to interfere in order to block a house property tax of, say, 5 dollars, and if he did, the Congressman would feel 5 dollars beneath his notice. But 25 rupees in Bihar would be a lot of money to a lot of people; many individuals would be willing to make several visits to a member of the Legislative Assembly to gain Rs. 25, and many members might be willing to go and see an official to help a constituent for such an amount.

The position is made worse in many ex-colonial countries by everybody's memories of the colonial past. The official unused in the past to any political control over his actions, may resent as unwarranted interference a quite proper concern by a M.P. in the interests of his constituents—a complaint that the police are harassing motor drivers, or that forest contractors are not paying their labour properly, or that somebody's pension has not been sanctioned in time, or that disciplinary proceedings taken against a clerk have been irregular. Normally, however, the fault lies not with the official, but with the politician, especially the lower-grade politician, the backbencher or the member of a local Assembly; bottom, of course, as everywhere, is touched with municipal councillors, who will interfere over the location of a street lamp, or the condemning of putrid food, or which lane should be paved first. The politician has the same need to make friends in underdeveloped countries as elsewhere; there are influential men, and still more, influential sections of the community, to be kept happy; there are election funds to be raised; there is a following to be created. And one of the easiest ways of doing it is to do favours. This is true everywhere. Probably more favours are done in the U.S. than in India. Nevertheless, in some ways the position is worse in underdeveloped countries where the politician and the civil servant have until recently been on opposite sides of the fence; where one of the major weapons of insurgent nationalism has been campaigns against police oppressiveness, or forest regulations, or payment of land revenue, the average politician cannot be expected to forget his prejudices in a year or two. He is very quick to believe allegations that, say, forest guards who are trying to enforce a system of rotational grazing have really been trying to obtain bribes from owners of goats, or that police using only that amount of force which is necessary to evict a contumacious non-payer of taxes have been giving innocent citizens an unconscionable beating. Politicians are thus perpetually being deluded into conducting crusades for crooks.

The result is particularly unfortunate, because in under-developed countries so many of the ideas on which development is based are imported from outside and have no roots in the day-to-day knowledge of the public. The ordinary villager does not realise that rotational grazing prevents erosion. He merely knows that his goats are now being kept out of forests and hillsides into which they have been allowed for centuries; and he resents it. The ordinary house-owner in a municipality may have no great awareness of why water-borne sewage is necessary; he may only see that the rates have gone up and that he cannot afford them. The best method of curing this ignorance is education, but education takes time, and, quite often, the reason for passing a lot of regulations in the first place is that the community cannot afford to wait to educate all its members to the stage where no coercion is necessary. Since underdeveloped countries are thus very frequently in a position where they have to use compulsion to back up persuasion, they must be quite sure that the compulsion is effective. If forest guards are punished for enforcing rotational grazing, or policemen for distraining on people who will not pay their rates, not merely will there be erosion and no sewage system, but the respect for law will be destroyed into the bargain. By refusing to accept a limited, democratic coercion, the community may make necessary for itself the unlimited coercions of totalitarian Government.

This politician's suspicion of the bureaucrat has a corroding influence on the public service in yet another way. In every large organisation, business or civil service or military, one of the great difficulties is getting proper discipline and loyalty, while at the same time avoiding the encouragement of yes-men. People must do as they are told, or the organisation will collapse; but they must not be afraid to say what they think, or it will stagnate. The problem obviously becomes much more difficult when the men at the top, the politicians, believe that those below them do not share their ideals, that the advice which is being given them is based on ideals they in their turn do not share, and that the policies they have decided on are being sabotaged in execution. The temptation is then very strong to give promotion, not to those who are capable administrators, technically competent, but to those who agree at the right times and show a becoming missionary spirit in carrying out the politician's pet ends. Then, instead of giving the appointments on a nationalised board, for example, to men who can run a factory, or market a product, or conduct labour relations, they are given to men who believe in nationalisation—but who may mess up their office, alienate their customers, and annoy their workers into strikes. Zeal is no substitute for competence; passionate zeal indeed normally destroys precisely that coolness and balance of judgement, that capacity to accept facts which go against his desires and beliefs, which is the hallmark of the good bureaucrat.

When politicians do not realise these facts, and they are not easy or pleasant for politicians to recognise, bureaucracies run badly. And when bureaucracies run badly, economic development becomes very difficult. Import licences are refused when they should be given, railway waggons are not available when needed, permissions to issue capital, or power to acquire land, or licences to expand, are delayed until the entrepreneur feels that the tide which leads to fortune has ebbed; honest firms find themselves undercut by tax-evaders, Government contracts go only to people who bribe the purchasing officers, prices are rigged to make fortunes for insiders; the scandals of Farouk's Egypt and Chiang Kai-shek's China or Gomez's Venezuela, show what can, and does, happen. These were all cases of dishonesty, but equally disastrous results can be obtained by plain incompetence; many troubles would have been avoided in Indonesia had the new Republic had available at independence as many trained and experienced civil servants as India had in 1947.

An incompetent bureaucracy can upset development in any country; there is the famous example of the distortion of the development of Italian industry under Mussolini, with its overemphasis on then quite uneconomic steel industries and engineering; there are the periodic revelations the Russians make about themselves. But the results are quite peculiarly serious in the underdeveloped countries of Asia, because there are so much of the society's own economic initiative is governmental (though there may also be a large private *foreign* initiative, as in the oil-bearing countries), and because an undeveloped country nowadays almost always tries to develop to the accompaniment of planning and controls. In India, for example, even in the 1930s, Government's capital expenditure has been estimated at one and a half times that of private enterprise, and it may now be two to two and a half times; in Pakistan the disproportion is greater still; in Burma or Iraq or Iran most of the investment which is not being made—or has not in the past been made—by an oil company, is governmental. In Thailand the Government is much the biggest entrepreneur, and so it was in Nationalist China; yet neither Marshal Pibul nor Generalissimo Chiang have ever been suspected of Socialism.

This dominance of the Government in underdeveloped economies is due to the fact that nobody else within the society, as distinct from foreigners, either had the money or could recruit and train the technical staff, or had the experience of large-scale organisation, to conduct really major works, particularly public utilities. If, with or without foreign help, the Burmese Government does not run the teak and the river steamers, and the export contracts for rice, and the oil and the mines, they will have to be run by foreigners, as they were before the war, or not run at all; the private Burmese citizens with the money and knowledge to do it just do not exist.

The dominance of the Government is, therefore, natural enough; and in Asian countries it is backed by a traditional tendency to look to Government for initiative and help. Problems, the private citizen considers, are for Government to solve. There is none of that suspicion of Government which makes the American columnist the U.S. public's way of finding out what Government is doing, so that they can make it do something else. But, precisely because Government is so important in Asian economies that the assets of the Indian Government are worth perhaps three times as much as those of the whole of organised private enterprise, precisely because Asian societies look so much to their Governments to give the lead, a properly functioning, uninterfered with, bureaucracy is of crucial importance. Large organisations like Governments must work in a hierarchy, with authority decentralised according to well-defined rules. The allocation of a railway waggon at a particular railway station must be the work of a definite officer, acting on known principles. That does not, of course, mean that the officer making the decision, or receiving the complaint, should be so tied down by rules that he has no discretion. It does mean that the discretion must be exercised consistently, that the same applicant, for the same purpose, and with waggons equally easy, will not get his waggon one week and have it refused the next, or get it from one station-master and, when he is transferred, have it refused by the next. Discretion there must be, or the whole railway will bog down in red tape, but the way in which it will be exercised must be predictable by anyone who requires waggons regularly.

It is exactly this predictability which ill-judged political interference destroys. Those who go to the politician are either those with political influence, or those with a hard case, or those who do not accept the rules. If the way to a waggon is through knowing a M.P., the inevitable result is first corruption, and then, in countries with a tradition of political honesty, like India or Pakistan, a widening resentment at the party in power, and, quite possibly, even at the whole system of Government; no Asian democracy today can afford to permit much corruption or undue influence if it is to compete with Communism. If the rules are to be broken for hard cases, then there is chaos; hard cases make bad law, on the railways as elsewhere; a businessman who knows exactly how an Assistant Transportation Superintendent will use his discretion, will find it quite impossible to prophesy what a lawyer-politician, with knowledge neither of business nor of railway operation, will consider a hard case; the premium is obviously on plausibility. Finally, if the politician listens at all often to those who want to change the rules the result is likely to be a very rapid deterioration in working. The rules quite often do need changing; but changing them is a matter for skilled investigation and long consideration.

In any large organisation, the rules all fit together. Changing a couple of apparently not very good ones may upset a whole series of unquestionably satisfactory ones. Again, in any complex organisation, there are more rules than anybody can remember, so people like goods booking clerks and clearing clerks work to a routine. They keep, not the rules, but a procedure, in their minds. If they want to book goods, they must do this, this and this, in this order. The smooth running of the organisation depends on this routine being automatic. If nobody is quite sure what the rule is now, if everybody is looking up the book all the time, there is complete disorganisation. An imperfect rule, which is known, is very often better than a perfect one, which is new. Changes must be made gradually, at a pace at which they can be absorbed by the goods clerk. It is this fundamental principle of all bureaucracy which the amateur critic of bureaucracy does not realise; and, although they rarely talk as if they realised it, professors, businessmen, newspaper editors, and politicians are all amateur critics. The politician's function is not himself to change the rule; it is to tell his officials where the rules pinch his constituents, and to insist on *their* easing the pain.

This comes out very clearly with controls, of which the underdeveloped economies now have very many more than the developed ones, because they suffer permanently from a desperate shortness of resources with which to do all they want to do, a shortness from which the developed economies suffer only during war and its immediate aftermath. The bureaucrat's first question on any control must be: is my control really necessary? And this is true whether the economy is free, planned, or wholly Socialist. It is a matter not of ideology but of efficiency. Ideology only comes in in the definition of 'necessary'. More controls are necessary for a planned than for a free economy, and more still for a Socialist one. But in none of the three should any control ever be imposed which is not essential. When in doubt the rule is always not to control; nothing is more fatal than the love of so many bureaucrats for a combination of power and provision for every contingency.

This love is fatal for a quite simple reason. The major problem in all economic activity is uncertainty; no one ever knows what tomorrow will bring. Crops may fail; public tastes may change; a new invention may make one's machinery obsolete or one's product superfluous; increased development may make one's labour too expensive; more simply still, a key manager may die before his second-in-command is ready to replace him, or a key bridge on one's local railway line may be blown down in a hurricane. It is these uncertainties which make development so risky, and which have meant that so many entrepreneurs have always been men of vision or gamblers rather than cautious city men actuarially calculating risks. If Rhodes, or the pioneers on the *Mayflower*, or Vasco da Gama had calculated their risks with a proper allowance for contingencies, they would have stayed at home. If Ford had had a bank manager's conservatism, he would never have gone in either for mass production or for high wages.

Since uncertainty is the major obstacle to development—and crops fail, new inventions are made, and skilled labour becomes unexpectedly scarce in Communist as in capitalist societies—it is obviously most unwise to add to it unnecessarily. Yet every control does add, by the mere fact of its existence. Say that one wishes to build a chemical works, which can begin small, but which will, if successful, need in due course to be very considerably expanded. With controls one can never be sure that when the time comes one will get one's cement, or steel, or permission to issue capital. Or say one wants to manufacture lipstick, or nylon sandals, or fancy leather belts; one can never be sure that just when one is growing and short of working capital, a directive will not be issued to the banks to tighten up on their loans to non-essential industries; and the definition of what is non-essential will be made by some bureaucrat in his office, who may well be of an austerity of nature which makes him quite incapable of appreciating how important lipstick and nylon sandals and fancy belts are to the mórale of women and the pleasure of men.

More serious still is the delay which controls create. Most Governments have grown up in a law-and-order tradition where it is more important for a decision to be right than for it to be quick. If one is fixing land revenue for thirty years, six months' delay does not matter; pitching it too high or too low does. If one is being tried for murder, it is unpleasant for an innocent man if the case lasts two years before he is acquitted; but it is even worse if, in his determination-to get it through in a week, the judge hangs him by mistake. With economic activity this is not so. Speed is of the essence, and it is often better to be wrong than to delay. If a primitive hunter was following the tracks of two beasts, and the tracks separated, it was better to follow what might in the end turn out to be the smaller animal than to weigh the chances so long that both got away. If one does not know whether the cotton market is going up or down, it is better to take a chance of loss than to wait so long before buying that one runs out of cotton altogether and one's mill shuts. If one is selling in an expanding market, it usually is better to take a chance and expand rather than to spend too long considering whether machinery might not perhaps be cheaper next year; maybe it will be, but maybe also somebody else will have got in his expansion and taken the market first. A businessman must make the best calculation he can, and, having made it, act on it. He cannot be perpetually waiting in the hope that tomorrow he may be able to make a better calculation; or he will do beautiful calculations, and no business.

Delay is thus a prime enemy of development; yet delay is inherent in controls. One sends in an application for a licence; then come the hold-ups; the officer concerned may be away on tour; or he must refer to headquarters for orders; or he is a buck-passer; or he is overworked and the files simply pile up on his table; or he has clerks who are incompetent or corrupt and keep one's application at the bottom of the heap, because it is difficult, or in the hope of getting a bribe. Even in a well-run Government, like that of India or England, there are a hundred possible causes of delay. In a Government whose bureaucrats have less experience, like that of Indonesia, or are corrupt, as in Wafd Egypt, the delays will stretch into months and disposal which is both prompt and honest becomes virtually impossible.

The application sits about, or is argued about in the Government office, and meanwhile one's building work stops for lack of cement, or a whole department shuts for lack of some vital replacement, or one shuts down altogether for want of some necessary raw material. Costs and uncertainty go up; employment and development go down.

Once again, this is true whether the development is being done by Government or by private enterprise. A Government is not one monolithic structure. It is a series of departments, services and people; and every extra control is an extra opportunity for departments, services and people to disagree. If there is exchange control, or import control, or steel control, the Government Department has to get its allocation just like anybody else; sometimes it may be favoured, sometimes if it is a department whose political weight is small, it may be neglected; but in general it is affected in exactly the same way as the private individual. Whether the Public Works Department or a private contractor is building a dam, if the cement allocation is late, or the waggons do not arrive, the building will stop. Whether railways are Government or privately-owned, if the Steel Controller cuts down on the railway's steel requirements, there may not be enough waggons, or line capacity may be reduced because speeds have to be cut; the nationalisation of the British railways only made it easier for the Government to give them too small a share of the national resources of capital and steel. Whether the railways are nationalised or not, whether works are executed by private contractors or not, if exchange control does not think exchange can be found for locomotives or bulldozers, or the Industries Ministry argues they must be produced at home, or the Labour Ministry objects to labour-saving, projects may be delayed or trains left unhauled.

To perform all its functions properly, an Asian bureaucracy must not merely be on proper terms with its politicians, it must be competent, honest and have a proper *esprit de corps*. It is an advantage if it also has some passion for the country's advance.

Once again, the need for these qualities may appear obvious. What has to be done in order to ensure them is not quite so obvious. Let us take what has to be done to get competence, for example.

If the whole of a bureaucracy is to be adequately competent, its members must be recruited by methods which enable the little man's son with no influence to get in as easily as the Prime Minister's or the Chief Secretary's son. There must, therefore,

be a properly organised public service commission and properly
organised entrance examinations, with not too much importance
attached to interviews. Intellect cannot be created; it is born. If
a man does not have it when he joins the service, he cannot be
taught it. Social ease, on the other hand, which is so often what
matters at interviews, is teachable. Next, it must be recognised
that the young man, when he gets into the service, knows
nothing. If the recruitment has been properly done, he should
have the capacity to become a good bureaucrat. But what constitutes being a good bureaucrat is something he has still to
learn, and it can only be learnt by experience, for it is a lot of
things which never get into books. He must, for example, be
prepared to work hard. Most Asian countries cannot afford a
civil service of adequate size, and, if they are developing quickly,
are inevitably particularly short of trained men in the middle
and upper ranges. The Asian bureaucrat must, therefore, be
prepared for the 12 and 14 hour days which are so frequent in
India, for instance.

Then, he must learn how to deal with people. The administration in underdeveloped countries, and particularly the economic development part of the administration, cannot be conducted on paper or at a desk. It must be carried on in the field,
by talking to people; and talking over a very wide range of subjects, from contributions for a new school for the village, to the
use of a fertiliser of which the villagers have not previously heard,
or the need to build a road to the local market. Government
land may have to be given out and those who do not get it persuaded that the reasons for their not getting it are valid. Two
quarrelling groups in the community may have to be reconciled
and their points of view persuasively put to each other. Persua-
sive officials mean fewer communal riots, whether over religion
or over group factions; and in Asia loyalties are very often to a
tribe, or religion, or local language, or even village faction as
much as to the nation as a whole. One of the bureaucrat's main
functions is to help in the process of amalgamating all these
minor groups into one major group.

He must learn when to act and when not to act. There are
occasions when a violent mob is met with violence, and everybody runs away, and the whole trouble is over. There are other
occasions when it is better to let the police have stones thrown at
them for hours because to shoot might merely mean a bigger riot
the next day. There are occasions when it is best to be rough
with a prejudiced or selfish group; others when persuasion is
desirable, either for practical reasons, because the group is too

powerful to be treated otherwise, or for reasons of principle, because the group has become too unsure of itself to be amenable to reason.

Finally, the bureaucrat must learn the rules, for unlike the ordinary private citizen, the whole of his life is conducted in accordance with rules, most of which have the force of law, and all of which bind him. If he keeps to them he can call in all the force of the State, if he breaks them his acts are no longer valid and he himself may finish in gaol.

Honesty, again, is for a bureaucrat a much wider term than for a private citizen. It does not merely mean that he must not take money to do that which he would otherwise not have done, or that he must not talk about Government's secrets to those who may benefit financially from his talking. There are countries in both Latin America and the Middle East where conformity even with these elementary principles is rare; but that is, on the whole, the exception. Where bureaucrats more often fail is in their observance of the wider and more indefinable meanings of honesty. Of these the most important is the various varieties of nepotism. Nepotism is perhaps the most widespread of all bureaucratic sins, for it contains in it so much that is good. Indeed until the introduction of the competitive system in the British civil service a century ago it was universally regarded as a virtue; the provision of his relations with lucrative sinecures at the State's expense was an equally proper occupation for a Chinese mandarin and an eighteenth-century British M.P., a Moghul noble and a French courtier. Since charity can never be quite universal, it is at least something that most men recognise the obligation to help their families and their friends, people from their own part of the country and people of their own faith. In private charity it may indeed be accepted that, though these limitations are bad, since religion requires one to treat all men as brothers, they are also inevitable, and that their removal might well mean only that one would make as few sacrifices for one's family as for strangers. The Welfare State is also a State where filial obligations are sometimes less scrupulously observed, and it is not always easy to collect enough to give a clergyman a proper stipend. Certainly, in Asia the disappearance of the profound sense of family duty which characterises India or Pakistan would throw upon the State and public charity a burden they are quite unprepared to bear.

These private virtues are, however, the worst of sins when they are applied to the work and charity of the State. This is especially true in endogamous societies, societies divided by religion

or caste or class or tribe into small groups which do not inter-
marry, so that certain sections can never hope to be relations of
certain other sections. In such societies, if the sections in control
of the State follow the normal private rule of helping their own
first, the whole society is put under intolerable tension. The sections out of power then have no hope of rising, or getting their
fair share in deciding how their country is to be run; the extreme
case is South Africa, where preference for one section has been
raised into the primary principle of Government; but Pakistan's
discrimination in favour of Muslims, Ceylon's in favour of those
of Ceylonese origin, are equally examples, though of a much
lesser order. When this happens, the society becomes unstable,
for sooner or later, the discriminated against section turns to
violence to get what it has lost hope of getting by law; Ireland
and the Hapsburg Empire both provide many notorious instances. When the discriminated against are a majority, as in
parts of Africa or South America, or in Asia when it was colonial,
then the instability in time becomes so great as to be positively
explosive. And nothing slows development down so much as the
fear of explosion.

Therefore, the bureaucrat and indeed the politician too, must
never give, or even give the impression that he is giving, any
preference to those of his own religion, or caste, or family, or
class. The range of possible preferences is wide, and they must
all be guarded against; indeed, nowadays they must be doubly
guarded against, for the State now does so much more than it
did in the nineteenth century, that those who do not get their
fair share of the State's favour now feel triply and quadruply left
out. In Asia, the State is often, particularly for the middle class,
the primary source of jobs (as teachers or engine drivers or road-
repairers as well as civil servants or army officers), of loans to
start a new business, of assistance for an old business in difficulties, of water and electricity and land.

All this demands of the good bureaucrat an almost super-
human indifference to all his old connections, an almost super-
human capacity to stand apart from all the old differences of the
society around him, and the pleasures of family and friends and
group. It can be done, as the Indian Civil Service has shown,
and though it may, perhaps, be argued that it was relatively easy
for the Englishmen in the service to be impartial in a society of
which they were not members, this argument does not apply for
the Indians. Yet the vast majority of them always showed exactly
the same impartiality; and they have had their reward; their
impartiality, more than any other single factor, has made the

administration in India better than that of any other under-developed country.

Most controversial of all the qualities required for the bureaucrat is *esprit de corps*. He must be proud of his Government and proud of his service. Such pride admittedly occasionally leads to unnecessary interdepartmental jealousies, to undue emphasis on dignity and attaching an excessive importance to precedents, but these are unimportant compared with the high quality of the recruits and the profound sense of duty which an established position and a proper *esprit de corps* will produce. If an Asian country wishes to have bureaucrats of the type one gets in the administrative branch of the British Civil Service, or in the Indian Civil Service,[1] then it must give its upper bureaucrats the same position, the same feeling that they do a special job in a special way, the same sense that they all belong to one great tradition. The alternative of recruiting everybody as low down as possible, of making one's civil service an undifferentiated mess and giving it a minimum of prestige will only produce the second grade bureaucrats of Australia. These may have a use in societies where all the major initiatives are taken by the private citizen. They are not good enough for Asia where it is so often Government which takes the lead.

The requirements of a good bureaucracy are many everywhere; they range from incorruptibility to the will to work, from no political interference to a fair share of the nation's best brains. In Asia the requirements are doubly severe; the politicians are so much less practised, the electorates so much less educated, the group tensions so much greater, the tradition of nepotism so much stronger, the need for the State to give a lead so much greater, than in England or Scandinavia. Good bureaucracies are rare everywhere; in Asia they are inevitably doubly rare. The State of Bombay, however, has a bureaucracy whose standards are high down to quite junior levels; both India and Pakistan have superb top services. These men should be valued above rubies, for, in Asia today, without good civil servants little development is possible which is not foreign. One can have the oil production of Saudi Arabia with no bureaucracy at all, but the Indian Five-Year Plans require the Indian Civil Service.

[1] Since 1947 the Indian Civil Service has been replaced by a new service called the Indian Administrative Service, though existing members of the I.C.S. continued to be I.C.S. The new service is, however, being built on the methods and traditions of the old.

Chapter 11

PROBLEMS OF FINANCIAL
ADMINISTRATION

WITHIN the civil service of a country there is no problem quite so difficult as the proper relation between the Finance Ministry and the other ministries. Every Government needs to do more than it can afford; and for many of the purposes on which Governments have to spend money, there is no such simple guide to what should be done first and whether it is worth doing at all as profit provides for the private businessman, and should provide for government's productive enterprises. The criteria upon which one decides the size of an Air Force or the number of years of compulsory education for children are very much more complicated than those on which one fixes the site of a new soap factory.

This always difficult relation between the Finance Ministry and the rest of the Government becomes more difficult still when the Government is also engaged in development. For then the Finance Ministry has to apply two quite different sets of criteria according to whether the scheme under consideration comes under one of government's traditional preoccupations like defence, or is in effect a business enterprise. In deciding on whether a new squadron of night fighters is required, it has to make the intangible balance of safety against comfort; but in deciding whether a new railway line is required, it has to make a calculation of profit just as tangible as that made by a private firm.

Finance Ministries are quite good at deciding how many squadrons of aircraft the Air Force can be allowed. That is a decision on how much of its income society can afford to spend on its defence, and what risks it should take for the future in order to live tolerably in the present. Finance Ministries have been taking decisions of this type ever since they began; many a medieval king had to decide between clipping the coinage and being overrun by an enemy. The problem is one which comes within the true traditional limits of finance, to decide how much money it can raise, and in what way, without damaging too much either the economy or the patience of the electorate, and then to lay down according to what priorities the money so raised should be spent.

Even with such problems, however, Finance Ministries are inclined to overstep their proper limits. They are far too inclined to go beyond setting priorities and fixing the totals of what can be done to telling other departments how they should do their jobs. The besetting sin of Finance Ministries is intellectual arrogance, imagining that because they can say 'No' to a sewage plan, they know more about sewage than the sewage engineers; they are always telling journalists how to run information services and engineers how to build railways. Sometimes it may be necessary, but then the solution is to get new journalists or railway engineers, not to let Finance do their work for them—badly.

This tendency is particularly dangerous in development, for which the normal government split between Finance Department, Administration Department and executive agency is often quite specially unsuitable. The Damodar Valley Corporation's slow start, for instance, was quite largely due to too much remote administrative, and still more distant financial, control.

In private industry, on the whole, those who run the business and those who make the financial decisions are the same people; the accountant makes cost estimates, he does not say 'Yes' or 'No' on other people's estimates. It is for the Board as a whole, to say whether the proposition, as a whole, is worthwhile or not; it is their collective judgement, and not that of the Financial Director alone, which decides whether they can find the money and whether the scheme is likely to make enough profit to justify the risk. In Government every proposition has to be put before a Finance Officer. Yet in most Governments very little is done to see either that the Finance Officer has and will have that intimate knowledge of the whole subject under discussion that the Financial Director in the ordinary business has, or that he will not interfere in what he does not understand. On the contrary, in most Governments, senior finance officers, on the expenditure side particularly, deal with so wide a range of subjects, sometimes covering two or three whole departments of State, that they cannot possibly know in detail about all of them. It is most unlikely that the same man will be intimately acquainted with the economics of putting up extra warehouse space in the countryside, the discount terms that have to be given to agents selling fertiliser if it is to be effectively marketed, and the proper tax to be levied on tea exports in order to finance tea research.

What he should do, therefore, is to restrict himself to the application of general principles to the problems that come before him. What he, in fact, very often does is to try and tell his Director of Tea Research how many laboratory assistants he requires, his Director of Storage how many warehouses he should put up per 100,000 tons of crop, and his Director of Fertilisers how to squeeze another ¼ per cent out of his agents. And his tendency to do so is made very considerably worse by the fact that he is sometimes right, since the finance side of most Asian Governments is better staffed than their executive side. His occasional rightness is, however, no excuse for lack of self-restraint. He is unlikely to save more than a very limited amount of money when he is right; and he wastes an enormous amount, usually in rather invisible ways, in profits not made rather than on losses incurred, on the occasions when he is mean at the wrong time or at the wrong place. And, so long as he is allowed to overrule executive officers with the arbitrariness which most Asian Governments, particularly those which have inherited the British tradition, permit, those officers will never acquire a proper sense of responsibility. This is doubly serious. First, money cannot really be used to the best advantage unless the executive officer is just as interested in its proper use as the Finance Officer; secondly, it becomes increasingly difficult to get the best men for top executive posts if they are always frustrated by finance officials.

This is not to say that a Government can develop its country economically without a Finance Ministry, or, what often causes even more trouble, Audit. The Governments of the United States and France, both of which have quite strong Finance Departments but in both of which the legislature votes expenditure and revenue separately, by this mere division tend to find themselves perpetually in deficit. Governments which do not keep a tight financial control over their technicians very soon either go bankrupt or have an inflation, as so many of the new European Governments discovered after 1918. Engineers know when a dam will not fall down, or when an aeroplane will fly at 700 miles per hour; they do not necessarily know whether the water rates on the land under command will pay for the interest on the money it costs to build the dam, or whether the aeroplane will carry enough passengers to pay for itself. Still less do they know whether there are other schemes, put forward by other engineers, which would be more profitable, or which, like Defence, the electorate may consider more socially necessary; nor do they know whether, profitable or not, necessary or not, the money for their pet schemes can be found at all. And what is true of engineers is equally true of soldiers, University heads and curators of museums. Somewhere in a Government under the Cabinet there must be a co-ordinating authority which decides first how much money can be obtained from the taxpayer (or consumer of a Government service) and how much is best left to fructify in his pocket, and then how that money is to be split up between necessary schemes, profitable schemes, and schemes which are neither necessary nor profitable, but which the electorate or some politicians consider either moral, like prohibition or the suppression of street-betting, or ornamental, like American-size Embassies or Guardsmen's bearskins, or perhaps merely cultured, like municipal art galleries and the opera houses of European towns.

These are wide functions. Where Finance Ministries go wrong—and it is a sin from which they all suffer—is in trying to make their functions more extensive still. It is for Finance to say whether a particular scheme has a high enough priority for the money to be found for it; it is also for Finance to lay down service conditions and to cut out obvious waste. It is not for Finance to teach the technical departments how to do their job. The worst hold-ups in Government, the most severe set-backs to development, come when Treasury officials try to explain to road engineers that the road would be just as good if it were 2 ft. narrower, or the dam just as effective if it were not quite so thick, or the department just as efficient with three clerks less. What is reasonable is to say that so much money cannot be found, and to enquire of the technician how he would economise in order to bring himself within what can be found. But few Treasury officials are content with so humble a rôle. They like to do the clipping themselves; and the result is delay, inefficiency, and the destruction of the will to economy in the administrative department itself. When one knows one is dealing with a Finance man who will give one exactly half of what one asks for, one simply doubles one's initial demand; that may be necessary, but it is not an effective way of getting either properly balanced development or proper teamwork between Finance and the rest of Government.

Finance officials, moreover, in general, cannot justify their detailed interference on the plea of being good businessmen. They tend, for example, to be unprepared when considering a road programme to balance against its cost the tax revenue it will bring in; and the forms of contract of which they approve are so one-sidedly in favour of the Government that the Government always in the end pays more to cover the contractor against the frightful risks he is compelled to run.

Audit can be even worse. The best business accounting nowadays conceives its function as presenting to management the facts upon which to base its judgements, and presenting them sufficiently quickly, even at some sacrifice of accuracy, for it to be possible to correct an error while it is still in the making. About mistakes which were made two years ago it is normally possible to do little unless there has been positive crime; one no longer knows who was responsible, or he has retired or been transferred; and nobody can remember how the mistake came about, or what needs to be done to prevent its happening again. But if one can catch the mistake which was made yesterday, something can be done straightaway; one knows who is responsible, and one can find out how he came to do what he did, so that the appropriate corrective action, whether it be punishment of a guilty person or correction of a faulty procedure, can be taken at once. Post-audit is excellent for getting embezzlers sent to gaol; management accounting sees that embezzlement does not happen, or else decides that a little risk of embezzlement is a lesser evil than incurring excessive expense and delay to get crook-proof procedures. So again, where old-fashioned costing takes an average of costs over a past period, management accounting tries usually to provide tomorrow's marginal cost, or perhaps to give a series of costs based on different assumptions about how much one will sell and how one will produce from which a judgement can be made about the best course to follow. This sort of information Government accounts departments are very rarely set up to provide.

Government audits are indeed painfully old-fashioned. That does not mean that they are not necessary, as engineers and politicians in their exasperation sometimes think. If there is no audit and no rules, there will be an infinity of waste, as one discovers every time the standard of audit goes down. Most people either cannot be trusted or have not the judgement to increase their establishment as they like, or to pay by merit, or to place orders without calling for tenders, or to pay more for greater speed. That way lies corruption, slackness, and empire-building. There must be rules to see that Government money, which is after all the taxpayer's money, is spent in accordance with proper sanctions, in a way that gives every citizen an equal chance as contractor or employee, and that does not allow Government's officers to get rich at Government's expense. Audit is necessary, as every report of a Public Accounts Committee shows. A Government that does not have audit finishes up like a mediaeval Sultan paying for soldiers who existed only in the imaginations, and the pockets, of his generals.

Many Government auditors, however, and this is perhaps particularly true in ex-British possessions, have more knowledge of the rules than sense. They sometimes come down just as heavily on a failure to call for tenders in a case where postage and tender forms cost twice as much as the purchase, as in a case involving millions. They are capable of demanding just as rigid an observance of the rules in an emergency when, if they are not broken, a large work may be held up for weeks for lack of a vital spare part that happens to cost more than the engineer's local purchase authority allows him to buy, as on an occasion when there could be no reason for breaking the rules except dishonesty. The only results of this lack of discrimination are that a great deal of Government money is wasted and that, in the general confusion, the dishonest get off as often as those whose actions have in all good faith saved Government money. Both ways development is severely hampered. The only cure is management accounting, for the auditor to ask himself whether the breach of rule was technical and necessary and economical of Government's money, or whether it was deliberate, corrupt and wasteful. It is important that the one should be overlooked; it is equally important that for the other somebody should be dismissed.

Good Finance Officers and good auditors are as vital for proper development as good engineers and good chemists. If control is inadequate, one goes back to mediaeval conditions of embezzlement and bankruptcy; if control is too tight nothing ever gets done. The right balance requires both that many of Government's best men shall be in Finance and in the senior positions in audit, and that, being so good, they shall nevertheless have enough humility to admit that an executive officer, on his own subject, knows more than they do. The difficulty of this combination is one of the worst problems development has to face. That is true everywhere. It is doubly true in Asia where money is so scarce, and the need for development so crying that every unnecessary delay, every waste of an anna, is a crime.

Chapter 12

COLONIALISM

(a) Colonialism and its alternatives

NOWADAYS politicians think nothing of promising their electorates a doubling of their standard of life within their lifetimes. The Indian Planning Commission hopes that its plans will double India's national income by 1968; in Western Europe an increase of less than 4 per cent per annum is considered failure. Indeed, any Government today which cannot promise its people steadily improving material conditions of life has a very poor prospect of survival.

This situation has become so much part of the background of everybody's thought today that it is forgotten how entirely exceptional it is. Before 1840 it was normal for economies to be stagnant, a wild exception for them to be dynamic. Doubtless the standard of life had taken a turn upwards when the wheel was invented, or agriculture introduced; but such innovations had usually been spread over centuries, and the increase in production was usually eaten up quickly enough by an increase in population. Englishmen in 1800 were probably poorer than Athenians in 450 B.C.; the Indian peasant in 1900 was certainly no richer than his predecessor under Asoka, more than two thousand years before.

The steady reduction of poverty which has characterised the West in the last century and a quarter is thus unique in history. Its uniqueness is not, however, in all probability, the result of accident. Rather is it the result of the coming together in Western society of a whole series of institutions and attitudes all of which were necessary to the nineteenth-century's outburst of economic activity.

It is therefore a priori likely that any underdeveloped society which wishes to develop will have to transform itself to be as like as possible in attitudes and institutions to Western Europe and its offshoots. Certainly so far no society has developed which has not done so. This does not mean that India and Africa and China have to become exact copies of the United States or Sweden. Some parts of Western civilisation, though it us difficult to be sure which parts, have nothing to do with economic development. Beauty contests and a taste for Plato, for example, are probably neither of them essential. Nor does it mean that there is something inherently superior about the way of life of the developed countries. Clearly it would be ridiculous to claim that there was any sense of the words 'higher' or 'civilisation' in which it could be said that the civilisation of Pittsburgh or Manchester is or has been higher than that of Israel at the time of the prophets, or the Athens of Aristotle, or the India of Buddha. All that can be claimed is that it is, and for a hundred years has been, an economically more efficient civilisation. There is no evidence that the national income of Israel or Athens, or North Bihar was any higher, at the death of Isaiah, Aristotle and Buddha than at their birth.

Underdeveloped societies which wish to develop have thus a limited choice of options. They can imitate; they can be compelled into imitation by a minority of their own people; or they can have a period as a colony (nobody of course chooses quite like that to be a colony; but at least there have been long periods when colonial peoples have been perfectly loyal). The term 'colonialism' must however for this purpose be given a wider connotation than is usual. It must be taken to include all government of people of a culture of lower economic efficiency by people whose culture is of greater economic efficiency, whether the governing people are foreigners or a minority within the country. For our purposes, the relation between the Spanish or Hispanicised minorities which rule so many of the Indian countries of Latin America and their Indians, or between the South African whites and their non-whites, is as much colonial as that between Frenchman and Arab in Morocco, or that between Englishman and Indian was. Moreover, the colonial relations which matter for our purpose are mainly modern, since so many past conquests represented economic retrogression—the fall of the Roman Empire, for example, or the nomad conquests of China. But the Romans in Gaul or Britain, the Normans in England, the Hindu empires with India's aboriginals, the Chinese in their slow push southwards, were all related to those they were conquering or assimilating in a way which has many resemblances with modern colonialism.

Simple imitation has been the usual method among the advanced countries themselves. Most of Western Europe took railways and Parliamentary institutions from England in the nineteenth century; everybody has taken mass production and a trade union interest in productivity from the Americans in the twentieth. But even in these simple cases, when the borrowing is not of a whole culture but only of a few missing factors, within a whole cadre of attitudes and institutions shared by borrower and lender alike, imitation has not always been easy. It has not been possible to rely upon the spontaneous adaptation of the community to meet its new want of greater wealth. There has had to be deliberate governmental effort—the German State Railways, the Anglo-American Council of Productivity. Sometimes there has even had to be war and revolution. Germany might not have developed so quickly without the Austro-Prussian War of 1866, or France without the Revolution of 1830.

Imitation forced on the country by an advanced minority has been the method chosen by a very few countries, for it requires a single-minded and ruthless minority, and one moreover united within itself in its determination to put material advance before all else. The obvious examples are Japan and Communist Russia; China is now following the same path.

In Japan a revolution put in power a small band of men of great ability, whose sole objective was to give Japan enough power for it to count in the world. They therefore looked where power was, and imitated everything that was imitable. They took French law codes and a German constitution and a British navy; they imported machines from everywhere and sent trainees to everywhere. They copied European imperialism and European top hats, and they built armed forces capable of fighting the Americans and an industry which in the 1930s was the West's most serious competitor. What they did not copy was Western freedom and individualism. The Japanese State continued to rest upon the Emperor's Divine Right, the Japanese individual to be bound by all the traditional onerous obligations to State and family and employer. So the imitation did not quite succeed. The armed forces lost the wars they began in Manchuria and at Pearl Harbour; and Japan is just ceasing to be primarily an imitator, adapting the innovations of others rather than making innovations for herself.

Communism is a still more obvious case. The Communist party makes no bones of the fact that it is a vanguard which knows what is best for the people; and the history of Russia for the last forty years is strewn with the evidence of the fact that many of the people, the peasants particularly, do not like what the party considers good for them. Nor does the party conceal the fact that its ideals are all Western European, and nineteenth-century Western European at that. The values are those of Victorian Manchester, with the important exception that Victorian Manchester believed, on the whole, in freedom. But Stakhanovism, the use of trade unions to increase production, the prohibition of strikes, the low income-tax, the high rate of saving and investment financed by regressive commodity taxation, even the heavy classicism of official architecture, the strict academicism of official painting, the increasing prudery of official morality and the lavish incomes but fettered positions of writers and artists—all would have appeared very proper to the Manchester millionaires who opposed the Ten-Hours act. When every allowance has been made for the fact that Marxism is a strictly Western European theory, the resemblance is far too close to be accidental. Marx was not a philistine; and he had a real feeling for the underdog. The rulers of Russia are philistines; and their State gives more than capitalist rewards to success. One can only presume that if one wants forced development, development at a pace faster than society would engender if left to itself, then one must put on top men like the Communist managers of to-day or the mill and mine owners of nineteenth-century Western Europe.

One can find in Europe itself, however, an example where the imitation by the minority was so long drawn out and so in accord in the long run with the wishes of the majority that, unlike Japan, the imitation was complete, and, unlike Russia, it required hardly any force. The example is Scandinavia, which has spent the whole of the last 1000 years acquiring the culture of its neighbours—Christianity, the Renaissance, the Reformation, the Industrial Revolution, even co-operation, all came from outside. The Scandinavians are nevertheless still very much themselves, not carbon copies of other people, and they have recently especially made notable contributions to the common civilisation of Europe. But their enormous economic development of the last 70 or 80 years, a development which has proceeded at a speed second only to that of the United States, would certainly not have been possible had their way of life remained that of the Vikings, whose interest in economics was purely exploitatory. It may be argued that this example is far-fetched; but many underdeveloped societies, especially in Africa, have cultures not so dissimilar to the Viking culture; and their whole problem is that they do not have the time to change at the pace most convenient to them which the Scandinavians had.

Imitation is thus not a very satisfactory answer for the underdeveloped in general. Japan was unique; and the underdeveloped countries do not want to go Communist if they can find another way; and they do not have the 1000 years Scandinavia had. Most of them, therefore, have taken their Westernisation (or whatever one prefers to call the adoption of the complex of attitudes and institutions which makes economic development possible) through colonialism; but colonialism too is only a half-satisfactory method, not merely because there is always a certain loss in being governed by others, but also because it can only do part of the job. At a certain stage when the people's most intimate habits have to be altered, it must be people of their own culture and background who do the persuading. At that stage independence is a necessity, but before it is actually granted, there is usually an unpleasant transition period of tension and agitation during which the economy is liable to go backward rather than forward. This is equally true whether the independence takes the form of the creation of a new State, or whether it merely means that within the country power passes from the minority to the majority.

Once again, it should be noted that the fact that a country (or a people within a country) may benefit economically from a period of colonial rule implies no judgement that the rulers are superior to the ruled except, at least temporarily, in the organisation of their society for economic ends. The great colonial powers themselves have all had a period under the Romans when it was they who were the colonies.

They were indeed colonies for longer, and their own cultures were more thoroughly obliterated than has been the case with any colony in Asia or Africa. Today they all consider the experience a necessary one. Without the Roman tradition of law and administration, of town life, and of good communications, without the Christian Church whose spread the existence of the Empire helped so much, without the Greek spirit of enquiry so largely passed into Europe through Latin, Western society might still be the congeries of tribes the Romans conquered, no more capable of development on its own than the tribes of the Congo in 1800. Yet at the time the destruction of their ancient tribal societies, the weight of Roman taxes and the Roman bureaucracy, and the special privileges of Roman settlers, must for long have seemed at least as grievous to many a Briton and Gaul as ever British rule in India did to the Indians; the Samnites before their final flare-up may well have felt about the Romans as do South African non-whites about their whites.

In the modern world colonialism, in our wide sense, has been the norm in underdeveloped countries, and it is still widespread. It applies, or has applied, to virtually all Asia and Africa—Japan has had an important dose of it since 1945, and China has had considerable partial experiences. It also applies to all

Latin America except the Argentine which has always been a relatively homogeneous European society, and Brazil, which is a special case. Finally, it has applied in various ways to Eastern Europe, not only to those countries which are now Russian satellites but also to those countries or parts of them which formerly were ruled by Germany or Austria-Hungary; this Eastern European instance is, however, again special, for it is by no means clear that the ruler always has been economically more efficient than the ruled—Czechoslovakia, for example, whether under the Austrians, the Germans or the Russians.

(b) Colonialism and independence

The economic advantages conferred on colonies have been so pooh-poohed of recent years, that it is worth remembering that they were commonplaces to the nineteenth century when Europe's economic expansion was new and wonderful and people still felt a missionary desire to give them to the whole world, whether the world wanted them or not. The nineteenth century went so far on occasion as to assert that no backward people had the right to sit on its territory and prevent its development if some more advanced people were prepared to develop it to the benefit of the world at large; which helps to explain, though not to excuse, both American ruthlessness to their Red Indians, and the determination with which China and Japan were opened up, despite the strong objections of the Chinese and the Japanese.

This nineteenth-century attitude was grossly over-simplified. It took little account of the cultural losses which frequently resulted from a too rapid development to which the local people had no time to adjust themselves; the South Sea Islands in Stevenson's day are a well-known example; the detribalisation of the South African urban native is another. It took even less account of the fact that while development normally meant an overall rise in the wealth of the world as a whole, it sometimes left the people in whose territory it took place poorer than before. Obvious examples are the Congo under Leopold II, or Spanish precious-metal mining in Latin America. Even where economically there was a great advantage to the local people as a whole, certain sections of them often suffered very severely. The importation of British machine-made cloth into India duty-free lowered the cost of living for the peasantry as a whole, but only at the expense of half-ruining hundreds of thousands of hand-loom weavers.

It is, moreover, now becoming clear as it was not in the nineteenth century with its belief in the white man's burden that the colonial relation is an inherently unstable one. Either the colonials cease to be dependent and become full citizens, or they revolt. The Gaul and the Briton become Roman citizens, India and Pakistan become valued members of the Commonwealth. But when Athens turned her allies into dependents, they revolted, and the Dutch lost Indonesia because they did not free it quickly enough.

Because this is so, one is faced with the dilemma that a country may not be able to start developing unless it has a period as a colony, but that its development while it is a colony will always be distorted, and that once independence approaches, development will become so distorted that only the actual attainment of independence[1] (and perhaps not even that) can restore it to its normal rhythm. The whole problem is further complicated by the fact that at a certain stage economic development merely by outside agency ceases to be feasible, an effort of the whole people becomes necessary. That stage may come in the full flush of unquestioned colonialism,[2] or it may come when independence is already near; whenever it comes, it requires an effort of local leadership which is normally not possible unless power too is in local hands.

We may here repeat our thesis that the institutions and attitudes of some societies are much more adapted than those of others to the bringing about of economic development. A society which listens to Samuel Smiles will get rich quicker than one whose only guides are Buddha or St. Augustine. Some of the necessary institutions and attitudes can be detailed. Modern economic development is not possible without a definite code of law which applies to all cases and before which all persons are equal,[3] or without a considerable habit of saving; or without people capable of using those savings to advantage; or without a willingness to accept innovations reasonably freely; or without society as a whole giving sufficient respect to material success for a fair proportion of its talent to be given to economic development; or without law and order; or a sufficiently large market to permit of economies of scale; or reasonable mobility between places and occupations, or a considerable measure of scientific and mechanical knowledge adequately spread through society.

[1] Always in our wider sense.

[2] As with swollen shoot disease in the Gold Coast, or with population control in Asia. The need in both cases goes back before the local independence movements had any importance; but alien rulers could do nothing much about either.

[3] Western readers will take this for granted, but it is historically an exception.

Development may even be impossible in a society in which the enquiring mind is too inhibited by a belief in magic and witchcraft.

Merely to list the pre-requisites of development in this way makes it clear why most societies, through most of time, have been stagnant, their periods of prosperity short, accidental, and often unrepeated. It makes clear, too, that it was not an accident that the Industrial Revolution occurred originally in Western Europe, largely indeed in Protestant Europe, and that in other parts of the world development has tended to go hand-in-hand with Europeanisation, whether enforced as in the colonies, or deliberately imitative as in Japan. Rome gave Europeans the idea of a universal law and the example of an efficient administration; Greece gave them the spirit of scientific enquiry, Israel a religion without magic; the mediaeval chartered cities contributed an environment in which merchants were respected, and wealth made in business safe from the rapacity of local lords; Protestantism added moral approval of hard work and thrift; the nation States provided wide markets; the Renaissance, the Reformation, and the eighteenth-century free thinkers combined to provide an atmosphere in which men were encouraged to think and act for themselves. No previous society had so combined the conditions necessary for risk taking and investment, for saving and enterprise; China in the third and fourth centuries, India under Asoka, Rome under the Antonines, perhaps came near, but all lacked something; all perhaps had too many bureaucrats and too many philosophers, not enough Lavoisiers and Stephensons.

One may speculate on why certain past societies did not produce the Industrial Revolution. It is clear, however, that in the nineteenth century it could have been produced only in Western Europe and its overseas descendants. No other society at that date had even the potentiality. Some, like eighteenth-century India, suffered from anarchy; others, like most of Africa, were still tribally organised, in a way that made innovation almost impossible and the division of labour only rudimentary. In most power was arbitrarily exercised, so that, although injustice might not necessarily be frequently done, it was at least impossible to know how justice would be done; and the maker of a contract must know how his contract will be interpreted if business risks are to be measurable at all. Above all, outside Western Europe, men were not free. They might be serfs, or slaves, or merely bound by an age-old and unchanging custom. The only people who were able to decide for themselves, or to think new thoughts, were the ruling classes; and they were prevented by the contempt for manual labour and for money-making typical of aristocracies from applying their freedom to innovate to economics. It was much more exciting to exercise power than to build up a business in the manufacture of cotton yarn. It is not an accident that the American South produced generals but no rails, or that Latin America had so many more revolutions than cotton mills. Nor is it an accident that in Russia under the Czars, or even in Imperial Germany, so much of the development that did occur was in railways and heavy industry rather than in consumer goods, or that in India the Government Ordnance Factories were for long the major part of the engineering industry. These meant power, which the governing classes understood. The complications of a rising standard of life, of more blouses for peasant women or more toys for artisan children, were normally beyond them.

The governing classes may often not have been interested in raising the national income. They were always interested in the consequences of its being raised, in the power and amenities that went with greater wealth. They envied English roads and French hotels, the British navy and the German army. Just as today, whether people like America or not, every society wants to have the wealth of America, so in the nineteenth century, whether people liked the Industrial Revolution or not, they wanted its fruits. And just as today, one can only have American wealth by accepting such American institutions as mass production, and a labour interest in productivity, and respect for the successful innovator, so in the nineteenth century, one could only become like Western Europe by accepting some of its institutions, an impartial law, for example, or a market unhampered by local and arbitrary tolls, or good communications, or the collection of taxes according to fixed and reasonable rules, or safety for the prosperous, or organised research.

One nineteenth-century society, Japan, through an enormous national effort, succeeded in imitating nearly all of these; the result was a unique economic spurt. Others, like the societies of Eastern Europe, had some of these ideas and institutions enforced upon them by their governors. The result was an uneven development which satisfied the lovers neither of the old nor of the new, neither Dostoevsky nor Lenin. Other countries were, until recently, incapable of even so much adaptation, either because they were already not independent like India and Indonesia, or because their governments and societies were unwilling or unable, to make the necessary effort, as in China or Latin America or tribal Africa. In these cases, a period of colonial rule, whatever its other defects, was the necessary preliminary to any development at all. It is perhaps that fact which explains why, even in proud countries like India, colonial rule was so acceptable for so long. The British in India provided the roads, the railways, the telegraphs, the law and order, the knighthoods for successful mill-owners, the safety of person and property, the codes of contract and tort, the banks and insurance companies and stock exchanges, the wide market for tea and jute and cotton cloth, the idea of the equality of touchable and untouchable, Brahmin and non-Brahmin, and the institutions of democratic Party Government, without which no development would have been possible at all. When the British went, India was able to go virtually straight into its Five-Year Plans. The basis is there, India has only to build on it.

An even stronger case is China. China has never been a colony, yet in all China's relations with more economically developed countries before 1947, one can see those countries bringing pressure to change China in ways that would make economic development possible. Extraterritoriality, for example, flowed from the businessman's need for a system of law which is predictable and taxes which are not occasional and arbitrary levies. The fight to get exemption from local tolls was the result of the need for a wide market. The insistence on prestige came from the need of mere foreigners and businessmen to be able to assert their equality against the arrogance of officials imbued with the belief in the superiority of Chinese to foreigners, bureaucrats to businessmen, and Confucians to everybody. The pushing of railway loans on the Chinese Government came from the perfectly correct apprehension that China's first economic need was railways, and that such railways were therefore likely to be profitable.

What the foreigner demanded in China was in fact quite reasonable. Had the aim of the Chinese Government been economic development, indeed, they would have wished to give what the foreigner was asking for to their own people as well, as the Japanese Government did; it is significant that by doing so, the Japanese Government was able to persuade the foreigners to give up their special privileges by the 1890s. The difficulty was that the Chinese Government's aim was not economic development, but the continuance of the traditional way of life; and economic development required change in China just as it had in England. So the Chinese resisted. The little development they got was despite themselves; indeed, in the only case where a great deal was done, Manchuria, it was imposed on the Chinese by a force they never ceased to resist. Nevertheless when, first under the Kuomintang and then under the Communists, the Chinese did finally accept economic development as an end in itself, it was not upon traditional Chinese society, but upon the so much resisted Western and Japanese innovations that they built their new order. The heart of the Communist plans is the railways and the Japanese-built industries of Manchuria and the graduates returned from foreign universities. Indeed, Chinese Communism like Russian Communism, is in one aspect an attempt to imitate nineteenth-century Western Europe by force. From the economic point of view, it is colonialism with the Communist party as the colonial power; but it is of course a more effective colonialism. The Communist party can westernise China more quickly than the British could westernise India, because it is ruthless, native, and single-minded, where they were relatively liberal, foreign, and split-minded about their objectives.

The most obvious example of the need for a period of colonial rule is, naturally, Africa. If Tunis, or Nigeria, or Ghana, can today hope to function effectively as independent States, it is because of their sixty years or more under Britain and France. Without those years, there would have been no central authority, no communications, no native élite, no legal system, no cocoa or groundnuts or phosphate mines. It is conceivable the people were happier under the old tribal systems; that one can never know; what one can be certain of is that modern States, capable of large trade and growing *per capita* incomes, could not have grown spontaneously out of disunited tribes.

With all its economic advantages, however, colonialism is fundamentally an unstable and temporary form of rule, in any case where the colony does not become assimilated to the colonial power, as Wales, for example, or Martinique, have done. There are two reasons for this. One is obvious. People like to govern themselves, in accordance with their own values, and are willing to make quite considerable sacrifices of efficiency in order to be ruled by people who talk their language and think as they do. This aspect has been made clear by every nationalist movement from Ireland to Buganda, and needs no expansion.

There is, however, another side, the side of the colonial power itself. If colonial rule is not to be pure exploitation—and normally it has not been—it must be justified by its success in changing the colonial society in ways in which it cannot change itself.[1] If the British change Indian society in such a way that India produces more entrepreneurs or more democrats than it did before, that may be some compensation to Indians for the loss of their freedom; if they leave Indian society as it was before, then, however good the government the British provide may be, it will still be felt as intolerable. Worst of all is the colonial power which attempts change without success. Thus the British opposed untouchability enough to annoy the orthodox, yet never took rigorous enough action to abolish it. The Northern carpet-baggers took enough action in favour of the negroes to create traumas among the Southern whites it is taking generations to cure, yet never were drastic enough to give the negroes a position of real equality. Another form of this is where the colonial power brings about the desire for change, and then opposes the change the desire for which it has itself brought about. The best known example is the way in which the British and the French have taught their subjects the merits of equality, democracy, and freedom, and then have proceeded all too often to refuse equality, postpone democracy, and argue they were unfit for freedom.

This ambivalence of the colonial power is not accidental. The people who support its changes are usually precisely those who wish to replace it in power; and its representatives on the spot tend to prefer the dignity of the old-fashioned, still secure in their own civilisation, to the insecurity of the Westernisers whom they so often resent as inferior copies of themselves. Tribal chiefs have nicer manners than clerical subordinates. But the growth of a society capable of economic development depends on the clerks, not on the tribal chiefs.

The result is that at the beginning colonial powers bring about very rapidly a whole series of the changes necessary for development. Manchuria in the 1930s, India in the second half of the nineteenth century, Rhodesia recently are all examples. Then the process slows down. There is, except in a few fortunate cases like Ghana, stagnation, tension, perhaps even economic retrogression. Politics replaces development as the centre of attention. Business confidence, that most delicate of plants, is disturbed. There is a reversion to older ways, a deliberate opposition to change. Whether the society can recover then depends on whether the local leaders are given the power

---

[1] I do not argue that this is necessarily a justification, only that no other justification is possible. The tribal societies of Gaul and Spain and Britain doubtless felt bitterly at the time about Roman exploitation and Roman destruction of their traditional values, however much at our present safe distance of time, we may feel it was all for our own good.

which will enable them to replace the foreign rulers as the engine of change; and on whether, when they get the power, they do or do not wish to use it in order to bring about the necessary changes.

A few examples may make these points clearer.

In India the process of economic change, from the building of railways to the creation of the tea industry, went on rapidly up to the early 1900s. Then came the nationalist movement. This had two consequences. The British became uncertain of themselves. They began to romanticise all that was old and loyal in Indian society, the princes, the landowners, the subsistence peasant, and to oppose all that was Westernising, the lawyer, the clerk, the Indian industrialist. They also lost confidence. Economically they stopped investing on the old scale. Few Indian loans were raised in London after 1919, and although British business already in India continued to expand, the only newcomers were a few great international corporations. Politically, they combined steady yielding on the legislative front with increasing social conservatism. Power began to pass to Indians, but the British no longer dared to abolish child marriage or polygamy as they had once abolished suttee, or to abolish the zemindars as they had once created them. All they could do was to use them to despair of the Indians with.

The result might easily have been a conservative British Government competing with a conservative Indian nationalism in trying to keep India static; there was a moment when Indians restored the pride hurt by perpetual European allegations of inferiority by claiming there were aeroplanes in the Vedas. Fortunately, the Congress party, under the leadership of Mahatma Gandhi, set its face firmly against any such obscurantism. Much of the Mahatma's economics was dubious. His insistence on hand-spinning, his passion for the self-sufficient village, his dislike of the machine, his objection to revenue from liquor as a fruit of sin, are making the growth of India's national income slower than it might otherwise have been. But even these have the advantage of making the peasant and the artisan the centre of the Indian Government's attention instead of merely, as they are in Communist countries, the people who pay the price of modernisation. And the rest of the Mahatma's ideas were unequivocally in favour of the sort of society which is required if there is to be economic development. Thus, he was against untouchability and caste discrimination; unbendingly he fought for the equality of women, and the education of the villager, and the idea that no job was too dirty to be below one's dignity; he would himself clean lavatories and live with untouchables, his own son made an inter-caste marriage. He insisted always that Indians should be proud of their past and stand on their own feet but should also not hesitate to adopt ideas from other countries that might be useful. He was a perpetual innovator, always, for example, trying to improve his spinning-wheel. He was friendly with businessmen, friendly enough to make Indian opinion for a time almost accept them as respectable. He was steadily in favour of land reform, and democracy, and freedom from arbitrary power for the common man. He was indeed in one aspect of him, one of the greatest of nineteenth-century liberals. It is not surprising that the Congress, his party, has since independence been engaged in all those reforms, from the equality of women to the abolition of rack-renting, which are necessary if India's Five-Year Plans are to succeed.

Mahatma Gandhi's rôle has been fundamental in preparing India for development. But something must also be said of Pandit Nehru, whose recognition of the importance of modern industry, whose insistence on planning, and whose appreciation of scientific research, have counterbalanced the Mahatma's Ruskinian insistence on the virtues of handicraft and the village. And, behind both the Mahatma and Pandit Nehru, making possible the effective carrying out of their ideas, is the corps of civil servants and technicians the British built up, who draft the reforms and run the railways and design the dams and make the contracts for technical advice.

India has been fortunate in its combination of a colonial power which laid the basis of a State capable of development with a nationalist movement ready to carry on the process of change where the colonial power left off. It has been fortunate too in a colonial power which realised not too much too late when the hour for it to go had struck, and in national leaders who have known how to lead instead of driving their people, how to push and pull them into change instead of shooting them into it. India is abolishing untouchability with the consent of the touchables, making women equal with the help of the men, getting rid of landlords with their own resigned acceptance, emphasising physics and economics rather than Sanskrit with hardly a murmur from the Pandits. Indian planning still shows an inadequate respect for business and the consumer, the Indian peasant still too often saves in order to spend on ceremonies rather than on investment. But on the whole Indian society has changed and is changing enough to make it probable that it can achieve development by its own bootstraps, that the Indian people are now interested enough in planning to raise their incomes to make the many sacrifices of habits as well as of money, which will be needed. From the purely economic standpoint one can criticise both the British and the Congress for many failures. The British, for example, hung on to power too long, did too little for primary education, spent too little on agricultural research, trained too few Indians too slowly. The Congress diverts too much attention to spinning, loses too much money in prohibition, does not appreciate the flexibility of private enterprise, places equality too high amongst the purposes of its taxation system. But these lists, and they could be lengthened, should not blind one to the greatness of the achievement which has made of India the leader among the great underdeveloped countries in economic development through democracy.

This analysis of the Indian achievement, however, in itself shows how special are the circumstances which have brought it about, how often is one or another necessary factor lacking in other colonial or ex-colonial countries. Thus, in much of Latin America, there is neither adequate law and order, nor any protection for the businessman from arbitrary Government nor any respect either for the slow money-grubbing or the perpetual innovation which builds up great enterprises. Much of the Middle East suffers from the concentration of too much power in the hands of a landlord class whose main interest is not development, but the preservation of their own privileges. Indonesia is terribly short of technicians and entrepreneurs. China has had no experience of elections, and before the Communists little recent experience of bureaucrats who were honest, obedient, and organised in proper cadres. In Rhodesia or South Africa the mining and farming techniques on which the economy depends are almost entirely unknown to anybody except the white minorities, so that development is perpetually slowed down at once by the fear of native advance and by the failure of the native to advance; the fear keeps out needed foreign capital and technicians, the failure prevents the native himself from providing a market, or providing adequate technicians, or taking a share in saving and investment and the making of innovations. Even in Pakistan, so similar in many ways to India, the very capable civil servants and soldiers who run the Government have been much hampered by the demands for an Islamic State, all too often interpreted by the ignorant as meaning purdah and the prohibition of interest.

In short, economic development is only possible in societies of a certain sort. Probably rapid economic development of the type the West has known since 1800 is possible only in societies like those of the West—Communism is not an exception to this, but an attempt to create such societies by force; whether it can in the long run keep its dynamic without Western freedom remains to be seen; so far Communist societies have on the whole been behind and imitating; if they ever catch up, so that it will not be so easy to decide to what ends the force should be used, they may well have to choose between freedom and being always just a step behind. Historically, however, Western society is a society of a highly exceptional type, which grew up because of a whole series of specially favourable circumstances and which as Hitler has shown, does not survive without perpetual vigilance even in its homelands. If the societies of the rest of the world want to raise their national incomes in the way Western incomes have gone up in the last century and a half, it is probable that they will have to transform themselves until they are very like Western societies. How far this transformation must go, which Western institutions are irrelevant to economic development, it is hard to say. The probability, however, is that the change will have to go very far, since even a society as like the American as the English is having to Americanise itself considerably in the desire for an income of American size. It is not necessary to jettison the study of Sanskrit for the study of Greek, or Buddhism for Christianity; but beyond such obvious examples it is difficult to think of any Western institution of which one can say with certainty that it has no relation to development. Western society is one whole, and its economic success has grown out of the whole.

Some underdeveloped societies have succeeded, or are engaged in Westernising themselves by themselves. But in such cases, Japan, Russia, China, the Westernising has been done from above, by very limited cadres. It has not yet been accepted by the whole people. It has also been external. Western material methods have been taken over without Western liberty. That has already led the Japanese to the defeat of 1945, and one does not know where it may yet take the Communists. There are therefore certain advantages for underdeveloped countries in a period of colonial rule, unpleasant though they find the experience. That way they can take over so much of the basis of Western society as they desire to absorb from the inside. Admittedly, that way involves losses, losses of old arts and values that may be considered superior to Western arts and values, losses too during the period of tension when everything is subordinated to the struggle for independence and during the period of hypernationalism which has so often followed independence. Nevertheless, it may well prove that it is the most effective way in the long run, the only way which permits a development in which the whole people share, a development which comes because the people want it and not because they are commanded into it. There is more hope in India, for all its slow start, than in China or pre-war Japan (post-war Japan has had its colonial experience), more hope in Nigeria than in Liberia or Ethiopia.

However valuable a catalyst colonialism may be, nevertheless, colonialism is not enough. There comes a stage when, if there is to be any further progress, there must be independence. This applies not only to the obvious colonial case, where the country is ruled by outsiders, it applies also to the subtler case, where the country is ruled by a minority class or race within itself. The groundwork for development can be laid by minorities and outsiders. They can build railways, develop mines, promulgate law codes, train élites. In the long run, however, economic development, if it is to be rapid, requires the co-operation of the whole people. Hence, the perpetual propaganda to their people of the Communist States, or the American insistence on the American way of life. The rich must save and create industries instead of buying land and Cadillacs. The peasant must adopt new methods, instead of concentrating on getting more acres and dowering his daughters. The worker must treat his machine with respect, and not in the way he used to treat the wheel of his oxcart. Women must come out of the home, the poor must have hopes of improving their lot. Such changes are more than foreigners and minorities can achieve. Barriers of language, of religion, of habits, of ways of eating and dressing, make the majorities they are trying to change look upon them as strangers, as 'they' and not 'we'; and people do not change their most intimate habits for strangers. The most striking proof is the amount of force the Russian Communists have had to use on their peasants, and the Russian Communists were always Russian, and sometimes ex-peasants. When a peasant has to be shown what crop to grow, or how to treat his wife and his neighbours, or what innovations to accept from his growing son, it must be done by people of his own blood. If at that stage power stays in foreign or minority hands, the whole process of development will be slowed down by what is in effect, though perhaps not in intent, the passive resistance of the majority. The misfortune is when that stage is reached while there are still not enough locals to be able to persuade the majority to the changes that are needed. Then the result, if there are enough to use force though not enough to persuade, is liable to be Communism; if there are not even enough for that, there can be only stagnation.

Chapter 13

LAND REFORM

MOST of Asia lives on the land. The proportion engaged in agriculture is rarely less than three-quarters. The income of the people depends, therefore, upon how productively the land is used more than upon anything else. Experience has shown that the land will not be used productively unless the man who does the using and who has to invest the labour, capital and knowledge required to create the productivity, reaps the benefit of his efforts. Who owns the land, therefore, is a question of vital import in every Asian economy.

Theoretically, there are three possible answers. The land can be owned collectively, as in Russia today and as it is soon to be in China. Or it can be owned by large capitalist farmers or landlords. Or it can be owned by the man who tills it, the peasant himself.

In practice, free Asia has no such range of choice. It must give ownership to the peasant. The peasant will vote out of office any Government that seriously suggests collectivisation. Moreover, what has happened in Russia suggests that while collectivisation and the mechanisation which accompanies it may be a good way of releasing labour to work in industry, of turning the terms of trade against the countryside in favour of the town, and of ensuring that the townsmen get their rations and industry its agricultural raw materials, it does not in any way increase the yield of land per acre; in annual husbandry it leads to a positive decline in output.

The advantages of collectivisation are not advantages in free Asia. The disadvantage that it does not raise yield is fatal. First, there is no need to use special measures in order to make available labour from the land for industry; the land has more people on it than it can effectively use; there could be a very large movement into industry, both from agriculture and from handicrafts, without any reduction in output in the occupations from which the surplus labour would move. Secondly, the democratic countries of Asia have no Marxist bias in favour of the proletariat. To them peasant and industrial worker are equal, voters both. There is no reason to give the town artificially favourable terms of trade, or to raise a disproportionate amount of investible resources by large turnover taxes on agricultural products. Thirdly, theirs are not siege economies. Hitherto, except in conditions of war or near-war, their towns and industries have been adequately supplied with food and raw materials by the ordinary operation of the market. It is simpler, as well as more sensible, for them to improve the output of their agriculture by better techniques than to take an increasing percentage of a static output by rationing and force.

On the other hand, the disadvantage of collectivisation, that it reduces the peasant's interest in what he is doing, is crucial. In free Asia, if the peasant does not look after his animals and make the millions of little experiments which are required to adapt modern knowledge to the special conditions of each little plot, nobody will. Theoretically, again, if one had large State farms run by a core of accountants and agronomists managing labourers, as seems to be the Russian objective, techniques could be improved and costs reduced more quickly than by millions of scientifically uneducated peasants acting individually. But in practice Asia has not got, and could not have for many years, the necessary agronomists and accountants while Russian experience suggests that in fact very often this system does not produce an increase in output, but only an increase in overheads.

Capitalist farming, despite its occasional successes, as on the Mitchell farms in Pakistan, is on the whole equally unsuitable for free Asia. The reasons are not economic, but sociological. In economic theory, there is no reason why the large landlord or the large farmer, with an adequate scientific training and ample supplies of capital, should not be able to increase the yield of his land much quicker than small holders with less knowledge and little capital, possibly can. The high yields of the English landlord and large farmer as against the lower yields of the French peasant prove that. But in Asia capitalist farming will not work for sociological reasons. Most of the land of Asia is today farmed by small owners or tenants; in India in the 1951 Census 66·7 per cent of those on the land returned themselves as owners, a further 12·3 per cent as tenants. In the democracies of Asia the tenant and small owner will not today accept the reduction to the ranks of landless labour which was enforced on the small English farmer over the years 1500–1820. Nor is large-scale mechanised farming possible, except in very limited areas, because it would only add to the problem of rural unemployment and underemployment which is already the nightmare of so many Asian governments.

Above all, the large Asian landholder is not a capitalist. His land is to him always a source of status and sometimes an investment. It is very rarely a business. This is because his property is not usually the result of past hard work or the successful taking of risks; it has mostly come either from conquest or from foreclosing on loans made at usurious interest or from religious grants. There are few Indian Brahmins or Rajputs or Banias— the three main landlord castes—who built up their holdings through good farming; and the big West Pakistan landlords usually began as tribal chiefs or Muslim saints.

Because he lacks the capitalist outlook, the Asian landlord does not save in order to be able to improve his land. The great majority live up to, and often beyond their incomes. The few who do save put most of their savings, like the Maharaja of Darbhanga, into industry and urban property. They are not interested in improvement. Asia has no Bakewells and few Cokes of Holkham amongst its landlords. The Asian landlord rarely experiments, except in a desultory way, with cattle breeding or fertiliser formulae; he still more rarely provides buildings or roads or drainage or irrigation for his tenants, as landlords so often do elsewhere. His interest is in spending his rents, and using his position to increase his power.

Such landlords are necessarily a very severe drag on development.

Their rents are high. An average for Asia may be half the crop, or several times the West European norm; and the Asian landlord provides his tenant with none of the fixed capital—the farmhouse and the farm roads, for example—which are so frequently provided in Western Europe. If he does make advances to his tenant, or let him have capital or fertiliser, these have to be paid for separately, until the landlord may in some instances be taking three-quarters or four-fifths of the crop.

Clearly, in these conditions, while the landlord will not invest, the tenant *cannot* invest. Yet, unless the law protects him, the tenant cannot escape from these conditions. Because techniques are so simple that every labourer knows them, because almost everywhere there are too many people on the land so that men will offer anything to get a piece of land to cultivate, and because the unit of operation is so small that every family can manage it, rents are driven up to a level which leaves the tenant not much more than subsistence. He has neither the surplus with which to invest, nor the leisure and education with which to find out what innovations he ought to adopt. Moreover, wherever the landlord is powerful, the tenant fears that if he does improve the land, his landlord will get rid of him in order to use his improvement to obtain a higher rent from someone else.

Landlordism interferes with economic development also in a more subtle way. It interferes also because so many landlords use their land primarily as a basis of political power. The big man is looking for power in the nation, and wants his tenants and labourers as voters or private armies. The little man wants power within the village, to be the person who arbitrates disputes, and to have his inferiors get up from their seats when he goes by. These attitudes inhibit development by both landlord and tenant. The landlord wants his tenants' votes, their support in village factions, their respect on ceremonial occasions; he must therefore not depart too far from their ideas, however old-fashioned economically they may be. But equally, precisely because the landlord wants from his tenant support and respect, he is not too pleased to see successful innovators, capable small businessmen arising among his tenants. A tenant who is a successful developer of new agricultural methods is all too likely to become a successful rival for the village council, or an organiser of other tenants against their landlords, or a challenger of a social system that puts the landlord's class (or caste) above his own. In societies where status is all, the possibility of a share for the landlord in the tenant's profits from his innovations is no compensation for so serious a potential threat to the landlord's status. Men who raise a riot if their tenants dare to imitate their forms of marriage display and who are liable to commit murder if a tenant aspires to their daughter, will not regard a small increase of income as compensation for having to accept tenants as equals. Keeping tenants in their place is a fundamental tenet of most Asian landlordism; and men kept sufficiently firmly in their place do not innovate.

If Asian agriculture is to advance, therefore, the landlord must go. Of the three possible methods of owning the land which we originally suggested, only one will work if what is desired is that methods should improve, and output go up. The tiller must own the land. That will not solve all difficulties. The tenant, who has become a free peasant, will still be small, and ignorant, and in no position to take any but the safest risks. However, given the State help and co-operation and education, discussed in Chapters 14 to 17, these difficulties might in time be overcome. The difficulties in the way of agricultural development through landlords or collectivisation can never be overcome, at least not in free societies, where those on the land have a vote.

Part Four

SOCIAL

———◦◦———

Chapter 14

EDUCATION

ECONOMIC development rests upon capital accumulated,
but the process of accumulation is not only physical, it is
also mental. Skill and knowledge are as important as
buildings and plant; and in a developing society, which is therefore a changing society, the sort of skill, the type of knowledge
which is required, is perpetually new, perpetually different from
those which the society is accustomed to teach and to which its
institutions are adjusted. Each new development means a new
educational curriculum. To make farmers out of peasants, they
must be taught reading and arithmetic, elementary biology and
some animal husbandry, perhaps a little botany and certainly
some physiology. Or, to take a more complicated example. A
railway needs not only money, track, signal-boxes and rolling
stock; it must also have created for it engine drivers and signal-
men, platelayers and transport superintendents, timetable
makers and labourers who can load a crate of glass without
breaking it. Each new line means a new educative effort and,
whereas money can be borrowed, skill must be developed in the
country itself if the native of the country is not to find himself
disinherited in his own land.

These may seem elementary propositions, but they are not
always fully appreciated either in the developed countries,
where the necessary processes of education have been going on
for so long that they are no longer thought about, or in the
underdeveloped countries, whose intellectuals do not always
realise that to make a main-line signalman out of an aboriginal
labourer is a longer process than for themselves to learn the
classics; nor is it always realised just how extensive the task of
education is in a society only beginning to develop. People may
know that one cannot drive an engine without training. They
do not always recognise that, for example, designing textile
prints is a skill to be acquired and not a job to be left to the

weaving master in his spare time; and hardly ever understand that even an unskilled labourer in a modern factory needs more than just to be shown what he has to lift or push. He is taken in at the factory gate in Leeds or Dusseldorf and put straight to work. Why should it not be the same in Bombay or Djakarta?

Nevertheless, it is not the same. However simple the actual work may be to learn, the ways of a factory are not, for a modern factory is a little civilisation in itself with its own rules and conventions and habits of thought. People who have never had to deal with anything more complicated than a wooden cart-wheel cannot be expected to know by instinct that too rough a jerk may wreck an expensive machine. People who have always regulated their lives by the sun and the growing of crops, cannot be expected to understand, unaided, that in a factory nine o'clock is a very different time from eight-thirty and that one cannot work harder for four days in order to make time to go to a wedding on the fifth.

Economic development thus involves a country not in one educational task, but in a whole series.

First, one has to create specific skills. People must be taught to mend a motor engine or work a drill or artificially inseminate a cow.

Secondly, one must create certain habits, attitudes, and ways of thought. People must learn to be urban, industrial and scientific instead of peasants living by ancestral saws and a long-tried rule of thumb.

Thirdly, the education has to be given at the right time; the clerks and the chemical engineers and the lorry drivers must be ready when they are needed or the society will be faced with the alternative of either accepting bottlenecks or importing people from outside who will tend, as in Africa, to become privileged and self-perpetuating minorities. On the other hand, they must not be ready before they are needed or there will be unemployment and the bitter discontent which comes from spending long years to acquire a skill which then cannot be exercised through no fault of its possessor. There are, for example, few under-developed countries which have not suffered from increasing their production of lawyers faster than they have increased their production as a whole.

Fourthly, the new education has to be grafted on to the old. The baby must not be thrown out with the bath water; the old education cannot be simply scrapped. The most primitive tribe has a culture of its own. Countries like India and China have civilisations whose art, literature and philosophy rank with the best Europe has to offer—neither Russia nor America can yet compare. If these ancient ways of life and thought are blown upon, ridiculed as old-fashioned, despised as unscientific, condemned as immoral, punished as savouring of witchcraft, then the society becomes disoriented. The old sanctions no longer apply; the sanctions by which Western society holds together are rarely taught and still more rarely understood. The result is the detribalised native, the native more European than the Europeans, or the Communist; and it is to be noted that of these only the Communist holds out any hope for the future. The detribalised native has lost the old without gaining the new. The Vietnamese who was completely French, the Indian who was completely English, had made a successful personal transition, but the process was too long and complicated and expensive to be possible for the whole of his society. The Communist by contrast acquires a complete Western outlook and does so in a sufficiently simplified and missionary form for it to be propagatable among the wide masses. The price is that he has to sacrifice everything else. China has jettisoned its classics; revolutionary Russia has produced no successor to Dostoevsky and Turgeniev.

THE FIRST TASK—THE SPECIFIC SKILLS

Of our four tasks, the first—the teaching of the specific skills—is the easiest. The Japanese solved it completely. They realised they had to learn and they learnt. A Europe which had forgotten its own beginnings laughed at them as ' copy-cats'—the superiority of the European attitude cannot be better expressed than by this schoolboy term—but they bowed politely at the laughter and in forty years were able to defeat Russia, in seventy-five to take on the United States. Nor are the Japanese alone. Every underdeveloped country whose Government has not taken the short cut of importing skill instead of creating it locally, has shown that this is a problem it can solve. Every railway system in Asia is locally run; and Asians today make as good pilots or irrigation engineers or physicists as Europeans, though there are not always enough of them to meet the needs of countries beginning to develop rapidly. The negroes of the Belgian Congo—and a bare half-century ago there was nobody more primitive—today drive locomotives. The theory of much nineteenth-century colonialism, which in its extremest form is the present day theory of many white settlers in Africa, that there are certain things a native is inherently incapable of doing, is simply démodé. All the facts since 1914 are against it. The frequent difficulties which still exist—the shortages of draftsmen or firemen or miners or good fitters or farmers who understand about erosion—are all due to failures of education. People have not been taught how to do these things or, perhaps even more often, they have been taught the husk without the kernel, the physical motions without the mental attitudes. In such cases what has gone wrong has been the failure to realise that in order to succeed in the first task, the teaching of specific skills, one must also succeed in the second, the creation of certain habits, of a certain outlook.

THE SECOND TASK—THE CREATION OF ATTITUDES

(a) Technique alone is not enough

The importance of training in how to conceive the job and not just in how to do it runs through every level and every subject. Thus, it has always been understood that to make a lorry driver, a man must be taught how to change gear and where the brakes are. It has not always been understood that to be a *good* lorry driver, he must have a feel for his vehicle, he must learn to nurse it, must learn that brakes are not there to be driven on and that gears must be changed before the engine pinks.

This is a very simple example and one which will be familiar to all who have had to deal with African or Asian drivers of motor vehicles. But its implications go deep. Western industrial civilisation is one whole in which techniques and attitudes act and re-act perpetually and the techniques cannot be acquired without the attitudes. One cannot teach a man how to make glassware of Swedish quality without teaching him the pride in his work, the feel for his materials, of the Swedish craftsman, as well as how to make glass. The biggest single difficulty in making Indian craftsmanship, for example, economically viable, is the tendency of the Indian craftsman to put good work on bad material and to be slipshod where he thinks it will not matter. He will make a lovely print and the dyes will run; he will take good sambhur leather and sew it with threads which snap. This need for the right attitude as well as the right technique is still more essential in heavy industry. Where accuracies of thousandths of an inch are required, it is not enough merely to know how to work the lathe which does the machining; a man's whole mind must be on his work, his whole self-respect must be involved in the quality of the result.

The problem is of a width which touches every aspect of education, every social attitude. Two examples will illustrate its ramifications. The first is the question of making manual labour respectable, the second the emphasis in Asia on the function of the Universities as a training for modern life, rather than as a nursery of scholars.

(b) The importance of using one's hands

In every agricultural society which has been able to afford a leisured class, the educated have stopped using their hands. Cincinnatus returning from his dictatorship to the plough is always an early story of the golden age; and in Asia this golden age is a very long way away indeed. Already for Manu, the great Hindu legislator who wrote nearly 2,000 years ago, agriculture was not amongst the respectable professions.

If Asia is to develop, however, the educated must learn to use their hands again. Modern society depends much less on the labourer's brawn than any society which has preceded it, because the machine can now do so much of the heavy work. It is, however, very much more dependent than were the European middle ages or than are today's underdeveloped countries, on the willingness to use their hands of the educated and still more of the semi-educated. The medical researcher, if he is to be sure of the accuracy of his results, must be able to look after his rats himself. The Works Manager must himself know how to run a lathe or boil a pan of soap.

This need to use the intellectual's hands comes hard in societies where for centuries clean hands and no sweating have been the reward of the arduous disciplines of education; it comes especially hard where the work is dirty as well as manual. In underdeveloped countries it is much harder to get nurses than doctors, foremen than clerks, Works Managers than laboratory chemists. The need for a new outlook is the constant wail of all who write on the subject.

Wailing, however, is not enough. There must be action. The Prime Minister must dig, so that people may know that digging is respectable. Engineering apprentices must have unnecessarily high minimum educational qualifications, a special pay scale and a guaranteed chance of promotion to make apprenticeship a Career with a capital 'C'. Above all, school life as a whole must place an emphasis on the manual job and the dirty job which is not necessary in, say, the United States. Much of the new Indian basic education, for instance, uses agriculture, the manual agriculture of digging and planting and weeding, as the craft through which other subjects are taught. Asian officers' training corps are often more valued by their governments for making undergraduates dig trenches and clean latrines than for turning out officers; and just as the medical student has to dissect bodies as well as read textbooks, so the engineering student must learn there is more to engineering than blueprints and mathematical calculations. In short, the campaign to make dirty work and physical work respectable is one which must be conducted all the time and at every level. It must not be confined, as is too often the tendency, to the academic report and the ministerial exhortation. It must cease to be a point of piety and become a hub of policy, for economic development is impossible without it. No society can build itself if the builders are ignorant and the architects stay indoors with their designs.

(c) What can be done—the example of the clerk

The change of attitudes Asia requires is so great as to be intimidating. Yet one can take heart from an example where success has already been achieved, the Clerk. What was done to make clerks, and the reasons why it was relatively easy to make clerks, point the path to what needs to be done to make the other technicians Asia needs.

Clerks are the fly wheels on which modern social organisation turns, a point sometimes forgotten by those who laugh at babus. Without people to keep the accounts, send out the invoices, look after the records, answer the letters, do the typing, work out the costs and remember the precedents, no factory or Government office or even private professional man could work effectively for a week. In the ancient society of Asia or Africa, however, clerks hardly existed. There were priests and scholars, lawyers and herbalists, but there were very few of what would today be called white-collared workers. India's revenue records before the British came were chaotic and even court decisions were rarely properly filed. Africa, or Sumatra, was worse still; in their tribal societies clerks did not exist at all.

Nor is making clerks in itself easier than making foremen or fitters. The clerk requires at least as many qualities as they do; and none of the qualities he requires come automatically to the son of a peasant or an astrologer. A clerk must be careful, exact, conscientious, punctual, regular in his habits and intellectually honest. He must be able to work with very little supervision; one must be able to rely on him to look up the precedents correctly, or to check a ledger which does not balance by going over the figures again, and not by fiddling them. A good clerk must, too, have a mind of some quality and with some academic training.

He must be able to decide, at least in simple cases, under which head a cost should be classified or in what terms a letter should be answered. Finally, any organisation of any size must be able to look for a considerable proportion of its officers (or managers) from amongst its clerks if incentive is to be preserved and if it is to have enough experience at the top. And in most Asian countries all this has to be done in a language which is not the clerk's own.

It is a very large bill. Nowadays one tends to forget how large a bill it is, both because the problem has been so successfully solved and because in Western countries the clerk's relative position has worsened so severely in the last twenty years. But if one looks at nineteenth-century Europe, one sees an enormous gap between the position of the white-collar worker and that of the manual worker, however skilled. This gap was at once the result of, and the reward for, the long list of qualities which the good clerk had to have. In other words, making clerks was so complicated that Europe, unlike Asia, found it more difficult to make clerks than fitters or foremen.

It is, therefore, important to consider why in Asia there has been so much more success with clerks than with almost any of the other categories an economically developing society requires.

The answer seems to be twofold. Clerking requires an education very similar to the traditional literary education of Asia; it flies in the face of none of Asia's traditional cultural values. Second, the real training for clerking was given not on the job, but before at the University or high school. It was his B.A., or at least his matriculation, not what he was taught in the office about the routine of the office, that made the clerk punctual and disciplined, enterprising and accurate.

(d) Culture and the fitter

What has been done for clerking must be done for every job which matters in development. Some reconciliation must be found between the requirements of the job and traditional cultural values. Otherwise good boys will continue to go for those jobs where the reconciliation has been made, and will leave the others severely alone, however necessary they may be to the country's development. If bright boys are to become fitters and draftsmen, foremen and overseers, and sales managers, the training for these jobs must be given something of the prestige which at present attaches to the acquisition of the society's traditional culture.

Education in a society's culture, the absorption of its civilisation, carries high prestige everywhere; nor is this surprising. A society's self-respect depends upon such education, upon the continuance of its own tradition, its own separate contribution to the world's civilisation. In most societies indeed the traditional culture is connected with the majority religion, and is thus stamped with divine approval also. The Hindu does not learn Sanskrit or the Muslim Arabic for their mundane value alone. The purpose of Asian education has in the past been as much to inculcate the canons of right behaviour as to produce, an appreciation of the classics. Inevitably, it has prestige. No science is in the end as important as theology. Nothing is more aesthetically satisfying than the classics.

This education will, however, produce only some of the people a developing society requires. It has made good clerks as we have seen; it has not hitherto made good plumbers or good mechanics. The clerk had the advantage that he needed an education of the traditional type. The classical masters of expression taught him lucidity, the moralists of the past gave him character. It is different when we come to a man who repairs lorry engines or supervises a roomful of girls packing soap. He needs less cloistered qualities, a knowledge of machines and of people, a sense of authority perhaps, a capacity for improvisation certainly. These require a different education, more practical, learnt more on the job.

The attempt to get the best boys to take this different education will, however, fail so long as it ranks below the traditional literary education. If to do a seven-year apprenticeship in an engineering shop is considered low, if the apprentice ranks a worse bride in the marriage market than the man who scrapes his B.A., then only those without an option will become engineering apprentices.

There are two possible, and simultaneous, cures for this attitude. First, the elements of the traditional education must be given to more people so that everybody who rises above the unskilled level has something of the formal culture of his society. Secondly, the specific training given for different jobs must show more respect for the academic leanings of Asia, and base itself less on the on-the-job methods of nineteenth-century Europe. There must be certificates for fitters which rank with matriculation, B.A.s suitable for draftsmen.

This perhaps requires some further explanation.

The present value attached to literary education and to being cultured are partly the result of the fact that in Asia education is still a rarity. Outside Japan even literacy is the exception. Culture therefore, though it may not help a man much in earning his living, makes a great deal of difference to his social position, to the people he knows and the families with whom his family can marry; and that in Asia is more important than money.

To denounce this emphasis on literary culture as wrong, as has for so long been so customary, does not help. It is doubtful whether it is wrong. Does an individual really develop his personality better by learning how to draw a blue-print than by learning how to appreciate Shakespeare or read the Bhagavad Gita in Sanskrit? But, even if it is wrong, so long as a man gives more pleasure to his mother by becoming a failed B.A. than a successful overseer, he will become a failed B.A. The way to deflate the value attached to academic education is not to deprecate it, but to increase the number of people who have it. More people must be educated; and to give practical jobs the same prestige as desk jobs, more of them must be taught academically.

The increase in the numbers of the educated is now very general. The number of children at school and of students at the Universities is going up very rapidly, and the effect of this increase is already being felt. There are so many too many of the literate for them all to have desk jobs, that the farmer's son who can read and write is now beginning to stay on the farm and to use his new knowledge to increase the family income through adopting improved seed for his wheat or artificial insemination for his cows. Similarly, there are so many too many matriculates and even graduates for them all to be clerks or accountants that now one can, at least in India, get graduates as salesmen and matriculates as skilled artisans. The answer to educated unemployment is not less education, but more, so much more that the educated will spill over into an ever-widening range of jobs, taking their prestige with them into the new jobs instead of being deterred from doing any but the old jobs because the new jobs have no prestige. And, as that happens, so economic development will become progressively easier. The graduate is, on the average, a better salesman than the matriculate, the matriculate a better overseer of works than the barely literate.

Giving an academic flavour to more sorts of training is more complicated, but quite as important. In Western society much importance has always been given to training on the job. The Works Manager began as an apprentice. The financial director began as an office boy. To begin at the bottom and work one's way up had, for a vital century, a Samuel Smiles glamour. But it is to be remarked that now that more poor boys can get themselves educations, starting at the bottom is losing its glamour in the West also. In Asia it has never had any. The fact that a man started at the bottom is remembered against him all his life; not even money makes him really acceptable and only a lot of money can make his children marriageable. Moreover, except in such not very highly regarded walks of life as speculation and shopkeeping, to begin really at the bottom and work one's way up is almost impossible. One may begin as a clerk, but not as an office boy, as a technical assistant, but not on the factory floor.

The reason is that the modern economy, like modern forms of Government, is in Asia an innovation, an introduction from the West. It does not grow spontaneously out of the society, like cotton mills in Lancashire. It must be learnt; and what must be learnt is more extensive than in the West. To succeed in China one must learn Marxism, to get on in India one must know English. However low one may have started, to acquire either Marxism or English makes a man an intellectual, cut off from his less educated fellows in a way the nineteenth-century millionaire who acquired money but kept his Lancashire accent never was. Education, therefore, keeps a prestige and also a usefulness which training on the job cannot give. A B.A. is not just a sign that one has passed an examination of a certain level, it is a symbol that one has acquired a modern attitude of mind, that one is no longer a peasant following the rules of his ancestors, but a man capable of acting and adapting in a Westernised and industrialised world, and, where the technical books are still, as in most countries in most subjects, in a foreign language, it is also a guarantee of the knowledge that makes more knowledge possible. In Asia, as distinct from nineteenth-century Europe, the self-taught must teach themselves more than just how to read.

Since, therefore, training on the job alone is not enough, one must have more courses. The model must be nineteenth-century Germany or twentieth-century America, with their courses in everything from journalism to carpentry, not England or France with their belief that the academic must be really academic. One must perhaps be able to get a diploma in engine-driving, a degree in the mechanics of the internal-combustion engine. Since people of talent will not go into jobs at fifteen, they must be made fit to go into them at twenty; since one must have an academic distinction to get a wife, one must be able to get the academic distinction in the field in which one can earn a living.

In this process of giving academic and cultural sanction to the knowledge and outlook development requires, no institution is as important as the University. It is the University which has made chemists and lawyers, clerks and doctors as respectable as astrologers and priests, philosophers and theologians. Every time the University provides a new discipline with academic sanction, the problem of getting recruits to it is solved. That is why so often nowadays the worst difficulties in getting the skills which are needed comes not at the top level, where they have been sanctified by doctorates, but at the middle level, where they have not yet been given diplomas.

It is worth seeing in more detail how this has worked.

(e) The function of the University

Much scorn has been expended on the allegedly half-educated and parrot-like products of Asian Universities. Certainly their academic standards are sometimes low, though no lower than those of the pre-war Cambridge pass degree. The scorn is nevertheless misplaced. The low standards are deliberate and appropriate.

The reason is not that Asian societies are less well endowed in the academically brilliant than Western societies. Admittedly, less original work is done in, say, the sciences, but the cause is lack of money and the newness of the disciplines rather than the impossibility of getting good men.

The reason is that the social task of the Asian University is not fully comparable with that of Cambridge or Harvard. What Asia needs at this stage is less scholars than people who have the basic knowledge, the fundamental attitudes which are needed to live and work successfully in the modern world. The University's job, therefore, is not so much to turn out double firsts, who can in any case only be few, but to mass-produce the equivalent of American junior college graduates. The really brilliant can be finished abroad or in special institutes; it is noteworthy that India's new chain of scientific research institutions are none of them attached to Universities. Nor does it matter if, for the time during which the Universities are performing their immense task of assimilation, Asia has to rely on more developed countries for most of its scientific advance. Penicillin does not cure an Asian pneumonia less effectively because it was discovered in England; and no Asian country could afford to spend the 300 million dollars on research which the Salk vaccine cost.

What the Asian University has to do is to create an educated class with a modern outlook. 'Modern' is, of course, a vague word, and the outlook which has to be created is not altogether easy to define. The willingness to accept new ideas and the results of scientific experiment are part of it; democracy and nationalism and the value of hard work and using one's hands all come into it somewhere; even love and choosing one's own wife may have a place.

For this task many Asian Universities are ideally constituted. Their whole purpose was to bring Western knowledge to Asia through the institution which the West had found most effective for that purpose. The Asian tradition had on the whole been that of the teacher and his disciples, which is admirable so long as knowledge is sufficiently limited to be encompassed by one teacher. But once specialisation begins, it is not enough. One must have a team of teachers, one must have laboratories and libraries, one must have an organised programme of research so that each researcher is content to add his little bit to knowledge instead of trying, as in the European and Asian past, to write a new commentary on the whole of what was already known. The University performs all these tasks to perfection—it had perhaps also done so in the Asian past, at Nalanda and Taxila, but in 1850 that tradition had been dead for a thousand years—and it is, therefore, natural that the University, like the railway, is an institution every Asian country has borrowed from the West unchanged; whether one looks at still colonial Malaya or at democratic India or at Communist China or at military-dominated pre-war Japan, the structure of the University and the essential of what it is trying to do are the same, though the spirit in which it works, the freedom with which it is allowed to work and, therefore, also the quality of its work, vary a great deal.

The University was, in conception, an instrument for the dissemination and broadening of knowledge. Because modern knowledge cannot be acquired without the attitudes which lie behind it, or science without something of the scientific mind, the University has turned out men whose capacity to modernise, to change, and to develop their societies is of a quite different order from that of men trained in the Confucian classics or the Commentators on the Koran.

Let us take once again our example of the clerk. The routine details of the clerk's job are often not difficult to learn on the job; if he is put in a good section he will pick them up in a few weeks. It is admittedly desirable to have in addition courses in such subjects as shorthand and typewriting or elementary book-keeping, and underdeveloped countries, in their excitement about atomic energy or clinical medicine, tend to give far too little attention to these little courses. But it is only a matter of giving them attention. They are neither difficult nor expensive to provide; the fees do not have to be high and they do not take long out of the life of the student.

The difficulty lies in creating the attitudes which enable a boy or girl to take advantage of his or her book-keeping or typing course. One cannot go straight from a village to such a course and within three months be fit to go straight into an office. These are habits of mind to acquire, hard work, punctuality, care, ambition within a hierarchy; there are modes of thought to learn, the willingness to accept innovation, the interest which makes suggestions possible, the understanding that rules must be obeyed because that makes the organisation work more easily.

These attitudes the University gives, for the University combines freedom of thought with a severe mental discipline; a training in organising one's thoughts for oneself with a realisation that there are others who know better than oneself; a willingness to try new ideas with a refusal to theorise unless one first knows the facts.

Even that much-maligned institution, the examination, has been invaluable to Asian societies, for in their tradition as in mediaeval Europe, scholarship was largely confined to those for whom it was a pleasure. A man became a scholar by being recognised as such by his fellow-scholars. That was not enough once one wanted to know just who was good for what over a wide range of employment. The advantage of examinations is that they enable one to grade at definite levels those in whom a certain amount of knowledge is necessary if they are to perform effectively some everyday function; e.g. a certain knowledge of English is necessary to be able to write a clear letter, a certain knowledge of physiology to be able to make a diagnosis. They permit the weeding out of those who are never going to be scholars at all, on anybody's standards, and, at the same time, they remind the student that the acquisition of knowledge is not just a hobby, that one cannot simply follow one's bent, that a subject is a whole, in which one must do the dull parts and learn the uninteresting facts too.

These are invaluable lessons, as one can again see from our example of the clerk, whose job requires him to treat every fact with respect and never to fudge a part of his work because it is routine. The University graduate is a better clerk than the matriculate and the matriculate, who has acquired some of the same standards, is a better clerk than the boy with a primary school leaving certificate, not so much because he knows more— his knowledge is inevitably in itself largely irrelevant to his work—but because, in order to know what he knows, he has had to learn those attitudes of mind which are needed to make a good clerk and which neither agriculture nor a village mother can teach.

What the University has done not only for the clerk but also for the lawyer and the doctor, the engineer and the physicist, has now to be done in all those other spheres of the national life where the supply of the skills which are needed is still desperately short. There, too, education for the job must consist in teaching not only techniques, but also attitudes, the attitudes which will enable a man to do the job competently and, still more, those which will make it possible for him to do it with pride.

Foremen, for example, must learn not only how the machines in their shop work; they must also learn that it is important for them to know how their men think and that the responsibility for the costs of their section is theirs first and other people's only afterwards; that theirs is a post of key social importance, the link between the men and the management through which information must pass constantly up and down if the factory is to work as a team and, therefore, effectively. Nor does teaching stop with the foreman himself. It is no use his having right attitudes if those above and below have wrong ones. The men too must see the foreman both as their link and as their line of promotion; the management must remember to see that he is never by-passed, that he is given the information he needs and that changes in policy are put to him in a way that will carry his agreement.

Such attitudes, in societies where the whole body of attitudes which go with industry are still new, can be learnt on the job only in the very best firms; and Asia has not got one hundred years in which to make mistakes as Europe had. The attitudes have therefore to be taught, though not necessarily in universities. Technical schools and personnel courses and Training-within-Industry will also have their part to play; for a problem so large, the answers must be many. But all the answers must base themselves on the lesson of the University's success. Society must be changed through its traditional values of learning and the quest for truth, not against them.

THE THIRD TASK—PLANNING EDUCATIONAL PRODUCTION

Because formal education is so important in Asia, the whole responsibility of seeing that the skills society needs are neither overproduced nor underproduced falls upon the educational system; and the penalties of bad estimates are heavy.

Overproduction brings about the educated unemployment

which at once makes the educated dissatisfied with the *status quo*, and gives them the free time in which to lead subversion. Underproduction produces a bottleneck everywhere at once. Public works are held up because there are no engineers and no overseers; Government functions badly because the clerks delay; the productivity and the standard of service of private industry go down because the new foremen and salesmen are worse than the old ones. There was in fact a deterioration of exactly this sort in the '40s in all the countries which were at war.

One must get the answer right. Yet it is an answer which it is very difficult to get right. From the time he goes to school till the time he finishes University it takes fifteen years to make a graduate, and before one can expand Universities, or run specialised courses, one must first train the teachers. To spread an idea like Training-within-Industry through industry may take a decade or more, to build up a good school of Economics may take a generation. One is, therefore, almost inevitably, always behind with the new skills and the new attitudes; new lines of development are always being held up for want of the people to carry them out. Every new venture means a training programme far larger than in Europe. If one wants to try artificial insemination of cattle, one must quadruple one's veterinary colleges; if one wants a new steel plant, one must arrange simultaneously to make steel workers and steel engineers. Public pressure is always to go more and more quickly; yet if one goes more quickly than one can train the necessary people, one may have such severe failures that the whole policy will be discredited; the man whose cow did not breed because somebody did not keep the test tube at the right temperature will not try artificial insemination again.

One never has enough of the new skills. Parental errors of judgement ensure that one always has too much of the old ones. The public have now had long enough to see that education is in the modern world the key to a job, to success, to prestige. The entry into the new, and rapidly expanding, middle classes is everywhere overwhelmingly through education. There is, therefore, a steady demand for more and more and more. The number of matriculates in India tripled between 1937 and 1950. But parents tend to be guided not by a judgement of the future, but by a reflection of the past. They do not ask themselves which walk of life offers the most opportunities for the next thirty years, but which has offered the most in the last thirty years. They look at the successful of today; they do not ask who will be the successful of tomorrow. If an ear, nose and throat surgeon is earning $25,000 a year because there is only one and there is need for two, twenty boys will make this their speciality, so that, by the time they qualify, though the need may have risen from two to five or even ten, there will still not be room for all of them. The most famous instance of this tendency is the overproduction of lawyers in countries like India and Pakistan and Burma. All through the nineteenth and early twentieth century the law was the way to fame and wealth, position and leadership. Therefore, too many people became lawyers, until one finished with the briefless barrister of the '30s. Then parents at last realised what was happening, and now in the '50s the supply has gone down enough for the first-class young lawyer to be sought after once more.

The parents are not altogether to blame. Exact prediction of educational needs is probably not possible. The scale of output which made graduate unemployment a major social problem in the India of the '30s, was hopelessly inadequate as soon as the war broke out; boys who would have been lucky to have been clerks lower division in 1938 were majors in 1944, and often quite good majors too. Since the war, however, in most of Asia it has at last been realised that in education as in soap-selling, one must make a guesstimate of demand before planning production. The errors of the future should therefore be less hopeless than those of the '20s and '30s. They can be considerably further reduced by various special measures.

First, more training can be done after a man has been employed. The Indian village level worker, for example, is given one year's course in such subjects as revenue law and agriculture after he starts work and after he has acquired the right approach through his general education. Thus, on the one hand, he acquires much more knowledge and much healthier attitudes than the old revenue accountant, who was pitchforked into the village and left to acquire his skill as best as he could; on the other hand, none of the training is wasted, for nobody is trained who has not got a job. Second, more vocational guidance can be given. In these societies which are being transformed as well as expanded, children and their parents mostly do not know where the opportunities are. The Indian Five-Year Planners have already recognised this as a problem; and it may also be one of the explanations why the direction of the educated to whatever work may suit the State seems to meet with so much less resistance in China or Russia than it would in a Western country.

Third, planning makes the whole problem easier. If it is laid down beforehand what industries are going to be developed, or how many villages are to have maternity clinics, then obviously one has a much clearer idea of how many chemical engineers (or midwives) one will need; one thus avoids the ridiculous situation which has happened so often in the past, where industry was looking desperately for chemical engineers of one sort, while chemical engineers trained in another speciality were looking equally desperately for jobs. Such planning has very serious defects; it greatly impairs the flexibility of the economy, its ability to adjust to what the consumer either of goods or Government services wants; once one has trained the midwives, it is no use the villager saying his wife can manage, what he really wants is a road. But it does marry supply and demand for the educated. That is one reason why planning is so acceptable to Asia's professional classes. It gives them a known future, a known set of opportunities, a known chance of employment if they acquire a known skill. For people into whose minds the fear of unemployment has bitten as deep as with a Durham coalminer, this is a great deal.

THE FOURTH TASK—TRADITION AND THE MODERN WORLD

(a) Traditional culture and the modern economy

The fourth of our problems, the adaptation of the society's traditional culture and ways of education to the knowledge and attitudes which are needed for economic development, underlies and dominates all the others. An old society cannot sacrifice all its values without losing everything that makes it a society, instead of just a zoo of individuals. But since most traditional cultures were geared to economies essentially static, it cannot cling to all its values either, except at the cost of stopping all development.

Certain of the difficulties of adaptation are well-known for Asia, and by no means unknown in Europe. Traditional education values culture—not so much the power to create but the power to appreciate. One must be able to put the correct value on a good example of Chinese calligraphy, applaud to the right extent a Bharat Natyam dancer. Development, by contrast, requires practical knowledge—knowledge of how to build a bridge or charge a blast furnace. Traditional education places great emphasis not merely on reading the classics but on knowing them. One must be able to pick up a reference to a hero of the

Mahabharata or quote Confucius. Development by contrast requires that one should have a large body of specialised knowledge in some particular subject; one must know how to treat depreciation in one's accounts, or have the balance of payments at one's finger tips, or have read all the articles in all the journals on experiments in food canning. Even if one started by knowing Confucius—or Shakespeare—one forgets.

Traditional education is a bringing out of the whole personality; the body is made healthy, the mind is disciplined, the taste is made aesthetic. The economy, by contrast, can manage with highly underdeveloped personalities. An accountant does not need to be able to tell Forain from Matisse; in fact, the ability to do so may be a positive disadvantage, for his colleagues may suspect that he cannot both do that and get his figures right. The English Victorian Age was the most tasteless in history, and its tycoons were distinguished neither for the discipline of their minds, nor the health of their bodies; but no country had ever developed so quickly.

A traditional education by the training it gives to mind and character, makes a man, economically, potentially useful; but he will not be actually useful until he has acquired some special skill. Thus a man who has acquired the philosophy of the Bhagavad Gita will in the end be a better Personnel Manager than one who has not; but he first needs to learn his Standing Orders, his labour law, the psychology of human relations, and the capacity to fit in with an organisation most of whose members will not have read the Bhagavad Gita, before he is of much use to his employer. Again, the power of analysis required to get a first in economics should in the end make a man a better sales manager than the salesman who works his way up; but before that happens he must learn his products, his area, his men, his dealers, and his colleagues; he must even learn that all of these are more important than being good at economics, and that his economics is only valuable in so far as it enables him to see further and sell more than the salesman who never learnt any.

The position of the educated is thus no longer what it was in the rural societies of old Asia, where the mere fact of being educated entitled a man to respect. In the changing modern world the educated must earn their respect by being good at their jobs. They must not expect to be Sales Managers or Chief Chemists in two or three years because they got Ph.D.s. They must realise that their degree is a beginning, a guarantee that they are qualified to learn their jobs, and no more. Most of the job has to be learnt while working, and they have to accept that they will in the end be valued by their superiors, respected by their colleagues, and worked for by their subordinates not for their knowledge but for the use they make of it, not for the brilliance of their conversation but for the ease with which they handle people and the effectiveness with which they get things done. It is one of Asia's difficulties that so many of its best qualified are reluctant to submit themselves to this second examination, and especially reluctant to enter such walks of life as business where brilliance is suspect and they therefore start with a handicap. Occupations which have always been staffed by people without academic qualifications do not easily absorb the highly qualified; those without degrees are so painfully prone to defend themselves against those with by pretending that in their particular occupation everything matters except qualifications.

Traditional education in Asia, as in mediaeval Europe, places its emphasis upon the attainment of truth. The most important subject in the end is theology (or philosophy), the highest form of life that of religious contemplation. In terms of absolute values, it would be ridiculous to argue that this is not correct. Nevertheless, it raises a dilemma which no society has yet solved altogether satisfactorily.

On one horn is the fact that neither theology nor religious contemplation helps on the material progress of which every society is now so desirous. Theology (and philosophy) are subjects so large that those who learn them rarely have the time to learn also some more practical art; religious contemplation exacts the abandonment of every material desire. A society in which all the best minds are engaged in contemplation or theology is unlikely to increase its national income.

On the other horn is the fact that no society can afford to have all its best minds give up theology and contemplation, or it will find itself living on its moral capital. The good and the true and the divine will no longer be reinterpreted by each generation to suit its own needs. The language of morality will no longer be refreshed, the symbols of religion will no longer be renewed. People will be good without thought, according to the rules by which they were reared. They will repeat old truths without questioning, because that is what they were brought up to believe. The failure to think will bring unbelief, the failure to question cynicism. And unbelief and cynicism together will bring a selfishness which slackens all the bonds which hold society together, until the lack of civil peace holds up development more seriously than ever otherworldliness did.

Everybody, after all, could hope to be good, and the possibility of mystic experience was open to all prepared to accept the rigours of its way. By contrast, the adaptability, the willingness to take risks, and the power of innovation needed to become rich are given only to a minority; and a minority moreover which a society can often only admire at grave risk to its morals. The Americans reduce the resultant tensions by equating riches with successful adventure and the successful improvement of everybody's standard of life, but this solution will not do for Asia; the equation too often flies in the face of the facts.

Thus we come back in a circle. If religion is forgotten, society dissolves. But if every man of worth is intent on sainthood, economic development is not possible. Between these two the balance is not easy to strike, either in providing society with an ideal of the good life, or more narrowly, in choosing an educational curriculum.

(b) The curriculum

The educational reformer must today find room in the same curriculum for a general cultural education and for those special forms of knowledge the economy needs. He must make the room he needs by dropping everything that is merely intellectual snobbery and the class consciousness of the cultured; yet he must be careful not to drop with them the values and ideas which give purpose to men's lives and make them good.

Thus to state the problem is easy; what should be done is not so obvious. Indeed, even the attempt to look for an answer meets with inhibitions in educational circles, for these are largely composed of people soaked in the traditional ways of thought; most teachers are, very properly, people whose whole bent of mind leads them to attach greater importance to cultural than to material values. They are far more eager to see that Sanskrit or Latin is not dropped from the curriculum than to have, say, civics added to it.

The choice between Sanskrit and civics is only one example of many possible alternatives. It does, however, highlight very prettily the dilemma which faces the Eastern educationist. He has to adjust educational systems created for a quite different purpose to the needs of economic development. Yet both he and most of his fellow-citizens feel that the changes which are necessary may make for quicker material progress, but will do so only at the cost of much that is valuable in the national life.

To take our example. Sanskrit is as good an intellectual discipline as Latin. It has a rich literature. In it are written all the great books of India's main religion, Hinduism. From it are derived most of India's main languages, and all of them turn to it for the abstract and technical words of which they stand in need. A knowledge of Sanskrit greatly increases any Indian's understanding of the individuality and the growth of his society. Civics, by contrast, has in some ways very little to offer. It is impossible to use it to teach students how to think. It provides them with nothing which will subsequently enrich the content of their leisure. It adds little to their understanding of why their minds work in the way they do, or what it is which makes that way different from other people's.

Its usefulness is that it can be used to do something else, something which Sanskrit cannot do. It can be used to inculcate a code of behaviour, a set of attitudes, which will be more suitable to a developing community than the traditional code of the static and self-contained village. Children can be taught that to give money to a clerk to find their papers is not a tip, but corruption; that they owe a loyalty to the community as great as that to their family, and that to use a public position to find a job for a younger brother is not meritorious, but wrong; that spitting may not have mattered in a village field, but is most unhygienic in a town tram; that woman's place is no longer confined to the home; that one should give one's vote according to a candidate's programme and personality and not his caste or religion or race. All Asian societies are today led by men who have a much more advanced sense of the changes which are necessary than their people have. A proper civics curriculum, taught by teachers with a deep enough belief in it, can be a means of importance in enabling the people to catch up with their leaders.

Sanskrit necessarily pushes in the opposite direction. The Sanskrit classics are the incarnation of the old values, the very sources from which they were derived. In reading them, the student will confirm his narrower loyalties to caste and family; from them he will get no guidance on such matters as vaccination and hygiene and the importance of buying savings certificates.

This particular Indian dilemma may be solved by somehow finding room in the curriculum for both Sanskrit and civics, possibly by teaching both rather ineffectively. But the dilemma as a whole cannot be solved so easily. In Asia, as in Europe, the traditional curriculum was a fairly full one. If place is to be found for new subjects, something must go.

Place clearly has to be found for new subjects. If, for instance, the new nations are to have the unity without which the sacrifices which are required for development will not be made, then people must be able to talk to each other. The Sinhalese in Ceylon must learn Tamil, the Tamil Sinhalese; everybody in India must learn Hindi, everybody in Indonesia Basha Indonesia; everybody in Pakistan may yet have to learn both Bengali and Urdu.

Again, Asia, even Communist China, is a place of small businessmen. Its population is overwhelmingly made up of peasants, artisans, and shopkeepers each of whom, in effect, is running his own little business. If the peasant is not to get into debt, he must be able to work out what his real income is; if he is to adopt improvements quickly, he must be able to work out rather more closely than he can at present whether or not they will pay; he must in short know some elementary accounts. So too, the small shopkeeper would both have less trouble with the sales-tax authorities and would be able to keep a better control on his stocks and margins if he understood double-entry bookkeeping. The peasant's or shop-keeper's son would benefit more if his primer contained lessons on running a co-operative society or on the law of promissory notes than he does from its present concentration on the geography of Australia or the life of the Eskimos.

The difficulty is that, while there is no great dispute about this need to add, few are prepared to agree on what should be dropped. The Communists have solved their problem by putting first everything the Communist State needs, and leaving out both the classics and training people to think for themselves. These are, however, answers not available to democracies who are proud of their pasts and whose citizens must learn to think for themselves in order to be citizens. They can only fumble and argue, and experiment, until by trial and error they get some answer which works. It is no accident that in all the newly-free countries the least satisfactory part of policy is education. Nobody quite knows what he wants; and when he does, he never quite agrees with anybody else.

The answer must be to try everything, or at least most things, and see what is successful. Until that is done, in these societies which are only at the beginning of their development, nobody can be quite sure what will work and what will not. As they develop, however, by watching who gets the jobs, and who does them properly when they have got them, parents as well as teachers will learn what is the most effective way of training children to take their part in development. Once that is clear, the insistence of the parents will in due course do the rest. Already some trends have been established, the switch from law and arts to economics and engineering and the sciences for instance, or the widening range of jobs the educated will take, or the value of craft education through agriculture for the village child. The rest will come; and if it comes more slowly than is desirable, that is perhaps not too high a price to pay to avoid jettisoning Asia's old civilisation, to avoid too the tension between the generations and within families that Communism so encourages. Social harmony and the classics are worth a few per cent off the national income for a few years. Revolution would be more expensive still.

Chapter 15

DEVELOPMENT AND THE SMALL
PROPERTY OWNER

ASIA is a continent of small property owners. There are few rich, few totally without property. In India, for example, only one person in 500 pays income-tax; on the other hand, when the Indian land reforms are finished in a few years' time, there will be four or five people who own land for every landless agricultural labourer.

This is a social structure quite different from anywhere in the western world except parts of France and Scandinavia. In most Western countries the typical citizen is an employee, not an independent businessman. He may be the managing director, he may have quite considerable private income; his attitudes of mind are governed by the fact that most of his life is spent in working for someone else, that his efforts benefit himself through promotion or prestige rather than immediately in his income, that he is one of a team and not on his own.

In Asia, by contrast, the typical citizen is the small peasant, the small artisan, or the small shopkeeper. His distinguishing features are quite different.

First, he is a businessman on his own. When he makes a correct judgement, he makes money, when he makes a wrong judgement, he loses it. If the peasant uses the right amount of extra fertiliser and crop prices are right, he may make enough money to be able to dig a well or find a better husband for his daughter. If he signs a promissory note without reading it, or sows a crop which needs rain in a year when there is no rain, he starves or loses his land. The nightmare of Western society, unemployment, does not weigh on Asia's small property owners. He is, however, far more often underemployed than in the West. If he is selling cigarettes on a street where there are ten sellers of cigarettes, he may have to be content with a dozen customers a day. If he has only two acres of land, he may not have, at his level of technique, enough to keep him occupied for more than 200 days in the year.

Secondly, he is on the whole unqualified for his job. If he is a farmer he knows the traditional peasant methods of getting a crop from his land, methods often very elaborate and rarely to be ignored with safety; but he knows very little about the modern scientific discoveries, from pest-killers to new seeds, that would enable him to get more out of the same land with relatively little extra expenditure of money or effort. If he is an artisan, he knows how to exercise his craft in the way his fathers did, to produce in the better cases exquisite results. What he does not know is either the taste of that majority of his consumers who can no longer buy from him direct, or what new materials or sources of power are available to him to improve his work, or how to market to anybody who does not live round the corner. If he is a shopkeeper he understands the importance of low margins and quick turnover, and he may be quite good at bargaining, but he usually does not understand either the time saving function of the fixed price, or the value of window-display, or how to help and guide his customer in making his purchases.

Thirdly, Asia's small property-owner is a little man in a world which even in Asia is no longer composed exclusively of little men. The railway which carries his goods, the factory which sells him fertiliser or cigarettes, the mill or exporter which buys his cotton or rice, are of necessity big. They know what they want, and they are able to express it with reasonable lucidity .The little man does not always know what he wants. When he does know, it is not necessarily good for him. Because he has no margin, he is always sacrificing his long-run to his short-run interests. Even when it is good for him, he may not always be able to express it in a way which convinces other people.

Fourthly, against these disadvantages he has a lot of votes. An Asian Government will listen more quickly to the inarticulate case of a farmers' union than to the best argued brief of a big business.

Fifthly, he tends to be suspicious both of progress and change. The world is altering around him. He ought constantly to be changing his methods, his markets, and his products. He feels himself, however, quite incapable of achieving the changes which are needed. He regards himself as too ignorant and too poor; so he asks for protection.

Sixthly, however willing Governments may be to listen to him, they find this protection difficult to give. The poverty-stricken budgets of Asia cannot afford to be lavish with the half-adapted as Western countries are with their farmers. On the occasions when they are lavish, as India is being in subsidising its handloom-weavers, it is at the expense of other developments equally urgent and economically more useful. The subsidies have to be given at somebody else's expense, and because the somebody else can never afford them, they create tensions and resentments.

Seventhly, he is frequently in debt to an extent that makes his independence only nominal. His creditor controls every aspect of his life. He must buy his daily needs or his raw materials from him, he must sell him his crop or his finished product. In extreme cases he becomes a semi-serf, perpetually paying a constantly renewed debt, allowed by his moneylender only just enough of the fruits of his labour to keep body and soul together.

This small property-owner dominates Asian society. He is the typical citizen, he has the votes, he has the power to get from the State enough protection to see that he is not competed out of existence.

Short of revolution and more than Chinese liquidations every Asian society must do its economic development largely through and by him. The characteristics we have described, however, mean that at present and in general he is not a very efficient instrument. He is too ignorant either to know by himself or to learn quickly from others, how to increase and improve his production. He is too small to be able to take a risk on anything that gives him less than a sure 30 per cent. He is often too indebted to have any incentive to do work and take risks whose fruit will be taken away by his creditors. He is always too conscious of his own weakness to accept any policy by which free competition is used to weed out the inefficient and the inadaptable. He always wants protection against people who might exploit him and trends which may leave him without a market, or worsen his terms of trade with the rest of society. He is, nearly always, too short of capital to be able to do much improving or expansion of his operations for himself, and often too short of skill to know what to do even if he had the capital. His extensive spare time is not easy to use, for it is sporadic, dependent on his beasts and the seasons, or on the whims of his customers, and he is untrained for any alternative occupation except unskilled labour.

A man who has neither the knowledge to weigh a risk nor the capital with which to take one, is not a very promising prospect for Asian economic development; and the more backward the country, the more all development is an adventure into uncharted territory. Yet development must rest upon the small property-owner, or it cannot be done quickly enough. The heavy industry so beloved of the Communist takes years to build, employs relatively few, and can only find a market in an economy the whole of which is expanding. If the national income is to be increased quickly and equitably, then much of the increase must both come from, and go straight into the pockets of, the small men who are the overwhelming majority of the nation. Otherwise there will be injustice, tension, sabotage, and an inadequate supply of food and consumer goods to keep the population happy while it is building—in fact, all the disasters which have happened in Russia.

The task is clearly immense, much greater than in the West, where so much of the burden of advance is borne by the great corporations, who usually know what to do without anybody's having to show them, and have the habit of taking the risks involved in doing it. In Asia, the great corporations, the oil companies for instance, or the big plantation companies, have admittedly done an amount of leading quite disproportionate to their actual importance in the economy; but they are too few, and too often foreign, to do it all. If the economy is to move forward as a whole, the small man must move with it. He cannot be left, as with the English yeoman or handloom-weaver, simply to be pushed out of existence; in the countries without adult suffrage, there might be revolution first, in those with it, the Government would fall.

Fortunately, there are precedents which suggest that the change from independence to working for others which is seen at its extreme in Communism, but which also characterizes the major Western capitalist states, is not a necessary concomitant of development. In Europe, there are the farmers and handicraftsmen of Scandinavia, the fruit-growers and restaurant owners of France. In Asia, there are the farmers of Japan and the small lorry-owners of all the Continent to show that the small man can adapt. The lorry-owners created themselves out of an environment whose most complicated vehicle was a bullock-cart; the Japanese farmers more than doubled their yields between 1880 and 1930.

If the small man is to adapt himself successfully, however, his risks must be reduced and his knowledge increased. At present he carries all the burdens of severely fluctuating markets, of a system of credit and merchanting services characterised by the most imperfect of competition, and of supplies whose prices vary much less than those of his own product. The price of his crop, whether it is rice or rubber, can, and does, double or halve in a season. When the price doubles, there is an inflation and perhaps special taxation to limit his gains, when it halves, the prices of what he buys do not halve too. His land revenue and his moneylender's instalment probably remain unchanged, his cloth and steel plough go down, but to nothing like so great an extent as the cotton he sold to make the cloth, or the food he sold to the steelworker. Moreover, whatever happens to prices, the peasant tends to be at the mercy of the man from whom he gets credit, who is also quite often his merchant, selling him his requirements and buying his produce; many peasants are not in a position to shop around for the cheapest lender or the highest buyer, though this is a position which is improving. A recent survey showed that half India's peasants were not in debt at all.

The handicraft-worker's position is even worse than that of the peasant. The peasant may be able to sell in a state-regulated open market. The handicraftsman is usually utterly dependent on the merchant who advances him the raw materials. The peasant gains in an inflation; the handicraftsman often finds that in an inflation he can get no raw materials and in a deflation no customers. His methods are frequently so antiquated that only special protection will enable him to compete; the village oilman, for example, leaves 5 per cent or 6 per cent more oil behind in the oilcake than does a good mill, and oil is worth around five times as much as cake. Yet he has usually got neither the capital to improve his methods, nor the knowledge that would enable him to recognise a better method when he sees it. Only a few scores have been sold of the improved Haskell ghani (the container in which the oilseed is crushed) invented before the war, though there are perhaps 400,000 oilmen in India alone.

Units so weak cannot operate effectively by themselves in the modern economy. Under free competition they will be driven out, as they so often have been in the West. Such a result is, however, unacceptable in most countries of Asia. It must always be remembered that there the small men are the great majority of the electorate, and that the big men are frequently foreigners— not only European but, for example, Chinese in Thailand or Indians in Ceylon. Asian ideology, too, is often, as notably in India, strongly in favour of the independent small man as a more satisfactory basis for society than the employee.

The only possible line of approach, therefore, is to make the small man more effective, better able to hold his own. This means especially more credit, more knowledge, and better marketing. Two ways of doing this have been devised, and are slowly, very slowly, becoming standard practice throughout Asia. The first is co-operation, the second is State help. The two intermingle, for the State takes part in the co-operative movement, and the co-operative movement may suggest policy to the

State. In principle, however, they are separate. The co-operative movement enables the small man to help himself; at most the State, by helping the movement, assists him to help himself. The State's direct initiative comes when the small man is dealing with something completely beyond his scale, like agricultural research, or overseas marketing, or the competition of large-scale industry.

Of the two, co-operation holds the greatest hope for the future. State assistance is all too often merely a prop; Indian protection of handloom weavers, like French protection of the wine-growers of the Herault, may be merely a postponement of the day when it is accepted that much of their production is simply uneconomic. State help is most useful when as in the community projects, it takes the form of showing the small man what he needs to do to be efficient and then helping him do it. Co-operation, despite its many failures, is a way by which the small man can become permanently able to live successfully in a world too big for him. These two methods, co-operation and the community project, are so much more hopeful than any other that they are worth separate consideration.

Chapter 16

CO-OPERATION AND CREDIT

THE great majority of Asian co-operation has hitherto been credit co-operation. The primary function of the Co-operative society in Asia is still to lend money.

This is a perfectly correct choice of priorities. The first need of any business is capital. Not merely does the Asian small man lack capital; all his social habits militate against his acquiring any. The wedding of a child will cost a year's income; and there may be four or five to marry. The funeral of a parent may cost two months' income; and every man has two parents. In the close society of the village, moreover, what is spent on such ceremonies depends less on the financial position of the spender than on his status, on exactly which Joneses he has to keep up with. In many villages in Peninsular India, for example, the Brahmin lives better than the non-Brahmin of equal income; one reason is that marriages in the Brahmin community cost less.

Where ceremonies do not eat away a man's savings, crop failures may. Much of India and China particularly is subject to famine, and it is very hard for a small man to save up enough to provide against what may not be just one failure of the rains, but as recently in the Tamil Nad, four or five. It is easier to rely on the relief which the State has organised against famine, though not always very efficiently, for many hundreds of years past. Famines are thus doubly discouraging. They eat up such savings as may have been made, and induce the fatalistic feeling that it is no use saving anyway.

In societies of small men with heavy social obligations and uncertain returns, capital is necessarily scarce and regular payments of instalments on debts contracted is equally necessarily difficult. Nor can the peasant and handicraftsman make much use of the urban money in the banks. There will certainly not be a branch in his village, and there may not be a branch in his local market town. The nearest branch of even a small bank may be fifty or more miles away. Moreover, were the bank on his doorstep, it would probably still not lend to him. Asian banking has been based on the cautious solidity of the developed banking of Western Europe; it has none of the adventurousness of American mid-Western banking in the nineteenth century. Yet to lend to the Asian peasant and handicraftsman it would

have to be very adventurous indeed for, whatever the form of
the contract might be, the bank would in effect be borrowing
short and lending long; the small man may repay at harvest or
when he sells his cloth, but he will need the money again at
sowing-time or when he has to buy yarn, and if he cannot get it
his whole operation will stop. To some extent this difficulty can
be cured by special land mortgage banks, but these are really
effective only for medium and long-term needs; they are
appropriate when the peasant wants to dig a tube-well, reasonably suitable when he has to buy a pair of bullocks, not suitable
at all when he wants one week to borrow a few shillings to buy
some food for his family, the next to borrow a pound or two to
buy seed with, and the third again to borrow a few shillings to
pay the women who weed his rice; when he wants also, to repay
in an equally scattered way, a few shillings when he does some
carting, another few when he helps in the harvest on a neighbour's field, a few pounds perhaps when he sells his groundnut
or his cotton. The overheads of having, say, twenty transactions
on a debt of perhaps $30 would be enormous for a bank; and
they are made more enormous by the extreme difficulty of any
form of self-protection. A mortgage means an investigation of
title, which is complicated even in those parts of India or Pakistan which have a good Record of Rights system and almost impossible in Ceylon where titles verge on the chaotic. The bank
might take a charge on the crop but then it must keep a watch-
man on the field, or the crop might be spirited away before ever
the bank gets to it. Once again the overheads go up.

The bank is not the answer. Nor is the State. The need for
credit is enormous. Indian agriculture alone could probably usefully use $4200 million as of tomorrow (present debts may be
$2250–2500 million); and each year the requirements will go
up, as the peasant learns to use fertiliser, or to replace cereals by
orchards, or to sink tube-wells. The State has not got so much
money. Moreover, even if it had, it could not lend so much to so
many people. It does not have the administrative machinery.
Many an Asian peasant only wants to borrow $7 to $9 in a
year; yet to lend him that much there has to be just as careful an
investigation of whether the money will be used productively,
whether he has any security of land or character, and whether
he will be able to repay, as for a loan of $600 or $850; indeed,
one may well have to be more careful with the smaller debtor,
for the big man may have ample security to offer, the little
man have little more than his signature. The little man, too,
is much more likely to be engaged in mere deception. He may

borrow officially for seed when what he wants is food, or for a
bullock, when what he wants is a husband for his daughter. The
imagination boggles at the organisation the State would require
under these circumstances, to lend hundreds of millions of
pounds to tens of millions of peasants, at a few pounds per
peasant, and a few shillings per occasion of lending.

The banks cannot do the job. The State cannot do the job.
The money-lender can do the job, as he always has done it. His
price, however, is high. The really good debtor in an area with a
businesslike tradition like Gujerat may get away with 6 per cent.
The really bad one, the man whose capacity to repay is doubtful
in the extreme, like the landless labourer of Tonkin, may find
himself paying 1,000 per cent. Between these extremes, the
usual man with a few acres in the usual area will probably pay a
rate somewhere between 12 per cent and 30 per cent. These are
high rates; but no honest money-lender will make a fortune on
them. First, where loans are taken and repaid in such small instalments, one has to consider not only the return on his money,
but also the remuneration for his time. A loan of $30 at 30 per
cent will bring in $9 a year; but for that he may have had to
spend several hours with his debtor. Secondly, there are always
defaults. A bullock may die, a daughter may get married, a
crop may fail, and that year the money-lender will not get paid
at all. Theoretically, the debt then runs at compound interest
and eventually the money-lender forecloses on the land. That
happened a great deal in the past, as witness the large money-
lender holdings in, say, Maharashtra or Lower Burma. Even in
the past, however, the money-lender quite often took something
less than his full dues to get his money. Today, virtually every
country in Asia has legislation which makes it extremely difficult
for the money-lender to get hold of his debtor's land, and often
in addition limits his interest, complicates his methods of recovery, and checks his books. The money-lender has to be relatively gentle with his clients, if he does not want to find himself with a series of tiresome and long-drawn-out court cases on
his hands. This is not a satisfactory solution either. If the money
lender is gentle, he may well finish with a net return lower than
he can get elsewhere, in shopkeeping for instance; so the better
men withdraw, and the business falls increasingly into the hands
of those who recover their money by the stick, the false weight,
and the forged account.

To rely for economic development on money from the money-
lender has yet another snag. The money-lender does not mind
for what the money is used so long as he gets his interest, so far

too much of his money is lent unproductively. There are many highly desirable schemes which will not pay 20 per cent or 30 per cent, and certainly will not pay the premium over 20 per cent or 30 per cent which the peasant or handicraftsman ought to get to justify his risk. A man with a starving baby or a daughter to marry will pay any rate of interest. A man borrowing for a productive purpose will calculate his risks. If the money-lender is charging 20 per cent, the scheme the peasant is considering must bring in 50 per cent or 100 per cent, to cover him against the possibility of a bad year or a fall in prices. He may not be doing very well without a well, but if he borrows for a well and then is unable to pay his debt he may be ruined; he must antici-pate an enormous return from his well before he will take the risk. Many a well does not get dug, many a handloom weaver does not exchange his throw-shuttle for a fly-shuttle, because the return does not seem enormous enough.

The money-lender may be the traditional answer to the problem of credit, the problem which is central to all development. He is clearly a bad answer. So we return to the co-operative society, which, for all its many failures, is the little man's only hope.

The credit co-operative is an institution by which people get together to provide themselves jointly with the credit and the creditworthiness they do not have singly. They come from one or a few neighbouring villages; they, therefore, largely know each other. The condition for joining is the purchase of some share-capital, so that the society will have some money to lend and every member will have an interest in it. Extra capital is obtained by taking deposits from outside or borrowing from banks, notably co-operative banks. The society is run by an elected committee, normally with the aid of one paid official, the secretary, who may be full-time or part-time. Borrowing is controlled both by giving each member a credit limit, and by checking the purposes for which he borrows. Recovery of debts is facilitated by a special legal procedure, and solvency should be assured by the fact that in the society's usual unlimited liability form every member is responsible for its debts with the whole of his property.

Obviously a properly working co-operative solves all the pro-blems of lending to the small man. It solves the problem of over-heads. It is on the spot in the village and its committee give their time for nothing. The costs of lending and recovering in penny packets are therefore not intolerable. It solves the problem of default. The limits up to which members may borrow are settled by people to whom the member's every circumstance is known, so that there is no overborrowing, or diversion of money to purposes other than those for which it was ostensibly borrowed, and therefore there should be relatively little default. It solves the problem of extravagance. The members are encouraged to limit their debts and increase their savings, not to plunge into debt as deep as their security permitted, as the money-lender always encouraged them to do. Lending for unproductive purposes is frowned upon and limited. It solves the problem of bringing the bank and the State to the village. Since the society can borrow in reasonably large amounts and has the security of all its members behind it, it is a suitable client for a bank where its members individually are not. It can borrow cheap and lend fairly cheap, usually at 6 per cent to 11 per cent. It is furthermore a suitable instrument for any assistance the State wishes to give the villager, and the State can help a great deal at low cost by subsidising the pay of the society's one official, the secretary, by auditing its accounts, and by contributing to the capital of the co-operative banks who do most of the lending to it.

These are very large advantages. They explain the great advances co-operation has made in Asia in the last fifty years. They are, however, the advantages of co-operation at its theoretical best. In practice the Asian peasant and handicraftsman is frequently as unsatisfactory as a co-operator as he is in his various other economic manifestations. Co-operative committees lend to their friends money they know will be irrecoverable; money officially lent for productive purposes goes on ceremonies and jewellery; debtors are not pressed enough while they are still solvent, so that their land has to be foreclosed when they become finally insolvent; the poorer people of the village are not allowed to join so that the benefits of the society can be kept to a limited clique; secretaries are often less than half trained, loans are not always made in time, there is not always adequate provision for lending for those unproductive purposes, like food or weddings, without which a man cannot survive physically or socially. The banks may not have the habit of lending much to the movement, and the State may have nothing to lend. Men who might be honest borrowers may not have enough money with which to buy the initial shares, without which they are not allowed to join; the village may not have enough men of even elementary education to be able to form an effective committee. The reasons why a society can go wrong are legion. That is why, in India until the late '50's, the societies only provided 3 per cent of all rural credit, though in the most advanced districts where the peasants are both businesslike and educated, like Broach, the figure rose to 40 per cent.

The answer is to bring the worst co-operative societies up to the level of the best, the villages which cannot run a society up to the level of those which can.

This requires State assistance. Such dependence on the State admittedly goes against all the original principles of co-operation, which was essentially a movement of self-help. In Asia, however, experience suggests that, if co-operation is to be a primary igniter of development, to a more than Scandinavian extent, then one cannot wait for the peasant and the handicraftsman to develop the education, the understanding of business, and the commercial integrity of, say, the Danish farmer. It took forty years to get to 3 per cent of what was needed in India; one does not know the corresponding figures for the other countries, but they are unlikely to be substantially different. Asia is in too much of a hurry to wait the century that might be required to turn the 3 per cent into 30 per cent if the co-operative movement were left solely to the initiative of its members.

The most elaborate plan for State assistance is that proposed by a special Committee set up by the Reserve Bank of India, and now being acted on by the Government of India. It is a scheme which has few specially Indian features; in its broad lines, there is no reason why it should not be as successful in Pakistan or Burma as in India.

The Committee starts from two hypotheses. Only co-operation can meet a problem as diffuse as the small man's need for credit; only the State help can make co-operation work.

The Committee's main recommendations therefore propose a much increased rôle for the State in the co-operative movement. The Committee are not trying to nationalise the co-operative movement, to substitute bureaucratic orders for the individual initiative which is the heart of co-operation. The purpose of their recommendation is to enable the State to help the co-operative movement to work by helping at all the points where the movement is weak, that is, primarily, in money and staff.

First, the village and artisan societies do not have enough money to lend their members. The State will therefore provide a proportion of capital to the co-operative movement, mainly to the co-operative banks from whom the societies borrow. This increased capital will not only directly enable these institutions to lend more to their constituent societies. This extra capital will also make them more creditworthy borrowers from the main banking system; they may indeed be able to borrow from the banks several times as much as the actual increase in capital, and what they borrow, they can lend to the primary societies. It is true that the commercial banks have always been reluctant to lend to them. The Central Bank, the Reserve Bank, will therefore step in to fill the gap; the Bank is in a better position to find the money than the State Governments whose constitutional responsibility co-operation is; it also is technically capable, as they are not, of building up an adequate organ of inspection of the co-operative banks.

Here it is perhaps necessary to explain that the co-operative banks normally function at two levels. There are the district banks, whose members are the village and artisan societies themselves. Then there are the State-wide banks—the apex banks—made up of the district banks. Hitherto they have got their resources mainly from the deposits of the Societies and from some outside deposits. The inadequacy of these deposits, and also of the bank's capital itself, has been one of the main obstacles to the rapid spread of co-operation. The reason for choosing the banks rather than the societies as the repositories of Government's and the Reserve Bank's money is that it greatly reduces the administrative problem—there is only one bank to perhaps a hundred or two hundred primary societies—and it preserves the Government from the risks of lending directly to its voters.

Second, the co-operative movement is weak in personnel. Loans badly made, potential members improperly refused, accounts badly kept, failures to recover when recoveries are due, all in the end are due to inadequate personnel; and if the State and the Reserve Bank are to provide more money for the movement, then there will have to be much better supervision than hitherto of how that money is used.

The whole movement needs better staff. The Registrars who supervise co-operation in each State, the inspectors who do so in the district, need to be picked officials, not members of a service people join if they cannot get in to the administrative service, the railways, the police, or even the posts and telegraphs. Pay and prospects are therefore being improved. The co-operative banks must have adequate boards of directors, good managers and inspectors. This the committee hopes to achieve through the interest the Reserve Bank will take, and through placing the branch manager of the new State Bank (India's largest commercial bank) on the local co-operative bank board. Finally, and above all, there must be good society secretaries, for without them the rules will not be followed, defaulting debtors will not be chased, accounts will fall into confusion; in short the societies will not work.

Here one comes up against a problem not only of training, but of cost. One of the committee's main solutions for the staff difficulty is more training, at every level from the Registrars downwards. The employees and officers of the co-operative movement must learn their job, not just fall into it. Getting good secretaries, however, is not simply a matter of getting enough matriculates and giving them a six months' course. That is not difficult; that Asian governments have so seldom done it in the past is a sign of their remissness, nothing more. What is difficult is the cost of the secretary. In a society with 200 members borrowing an average of $30 p.a., which in Asia would be a fair-sized society, a secretary earning perhaps $425 p.a. (the price for a good matriculate including pension rights) would add $7\frac{1}{2}$ per cent to the cost of the loans. That is too much. The cost must therefore be reduced. This can be done in two ways. First, the size of the society must be increased. The idea of one village, one society must be given up, and there must be a society for a group of villages, though this in turn involves difficulties in getting a committee which will work together and will know the circumstances of all the members. Second, the secretary must do something else. What the something else should be has not yet been finally decided in any country. The most appropriate combination is probably with the secretaryship of the village council, though that involves the risk of the secretary's having to steer his way successfully through two sets of politics, the politics of the society and the politics of the village. Some risks must, however, be taken. It is not proper that the State should permanently subsidise secretaries' pay; but if that pay adds more than, say, 2 per cent to the cost of borrowing, the society will begin to become nearly as expensive as the money-lender.

The Committee also makes two sets of suggestions where the role of the State is more indirect than it is for money and staff. They want to make the security for loans better; and they want to separate provision for unproductive lending from the society's normal lending for production.

The Committee's primary recommendations for making the security better is to shift the emphasis from a charge on the borrower's land to a charge on his crop. Using the land as security has two disadvantages. It concentrates the lender's attention on the adequacy of the security instead of on the purpose of the loan; and recovery from a defaulter is always difficult, because in a peasant community a man will adopt every expedient rather than part with a yard of his land. If the charge is on the crop instead, everybody's attention is concentrated on the purpose of the loan. A productive loan—for a well or ferti- liser—will automatically increase the value of the security, an unproductive one will not. Attention is concentrated too, on the character of the borrower as well as on his security; there are many ways for the dishonest to spirit away a crop. The com- mittee indeed recommends, to reduce this risk, a general system of co-operative marketing; the society would be sure of getting the crop because it alone could sell it. But, as we shall see in the next Chapter, co-operative marketing is a very much more complicated operation than co-operative credit.

It may be the answer one day; it cannot be the answer today. More useful is the Committee's proposal for a nation-wide sys- tem of warehouses, so that the farmer could at least borrow against his crop once it has come in, on the security of the ware- house receipt, and would no longer be compelled to sell at the low prices of harvest.

The Committee's fourth set of suggestions, on how to deal with credit for unproductive purposes, faces up to the hardest problem of all. So long as people must marry daughters, so long too as crops fail and they must sometimes borrow to buy food or starve, it is useless to say credit must not be given for unpro- ductive ends. That merely drives the peasant back to the money- lender; and since an unmarried daughter is, in Asia, a worse calamity than a field without fertiliser, in any clash of interest the peasant will have to give his loyalty to the money-lender and not to the society. Yet, if debt is not to pile up in a way which makes borrowing for productive purposes impossible because there is no security left, borrowing for unproductive purpose must somehow be limited.

This in only very partially something the credit system can solve. As with so many of Asia's economic problems, the real answer lies in a change of social attitudes. It must become fashionable to bury parents without fanfare, to marry daughters without clothes or jewellery or feasts for the village. Perhaps even it must become the rule to marry for love and not by ar- rangement. Certainly the form of women's property rights will often need changing. The Hindu rule, for example, by which her jewellery was a woman's own property, but the widow had only a limited interest in her husband's property, and a daughter had no interest in her father's property, goes a long way to explain the fantastic economic waste which goes on in India in the form of expenditure on jewellery. All these rules have now been changed by statute; over a generation, that will be more important in reducing unproductive expenditure than anything which can be done by the direct reduction of credit.

Meanwhile, the Committee has had an idea that might work, not only in India but all over Asia, by inducing a wider range of people to regard social obligations as something which must be saved for, and not just borrowed for. There is in South India an institution called a Chit Fund, which is not unlike some of the burial funds they used to have in Northern England. The members subscribe a fixed amount of money at fixed intervals to a fund; every time they subscribe there is a Dutch auction, and the subscriptions are sold to the person who agrees to accept the least money. Nobody can bid more than once and the money left over at each auction is added to the kitty. Therefore, the thrifty, who can wait till the end, get a handsome return on their money, while those with a wedding or a funeral hanging over them get both an opportunity to borrow at a reasonable rate and a compulsion to save back what they have borrowed. The Committee has suggested that the co-operative societies should run Chit Funds. This would enable them to confine their regular lending, part of the money for which is being provided by the State, to productive purposes without losing the loyalty of their members, since the fund would give the members the chance to meet a calamity or a social obligation without recourse to the moneylender. It would also make saving more exciting for them; there is about the Chit Fund a touch of the lottery.

There is another credit problem for which the Committee has provided an answer. Certain forms of loan—for land reclamation, say—are not suitable for the ordinary society, since they are necessarily long-term and the society cannot afford to tie up for the long term funds all of which are short or, at the outside, medium-term. Moreover, whereas the crop is the best security for the short-term loan, the land is the best security for a long term one, since it is for improvements to the land itself that long-term loans are normally given. The Committee's answer, therefore, is the answer which has already been successful in Egypt, the land mortgage bank, raising its money by debentures, with Governmental and Central Bank assistance, and lending for specific improvements for a term that may extend to twenty years.

The Committee has indeed covered the whole ground. There is, however, one idea which may be worth adding to theirs. Indonesia has long run a successful organisation of village pawnshops. Were it possible to run such pawnshops in addition to co-operative societies, they might relieve the societies of one of the most troublesome and overhead-creating types of loan, the small and very temporary loan for consumption. The improvident could be in and out of the pawnshop by pledging their wives' bangles without interfering with their credit limits in the society, or causing the secretary to worry perpetually about what they really did with the money they borrowed for a new bullock.

There are many snags to the Committee's scheme. There was bitter opposition to the abandonment of the idea of one co-operative society, one village. Many good co-operators hated the part given to government. It is not proving easy to find quickly the secretaries and the inspectors who will be needed. Governments will be tempted to over-expand, as has happened in the past, to create societies before there is either the staff to run them or an elementary understanding of co-operation among the villagers. Such societies do not merely die themselves, they discourage others from co-operation. The money-lender will try to tempt away the societies' members. Committees may be factious, or elections to them infected by politics. The warehouse programme may lag for lack of money. The societies may have nowhere to put the crops on which they have a charge, or may sell them ineffectively. Where one deals with so many millions of small men, there are corresponding millions of chances for something to go wrong. It is useless, however, to be discouraged by the possibility of failure. Everything else, from the commercial bank to the money-lender, has failed already. If the small man is to get the credit he needs to expand, to innovate, to improve, co-operation is the only possible way. The Committee's scheme is one by which anywhere in Asia co-operation *could* work on a much larger scale than it has ever done before, by which therefore the economy *could* develop much more rapidly than it ever has before. In an economy of small men, it is the small man's credit which counts. Certainly the government of India thinks so. By 1966 it will have put some £450 million behind the Committee's ideas.

Chapter 17

MARKETING AND CO-OPERATION

WHAT credit produces, marketing must sell; and for the Asian small man marketing is a newer and more complicated problem than production.

In the old days, his market was his neighbours. He knew what they wanted, and, if he did not, they told him. He did not have to compete for their favour, or consider too much the relation of price and cost. The village barber, paid in grain at harvest, did not have to advertise his shaves. His clients could no more go to a barber in another village if he shaved badly than he could ask for more grain at harvest because he shaved well. Making for a market of people unknown to the maker was confined to a few town luxury trades like silk brocades, and even there the artisan usually made to sell to those he did not know exactly the same designs as he made for his local rich whom he did know.

The Asian small man is, therefore, very unprepared to meet the problems of modern marketing, whose fundamental feature is that the producer never meets his customer face to face. He cannot talk to the customer about what the customer wants; he must find out by market research. If he has a new idea, he cannot infect the customer by vehemence. He must advertise, and window-display, and get favourable comment in the household advice column of the newspaper. Finally, he cannot wait till he knows what his customer wants before he makes it, for the customer cannot tell him what he wants. He must make (or grow) for stock; which means that he must have more capital, more credit, and that he must take the risk that the customer will not like what he has made, and will express his dislike, not as in the old days, by coming back and demanding an alteration, but simply by not buying.

Deprived of his traditional contact with his customer, the small man is lost. He may increase his acreage under cotton only to find that there has been a switch to nylon, or that every other peasant has also put more land under cotton, so that the price has plummeted. He may make a series of nine-yard saris ready for sale, only to have the merchant tell him that nowadays everybody is buying six-yard saris. Or, like the shoemaker, he may go on making to order, only to find his customers switching to ready-made factory shoes because they are cheaper and they can see the quality before they buy. The small man loses because he cannot give his customer the guarantee of a brand; a man who buys Lux Toilet Soap this week can expect to get exactly the same soap as he got last week, whereas a woman who buys a handloom sari today may get an article considerably different from the one she bought six months ago. The small man loses, too, because he cannot wait for his market. Come harvest, and he often must sell to pay his debts and his land revenue, even though he knows that if he waits six months he will get a better price.

The result of these incapacities of the small man is the enormous number of middlemen he has to carry. The small man cannot afford to make much for stock, so he must carry the overheads of a large number of people coming round frequently to collect his goods. The small man does not know his market, so the man who makes the money is the merchant who does. The small man has no brand (or, for crops, guaranteed grade), so the customer does not ask for them by name, the shopkeeper can sell as he wishes and retail margins are higher. The small man's quality is uneven, so the factory or the consumer will pay less for his products in order to insure themselves against rejections and imperfections. The adulteration of crops is widespread in Asia, short-staple cotton is mixed with longer-staple cotton or dirt with groundnuts; it is the peasant who in the end pays for the adulteration, for as a result he gets a price made lower not merely by the amount of dirt, but also by the cost of carrying the dirt to the mill, and by the tiresomeness and risk of the whole operation. The small man cannot advertise, so he is at the mercy of the shopkeeper; and the Asian shopkeeper wants quick returns and no trouble; he will not bother to sell a new ingenious idea to his customers, or to point out that producer X's quality is better than producer Y's; it therefore becomes almost impossible for the enterprising small producer to reap the reward of his enterprise in the building up of consumer goodwill. Finally, the small man cannot make large quantities at once, so that it is impossible for him to build up the really profitable mass, repetition market. This is particularly important for export handicrafts. There are many more people in the West than in Asia itself who can afford to buy the better Asian handicrafts. Yet the market is seldom built up, for all too often when a Western importer has succeeded with, say, one thousand gross mats, and comes back with an order for fifty thousand, he finds the fifty thousand are simply unbuyable. This ends not only that business, but many other potential businesses; in many Western markets, notably North America, small quantities cannot carry the cost of sales promotion.

As with credit, the solution of the problem of marketing to which most Asian countries are beginning to turn is co-operation, co-operation with the State very much behind it. It is, however, much less obvious that co-operation and State assistance are the answer for marketing than it is for credit. They will work where what is being dealt in is a standard and easily gradable article, like cotton. They will not work nearly so well where consumer preferences have to be considered, with cloth or shoes. They are, in fact, a better answer for the peasant than for the handicraftsman, and in either case, they will depend very heavily for their success on the capacity to sell and to understand the market of their committees and their paid staffs. The marketing societies will only succeed if they develop the sixth sense that tells a good marketeer that the villager might be persuaded to buy shorts, or that his wife would like to wash in a soap perfumed with jasmine.

Another pre-requisite of good marketing societies is a proper organisation of credit societies. When the handicraftsman can get adequate credit for his raw materials, he will no longer need to put exquisite work on poor cloth, or to use dyes that run. When the farmer has a warehouse-receipt in which to borrow, he will no longer need to glut the market at harvest time. When the farmer can borrow for improved seed, it is easier to organise grading.

Credit is, however, only a pre-requisite.

The heart of the marketing problem is good selling. The small man must know what to grow or to make, and in what quantities; he must get the premium for proper grading, high quality, or imaginative design, which so often means the difference between bankruptcy and a living profit for a farmer or handicraftsman. This is a big task, and the great question for Asia is whether marketing societies can solve it. They have done so elsewhere, amongst Californian orange growers, Danish bacon farmers, and Swedish craftsmen. Can they do in Asia for small men who are at once desperately poor and largely illiterate?

If they are to do so, the small man must be educated first.

The first necessity is literacy. If a handicraftsman cannot read a blueprint or a design, if a farmer cannot read a list of current market prices, if neither can read a pamphlet explaining to them an improved method nor keep accounts showing their costs and their returns, nor write an invoice or a business letter, then they are hopelessly handicapped. Anybody can exploit them, from the merchant to the corrupt weighman.

The next need is an elementary training in business methods. That means more than a training in such simple techniques as book-keeping or elementary stock control. It means for the handicraftsman, for instance, learning the importance of regular deliveries, of not borrowing too much, of changing designs with changing customer habits, of adapting one's quality to the prices the customer can pay. In the West many of these ideas are learnt automatically, in the shop or as a salesman. In Asia they have to be taught and retaught. To men who have been accustomed to borrowing as much as they can from the merchant and to making as their fathers did, at their own convenience, from their ancestors' designs, they are revolution. The farmer may have to learn more still. If he is to use sulphate of ammonia without burning up his soil, if he is to appreciate the full importance of using his cowdung on his soil instead of to simmer his dinner, then he must be taught some elementary soil chemistry. If he is to breed and feed his stock as they should be bred and fed, then he would be greatly assisted by some knowledge of biology. Agriculture today is no longer an art to be practised according to village proverbs and one's father's teaching. It is a science. The more the peasant knows of that science, the more able he will be to grow for the market what the market wants. In an area where people have always grown cereals, for instance, a man cannot turn over to fruit merely because his land is given water; he must also know something about fruit.

Behind the marketing society, therefore, there must be a practical, vocational bias in the elementary schools, and an adequate number of vocational schools at the post-elementary stage. There must be design schools, and book-keeping courses, and institutions from which market research can be taught. There must be courses in salesmanship, and courses in the qualities of the materials the handicraftsman uses. There must, in fact, be the whole range of evening classes and correspondence courses and simple manuals which exist in countries like England or the United States. The educated may sniff at them; they are perhaps not a way to culture, but they are the open sesame to something more important still, to the small man's acquiring the elementary knowledge, however crude, however potted, which he needs in order to be able to make a living.[1]

Because efficient marketing thus requires that so many millions shall learn so much, it cannot be too often repeated that it is the most difficult of all the problems which face Asia, in

[1] This problem is also discussed from the educational point of view in Chapter 14.

some ways more difficult even than saving. It is not a problem which can be solved quickly. Millions of people can only take the equivalent of millions of correspondence courses over years and years. Nor, apart from the vital point of education, can the State do very much. It can provide secretaries and credit for marketing societies; it can run grading schemes; it can make available crop forecasts and market prices; it can organise schools of design for handicraftsmen, create in the big towns corporations to export or sell to Government, set up institutes to research into the problems of particular industries and particularly into their markets. The decisions what to grow or to manufacture, to whom to sell it, and what price to ask, will still be the small man's, or his marketing society's and not the State's. Unless they learn to make them intelligently, in reasonable knowledge of the facts, the Asian economy will continue to combine under-consumption with unemployment, high prices one year with low prices the next, in the way it does today.

It is enough thus to state the problem for it to be clear that it is beyond the small man to solve it for himself. So long as he has to try, either he will go on being poor and exploited, or he will need the constant crutch of State help and discrimination in his favour, as American farm and small business policies prove even more clearly than Indian assistance to the handloom weaver. Who *can* solve the problem is something about which one cannot now be dogmatic. The marketing society is undoubtedly part of the answer. Cotton and rice, wheat and fish and oilseeds can all be sold successfully by co-operatives once the producer has a quite limited amount of education and economic understanding; successful cotton marketing societies already exist in Asia on a considerable scale. The marketing society may also be the answer for traditional luxuries and for the more elementary consumer goods, silk brocades or plain shirts or men's sandals, for instance. For the rest, however, for those goods where preferences are fickle or habits have still to be created, for detergents and radio sets, nylon bags and plastic glasses, the answer really is that the small man has no place. Asia, too, must become more a continent of employees. For marketing to be successful in the modern world it is not enough to co-operate in a marketing society once a product is made. There must be co-operation before it is made, a pooling of knowledge and skill on what to make and how to make it, a pooling of effort in the actual making; and that requires a firm, not a marketing society, the disappearance of the small man, not his propping-up.

Chapter 18

COMMUNITY PROJECTS

IF Asia is to develop, Asia's small men must become effective units of a modern economy. That is Asia's central problem. The community project is an attempt to solve the problem all in one go, by one comprehensive answer. In it are included co-operation and education, better means of production and better marketing, better communications and better health, 4H clubs and women's institutes, artificial insemination and maternity clinics. The State provides more staff than ever before; the small man himself provides more labour and money than ever before. The project is, in fact, a co-operative effort of State and citizen to bring about the changes in the ordinary man and woman's way of life Asia needs if it is to become rich.[1]

The community project scheme rests on the realisation that, if the peasant and the artisan are to become richer, they must be shown both what to want and how to get it. Riches by themselves are a vague idea, an end-product. It is no use a man wanting money in a general way. He must know and will the means to get it. And, when he has got it, he must know what to do with it if he is not to be worse off at the end than at the beginning. The peasants who shod their bullocks with silver during the Bombay cotton boom in the early 1860s were acting as those untrained in the use of sudden money always act.

The projects also start from another principle, one perhaps harder to inculcate in a continent where the educated believe in their own right to leadership as firmly as they do in Asia. It is that people will work harder for things they want themselves than for things that are merely pushed on them. The jargon is that one must go for the people's 'felt needs'. What it means is that, however ignorant a man or woman may be, they are far more likely to be successful in doing something they know they need than in doing something an official thinks is good for them. And that this is true even when what the official thinks is good for them is in fact better for them than what they actually

[1] The community projects are now becoming popular everywhere. In India every village is to be covered either by projects or by the more diluted national extension blocks by 1963; Ceylon is trying them on the Gal-oya project; Pakistan and Indonesia have begun on them. My personal experience of their working is however limited to India. What follows will, therefore, be based primarily on India.

want. Their need for education may be greater than their need for communications; but if they want a road first, and a school afterwards, the project idea is that they should be helped to have the road first.

Plainly stated like this, it is an idea which may appear incontrovertible. One has to put it into Western terms to see how revolutionary it is, how much further it takes the control of Government by the people than it has ever been taken before. Nobody asks the people of Kensington or the Bronx which they would like to have first, their local high street widened or a new laboratory for their local high school. The decision is made by the local council, often in fact by its officials. In Asia, the people are being asked to decide for themselves, and to back up their decision with acts. They do not just choose. Having chosen (or, normally, said what they want through their leaders), they must then either work or pay for their choice. If they want a road, they must provide the labour for it; Government only provides the culverts. If they want a school they must pay for $\frac{1}{3}$ or $\frac{1}{2}$ of it (the proportions vary); Government gives only the rest.

The third principle of the projects is that the villager's problem is one problem to be solved as a whole, not a series of little problems to be attacked piecemeal. His whole life must be changed. He cannot have education and health services without higher production to pay for them. He cannot have higher production without the education to know how to get it, and the health to do the necessary work. The attack must be on all fronts though above all on that combination of agriculture and education which is agricultural extension.

From these principles follow automatically the main administrative features of the projects.

The welfare state changing the life of its people cannot manage with the staff which was enough for the night-watchman state. The night-watchman state was only trying to protect them in the happiness they already had; the welfare state is trying to lead them to a level of happiness they have never before known. Therefore there is much more staff, educational, co-operative, veterinary, agricultural, and so on, than there has ever been before, and the key staff, the staff at the villager's own level, is much more multi-purpose than it ever was before. Most of the villager's questions do not need a highly-trained expert to answer them. The points which puzzle him are often quite simple and quite small. They are also, however, often very urgent. If something is wrong with his cow, a veterinary surgeon two days' bullock cart journey away is of very limited use. Therefore, in place of the old expert departments each working with limited staff in its own watertight compartments, there is now being substituted at the bottom level, in the village, one village-level worker, who will be able to answer questions on every subject, who will always be within call, two or three miles away perhaps instead of fifty or more, and whom the villager will be able to get to know as an individual. This village-level worker will not of course know the answer to all the questions. The complicated ones will always be beyond him. The complicated ones can, however, usually wait a little while for an answer. For them it will then be the village-level worker's function to know, as the ordinary villager cannot possibly know, first, the best place to go for the answer, and then how to adapt it—for it may be in somewhat abstract and technical terms—to the concrete circumstances of the farmer who posed the question.

Now that Asian Governments are trying to develop by changing the life of their people, their main attention must be on the villages, where their people live. The projects provide Government with the framework by means of which it can concentrate on the village and the development of the village.

In India, for example, the main arm of the administration has always been the Revenue Department. Traditionally, the revenue department collected the revenue, controlled the police and the excise, provided the criminal judiciary, and did what development was done. It was the 'ma-bap sarkar', the mother and father of the people—which included smacking them when the department thought they were naughty. Revenue officials are normally the most respected and most adaptable of all officials, the ones who understand the people best, the ones who are best able to achieve results. Community projects have, therefore, been made primarily their responsibility, and their other less important tasks have largely been taken away from them. Inflation has reduced the land revenue to a level at which it almost collects itself, while the separation of the judiciary from the executive which is now general in the Indian States makes it possible to appoint separate officers for the time-consuming judicial work. For the first time, Government's main department is able to treat development, not as a side-issue and a hobby, but as a full-time, or almost full-time job.

The result is that much more can be taken down to the people than ever before. Where the Assistant Collector of pre-war could allow himself half-an-hour to talk of improved seeds, the Project Officer of today can allow himself as long as he likes. The result is also, perhaps, less obviously, that much more comes up from the people than ever before. In half-an-hour a slow-thinking village audience did not always have the time to do more than twiddle its toes in discomfort at the thought of reform. In a whole day, it can collect its thoughts and put forward its orators to explain why its old ways are much better than any new-fangled ideas the Project Officer may have; and once the village begins to argue, it can sometimes show the official an angle he did not know.

The same applies to planning. When there was a limited staff and limited grants to be spent within the budgetary year, the officials had no option but to spend the money where they themselves thought it would do most good. Now, when Government asks in advance for village plans and district plans, when the whole of planning for the countryside is deliberately based on what the countryside itself wants, there is time to find out which village wants a seed-store and which a maternity home, which a bigger school and which a better road. There will not be enough money to provide for everything the villager wants; but in time the Project staff will know what the villager would like to drop if he has to drop something. If, therefore, everybody does his duty—and some inevitably will not; it is so much easier to decide everything for oneself than to find out what hundreds of villages want, so easy too to convince oneself that one knows better than these poor ignorant people possibly can—then the villager will have a plan he wants sufficiently badly to be willing to tax himself for it, whether in labour or in money. Thus one of the primary problems of Asia, the poverty of its Governments, will be half-way to solution.

There is another important consequence of the basic community project rule that the people must get what they want, not what the official thinks they ought to want. In the projects they are not lectured, they are shown. Instead of the Assistant Collector explaining to a village meeting that such and such a Pusa strain of wheat will give a 25 per cent better yield than their local seed, there is a demonstration plot in the village so that they can see for themselves. Instead of their being lectured on the merits of village industries, knitting classes are provided for their wives. Instead of arguments about the merits of drains, they are taken to see how much cleaner a nearby village looks that has already got them.

There is one aspect of this insistence on showing rather than telling which is especially important in Asia. It was named 'dirty hands' by Albert Mayer, the American to whom the community projects owe so much of their inspiration.

In Asia, because labour has always been ample, and because of the climate, manual labour has always been looked
down upon. To fell a tree in a cold climate is an invigorating
pursuit, one in which the late Duke of Devonshire could indulge
without anyone thinking it odd. In a hot climate it is merely
sweaty and exhausting, something no one would do if he could
avoid it. Development, however, involves manual work, and a
great deal of it. Without people using their hands, irrigation
channels cannot be dug, schools cannot be built, pump engines
cannot be mended. They must, moreover, more and more often
be skilled hands. The village can no longer afford to lose its
educated to the towns. It needs them to drive lorries, look after
tube-well engines, or run demonstration plots. Manual labour
must be made respectable.

This has long been realised. Under the British a Collector
would occasionally dig the first sod to set an example. But he
was a foreigner. His subordinates applauded and took no notice;
they could not afford to compromise their social position by
copying him. In India when a junior official wants to move his
chair from one part of the room to another, he does not carry
it himself, he sends for a messenger. In such an atmosphere occasional examples are not enough. Mr. Nehru gives such examples
regularly; but his administrators, especially the older ones in
the lower-down positions, are less emancipated than he is. They
cannot ignore society as he can. Therefore, they have to be put
in an environment where to use their hands comes naturally,
where it is a routine part of the job, taken for granted by themselves and everybody else. That is the point of the community
project insistence on 'dirty hands'. Here is a new scheme which
everybody knows is to rejuvenate India. The men in charge have
been put there as a compliment, because they are Government's
best. That too everybody knows. They have in consequence
some of Mr. Nehru's freedom of action. When they use their
hands, they do not lose prestige. They gain prestige; for they
are, by the very act of digging or building, pioneers creating the
new India; the more imaginative can feel upon themselves as
they work the eyes of the nation seeing itself renewed.

This particular doctrine of 'dirty hands' is part of something
wider and more important, the sense of mission which involves
so many of those who work on the projects. The Indian official
in most States has always had a high sense of duty. His morale
has, however, been somewhat depressed over the last thirty
years by constant propaganda that in serving the Government
he was betraying his country and that what he was doing was

not really nation-building. It is a great relief to him to be able to do a job of whose value to his country there can be no doubt, a job too where he can see with his own eyes the results of his efforts. It is an enormous satisfaction to a man to see a school finished and beautiful, dominating the countryside from its little hillock, if he knows that without his hours of persuasion, without his constant reminders that work needed to be done or money to be paid, the school would never have existed at all.

Every project official is not perfect. An astonishingly high proportion, however, are expending themselves without stint. They work 12 hours a day. They do 50 to 60 miles in jeeps a day. They spend hours talking to villagers to get them to decide what they want, and to act on their decision; and more hours writing to their superiors to get sanction for Government's part of what the villagers want to do. They are badly paid; their job may involve long separations from their families; the politicians sometimes try to take the credit for their work; they can rarely afford to lose their tempers and never to be tactless. Their work is done as well as it so often is because of a deep sense of dedication. Project officials do not look like missionaries. They are rarely eloquent. It usually embarrasses them to talk about ideals; they prefer to discourse on the percentage of their road grant they have spent, or the beautiful drains they have built. Their enthusiasm is seldom betrayed by anything more than the conjunction of the words 'beautiful' and 'drains'. Some are old and slow; others are young and still unlicked. But most are deeply keen on their work. It is this keenness which gives one hope for the future.

The community projects are still in their infancy. They are still far from fulfilling all the promises they hold out. They are meeting with many difficulties, the nature of which reveals what sort of obstacles stand in the way of economic development in Asia. There are difficulties in training, difficulties of getting the official to let the people decide for themselves, difficulties in getting co-operation from leading non-officials, difficulties over not letting the social services outrun the increase in production.

Although the projects have behind them a training programme bigger than anything which has ever been seen before, so that the ordinary village-level worker undergoes a one year's course, far too many of, especially, the senior people are still not trained enough. Especially, too few project officials have agriculture, the villager's life blood, at their finger tips. So some may lose the villagers' respect by committing obvious gaffes:

others concentrate on subjects they do understand, like schools and libraries, and do not give enough attention to the improvement of crops and livestock which is the necessary economic base for all other forms of improvement. For every project official to be thoroughly agriculturally trained is a first necessity.

Keen though the officials are, moreover, not all of them have freed themselves from the besetting sin of the educated, the belief that they alone know best. Getting a set of slow-minded and not very lucid villagers to decide for themselves what they want can be a frustrating business. Sometimes what they want is obviously silly; sometimes if one faction in the village wants a road, a second faction will want a school, and a third will want drains, simply in order to avoid accepting the leadership of the first faction. Sometimes the villagers may all agree on something, and then be evasive about giving either work or labour for it. The poor official meanwhile has targets of achievement to meet, and it inevitably often seems easier to him to decide for himself what they need—or what he has the money to help them have—and then to exercise Government's traditional gentle pressure to see that they do what he has decided they ought to do. In the short run this works quite well. He does not have to be oppressive. The villager is accustomed to responding to a Governmental lead, and he does not like to say 'no' to somebody who appears to have his interests at heart. The trouble is that work achieved in this way has no permanence. The school may be built, but the little girls may still be kept at home. The water-supply pipes may be laid and the villagers may quarrel for months over where the taps should be. Getting the villagers to want something for themselves is the long way round, but it is shorter in the end. A school they wanted is a school they will keep neat and clean, a school in which they will be eager to enrol their children. A water-supply they agitated for is a water-supply they will use. A road they felt they needed is a road they will mend after the monsoon wash-outs. Nothing threatens the whole community project idea more than any official tendency to meet official targets instead of those of the villagers.

The third difficulty in the community projects is the lack of co-operation from leading non-officials. Every project has its project committee, on which are put such leading non-officials as members of Parliament and of State Legislative Assemblies. These are people who, in their own areas, normally have more influence than any official. The official is an outsider who will be transferred after at most three or four years. The non-official is a native, whose life is spent in the area, and whose whole position is the result of his ability to influence the local people. He is, not always but very often, one of them; he does not need to learn their customs and habits of thought, he was brought up to them. He does not have to run headlong into their resistances to discover what they are; he is familiar with them amongst his own aunts and cousins. He knows which of the rich are always ready to give, and what pressures to apply on those who are meaner-minded. If he will help. he can be invaluable, as has been shown for example, by Mr. Paranjpye, a Congress M.P., who is running a little project of twenty-five villages almost single-handed near Latur in Hyderabad State.

The trouble is that he so rarely helps. He forgets to attend advisory committee meetings. He cannot find the time to go out to the villages. This may not be his fault. He has a living to earn. Asia does not have the large population of rentiers, vigorous pensioners, and middle class wives with time to spare, on which so much Western voluntary effort depends. In an ordinary Indian district the leading non-officials are men who probably earn $30 to $45 a week, and who have to use their whole time in order to do that. Moreover, though voluntary work in Western slums is not precisely comfortable, voluntary work in Indian villages is worse still. There is nowhere to stay, except perhaps in some villager's house; there is nothing to eat, except perhaps what the village may provide. There is no way of getting to many villages except in a bullock-cart or a horse-carriage. And if the reformer is keen enough to overcome all these obstacles, he will probably not find himself very welcome in the rôle of reformer. Asian villages are very close corporations, and do not change their habits too easily for a man from the next village or the local town, however willing they may be to vote for him at an election.

When every excuse has been offered, however, it is still true that the non-official does not do enough. Partly it may be the reaction from the effort of attaining independence; if so it may wear off as a new generation grows up which has not already spent years in going to gaol. Largely, however, it is the result of an attitude of mind which will work for political change, but is less conscious of the need for social change, and is hardly conscious at all of the importance of tube-wells, fertiliser and improved seed. This attitude is the inevitable legacy of the struggle of British days. Mahatma Gandhi always fought against it. All the Indian political parties are now fighting against it. The attitude is, however, so deep-rooted, it may take so long to change, that the village will in the end find its non-official leadership more quickly within itself, amongst its matriculates who do not go to town. This would be unfortunate in some ways, for it will make the process of change slower; people cannot be expected to accept advice as quickly from their own sons and nephews as from the recognised leaders of their district. On the other hand, advice once accepted from sons and nephews after long family argument may perhaps be more permanently assimilated into the village's folkways.

The last, and perhaps the most serious, big difficulty that the community projects face is the risk that social services will run ahead of the economic improvements which must pay for them. The Asian village's needs are so crying that once the villager stirs to the possibility of a better life, he wants, and is even willing partly to pay for, a whole series of amenities at once. He wants a school *and* a midwife, a road *and* a water supply. In the long run all are vital to economic development. If the women are not always being crippled by the after-effects of ill-managed deliveries, if men and women alike are educated and do not get dysentery from drinking bad water, the village will be both more responsive to new ideas and more able to do the hard work necessary to carry them out. In the short run, however, they have to be paid for, and they do not bring in any money with which anybody can pay.

It is therefore of crucial importance that agriculture should be improved even faster than other aspects of the village's life.[1] This is not easy. It is not too difficult to persuade the villager to use fertiliser; but one has to be careful he does not use too much and burn up his soil, or he will be put off for the future. When, however, one is trying to turn dry cultivation into wet in a region with no experience of wet cultivation, or to teach ploughing along the contours, the whole process can be very difficult indeed. The results may not be sufficiently spectacular for a man as little able to run risks as the average small peasant. Or the applied research to adapt fundamental results to particular soils and climatic conditions may not have been done. Or the improved methods may involve capital expenditure or wells or new implements or better beasts which the villager cannot afford. Or the weather may be wrong the first year, and the new methods fail.

Moreover, the improvement of agriculture is much more exacting, it requires much better organisation and timing, a much better business sense than the other objectives of the pro-

[1] The Government of India now wants the village level worker to devote 80% of his time to agricultural extension.

ject. If a school is a few months delayed in the building, or if a doctor cannot be got for a dispensary for a while, there is waste and damage, but they are temporary. If, however, a Government seed-store for improved seed does not have the seed when the farmer wants it, or if the money for fertiliser credit is not sanctioned before the fertiliser has to be put on the field, then at the very least the improvement must wait for another year, and at worst the farmer's confidence may be shattered for ever. Agricultural improvements are no different from new ways of washing up dishes in a Western society; they may be better, but the customer—the peasant—does not know they are better. He has to be told, he has to be shown, he even has to be bally-hooed if a new habit is to be substituted for the old one. And, once he becomes willing to try the experiment he must not be discouraged by any irregularity of supply. No advertising is of any use if the housewife cannot then go to her local shop and buy a packet. No demonstration plots will help if the technique is such that the farmer cannot adopt it without great difficulty, or if the materials he needs are then not available.

The project administration is aware of these risks. It is making a great effort to see that its seed stores are run in a businesslike way, that the peasant is shown new methods on a plot in his own village before he is asked to try them, that the project officials spend infinite time in persuasion and argument. But the administration is dependent for its success on the man on the spot; and there are cases where it is fatally easy for him not to be present when wanted, or to recommend something he himself does not really understand, or to use the methods of the bureaucrat rather than those of the advertiser. Therefore, there are failures, not fatal, but also not infrequent.

Changing the villager's whole life, that key and vital principle of the community project, goes beyond all that we have talked of hitherto, beyond agricultural improvement or more education into social change, change in the whole structure of village life. Here the projects are still to some extent feeling their way. So little work has been done on Indian sociology, so much of the territory to be explored is still uncharted, that the projects cannot but grope. The groping is temporary. The experience they will themselves accumulate, the sociological work now beginning to be done by Indian and foreign universities[1] will gradually teach them the answers. But for the time being

[1] See for example *The Indian Village*, by S. C. Dube, Cornell University Press 1955. *Economic Development and Social Change in South India*, by T. Scarlett Epstein, Manchester University Press, 1962.

they must feel their way.

Nobody, not even the villagers themselves, has any difficulty in deciding that the village must be educated and healthy, that untouchability must be suppressed, the village made clean, and everybody taught to read a newspaper. These are obvious and accepted objectives; their attainment is a matter of time and money, nothing more.

The changes required, however, are more extensive and also more indefinite, female equality for instance. Unless women become more the equals of their husbands, unless as much value is set on a daughter as on a son, female ignorance and female conservatism will be a perpetual drag on development. Unless, too, the adolescent boy and the young man cease to be quite so unquestioningly dependent on the father who runs the property and traditionally makes all the decisions, youth will never get the chance to make mistakes and try experiments which pays Western societies so high a dividend of successful innovation. The untouchable, too, must learn, not only that he has rights, but that he must be willing to fight and make sacrifices in order to enforce these rights, if his degradation is not permanently to deprive the community of his abilities.

These problems, and others like them, are much more complex than the simple question of whether extending the school or building a new road should come first. All that the projects have done to deal with them so far is to appoint social education organisers. They, however, are usually the most ineffective people on the project. Neither they nor anybody else knows what they are really trying to do. The effective reforms so far have been the result of State legislation—legislation giving women greater property rights and making it a criminal offence to deny an untouchable access to a well, for example; not of anything the projects have done. Much of what the projects need to do is nevertheless fairly obvious. They must drive for adult literacy. They must make the village a pleasanter place for a person of some liveliness of mind to live in. They must provide 4H clubs for the young and women's institutes for women.

As with so many of the changes Asia needs, the first necessity is adult literacy; once untouchables or women can read, their whole social position changes; the Brahmin's position originally rested on the fact that he alone knew the Vedas. The projects realise the importance of adult literacy. But they come up against the old problem, the key problem of all economic development in Asia. It is not enough for Government to provide; the people must also want. They must want education for all their children, not just for the sons of the better-off. They must want it too for themselves; without adult education everything will have to wait, for today's ten-year-olds to become fifty. Once people want education they will come after a hard day's work to learn their a.b.c. in a small, hired, room by the light of a kerosene lantern; where they do not want it, the hardness of the day's work becomes an immediate excuse for dropping off after the first few lessons; then not even electric light and a large, airy room will tempt the labourer.

The next necessity is diversion, more useful and pleasant occupations for the villager's leisure time. One of the main reasons the towns attract the cream from the countryside, in Asia as in Europe, is that there is more to do in a town. There are cinemas, newspapers, the ever-changing life of the streets. The village is dull. Even the factions that keep their elders interested do not amuse the young much; they are not important enough to be faction-leaders, and the brighter amongst them realise that factions are bad for the village. The young must be given something to do in their spare time; something to make their minds active, so that they will not stop being receptive to new ideas the day they leave school; something at which they can earn a little money, so that they can at once gain some business experience and get a little freedom from their elders. The women, too, need something to stir their minds, to make them better wives and more knowledgeable mothers, to enable them if possible to supplement the family income and obtain the respect which comes from earning. The men themselves need to be refreshed after their day's work, to be given something which will take them out of their poverty and their quarrels; their minds need to be diverted from the groove of their daily round, stimulated into the painfulness of thought; for those of them who have spare time, they need to be shown ways in which that spare time can be used to relieve the bareness of their life.

To this problem there is, of course, no one answer. That is one reason why the problem is so baffling for Government. It is so much easier for a large organisation like a Government to deal with one big answer than with fifty little ones. The fifty little answers, do, however, exist. They are even fairly widely known and if they cannot be applied quickly, it is only because a lot of little organisations take a long time to get going; recruiting and training the people to run them is much more complicated than when one is concerned with some single major service like road-building or forestry.

One answer which is being tried, so far not very effectively, is to adapt the American 4H clubs to the Asian village. These clubs do in fact do most of what is needed. They teach the boys and girls about farming and homemaking, giving them knowledge which it is hard to fit into a school curriculum but which they absorb easily in the mere informal atmosphere of a club. They provide the young with an institution of their own, which they manage for themselves and in which their parents do not interfere. They can be a means to a little independence; if a young man has learnt about vegetable-growing in his club, his father may allow him a small plot; if a young woman has learnt how to make preserves, a new art in Asia, her mother or mother-in-law may let her have the materials to make them. Above all, through the club outside ideas and techniques can be introduced, from the place of vitamins in the diet to the proper shape of a cradle for the baby. This kills two very large birds with one not very expensive stone. The village learns the new ideas; and the parents learn respect for their children as the children acquire knowledge the parents do not have.

If, however, the 4H Club is to achieve these objectives, what it is doing must be carefully related to the village environment. It is no use merely importing an American club and putting it as it is into an Indian village. The temptation to teach the girls how to embroider tablecloths, for instance, which besets so much Indian social work, must be sternly resisted. Embroidered tablecloths are not a high priority for Indian village homes, and the embroidery is not usually good enough for the tablecloths to be saleable. To teach the girls to sew and darn, on the other hand, is invaluable. Indian garments have traditionally been unsewn. The material is simply wound round the person who puts it on. The result is that the Indian housewife has none of the European housewife's skill in making and mending. Now, however, the shirt and the blouse and the child's frock have become everyday garments in the village. If the women could make them, or at least lengthen their life by mending them when they get torn, the economic advantage would be considerable. The golden rule in choosing what to teach is not to be too ambitious. It is the simple techniques which are most needed; how to grow and cook tomatoes, how to wash clothes without beating them, how to keep flies away from the food, simple first-aid. Embroidery and flower-arrangement can come afterwards.

What the 4H Clubs might do for the youth, some modification of the Women's Institute might do for the women. Once again, it is not an institution which can simply be lifted bodily and put down in Asia as it is. The Asian village lacks some of the essentials which have made English Women's Institutes so successful. Asian women do not have the habit of sitting on committees. Asian villages do not have squires' wives, parsons' wives, doctors' wives and rentier spinsters to provide leadership and funds. Asian women do not have the independence in managing their budgets and doing their shopping the English labourer's wife has; the husband decides what shall be spent, the husband often does the shopping, the husband may even decide the brand of soap or the quality of cooking oil. Finally, in the Indian village there are not as many special housekeeping skills and secrets to be shared as there were in the English village, except amongst some of the upper castes. Life is too simple and too frugal, everybody in a particular caste knows all the same recipes, and there are resistances to adopting the recipes of other castes.

To start a Women's Institute in an Indian village and leave the village to go on from there is, therefore, to ask for failure. The Institute will simply die, and the death will not even be lingering. The community project has to recognise that the institute is a foreign concept, which the Asian village could not possibly produce spontaneously. The plant is delicate, it must be watered and looked after. The project's Social Education Organiser must provide the new recipes, she must teach the new techniques, she must give most of the lectures, she must train the committee in how to work as a committee, she must look for the potential leaders and overcome their feeling that leadership is for men.

It is a large task; it is not a matter of a few evenings, talking to women who can then do the rest for themselves with the minimum of assistance from headquarters, but of ten or fifteen years of careful nursing. Indeed, to make a good committee woman, English squire's wife style, may well take generations. Institutes can be created, techniques can be adapted to Asian circumstances in months; for the members to learn how to work the Institute themselves, for their families to welcome the new techniques, takes years.

4H Clubs and Women's Institutes are very practical institutions. The village also needs less immediately useful cultural fare. It requires, for instance, a library, where it can learn what is happening in the world from newspapers, and from which it can borrow books. The man who reads a newspaper knows much more about what is happening in the market than the man who does not, and he learns much more quickly about innovations that may be to his economic advantage. The newspaper, and still more the specialised weekly, greatly reduce for the small man, his disadvantages of ignorance and isolation. The books too can be of great economic help. They should not be chosen primarily to improve the acquaintance of the villager with the classics. The classics often require a greater effort of the imagination than the villager is capable of at the end of a day in the fields. What he needs is, on the one hand, the little manuals and handbooks which will enable him to do his job better, and which in most Asian languages, will have to be written specially, and, on the other hand, a source of relaxation and amusement; and the projects will have to remember that in Asia as in mediaeval Europe, relaxation comes more often from reading the lives of saints than from detective stories. The Koran or the Mahabharata mean more in the village than the best psychological novel. It is indeed one of Asia's great advantages over Europe that the Asian villager still likes to be uplifted as well as entertained.

The villages need, too, forms of cultural activity which do not have the direct economic advantages of reading. In Bengal, for example, every village has its music society and its dramatic society. This is, however, rare, a reflection of the Bengali's exceptional artistic perception. It may incidentally be the reason why the Bengali villager sticks so closely to his village, and leaves the working class of Calcutta to be composed of Biharis and Oriyas. Almost every region in Asia, however, certainly every religion which has ever been touched by Hinduism, has its own tradition of dance and drama. These traditions, revived, can be used, as the Communists use them, to demonstrate simple lessons and drive home social points. Nothing is better than a play or a ballet to teach the advantages of thrift, or to make real to the imagination of the better-off the miseries of untouchability. Art must not, however, be used only practically. It must also be used for its original purpose of entertainment, to make the village a more livable-in place, a place where the young man and the young woman can enjoy themselves without going off to town. Art has also a social advantage. In the village leadership is too concentrated in the old and the men. Dance and drama spread leadership out. The best dancer is more likely to be young than old; plays more often centre round young heroines than old heroes. More plays and more dancing will help to give the women and the young the place they must have if change is not to be intolerably slow.

The biggest of all the changes the project must bring about

if Asia is to develop, however, is none of these. It is the change from a society based on inherited status to a society based on individual achievement.

Village society in Asia, like most societies everywhere at all times, is based mainly on status. What matters is not an individual's personality, but his sex, his age, his caste, his religion, his inherited position. This is a system admirably adapted to a static society; where little change is possible, it is well that people should be happy as they are. But the first requirement of a dynamic society, a developing society, is that people should not be happy as they are, that they should get new wants and be willing to change and to work in order to satisfy them. Hence the growth of individualism in recent Western history. This growth has strained Western society to bursting-point. Many Western societies, like France in 1789 or 1848, and Russia in 1917, have in fact burst; every Western society has been afflicted with great increases in social tension and personal maladjustment.

These results may be welcome to Communists whose aim is that the strain should become so intolerable that it can find release only in revolution. Democrats must, however, hope to avoid them. That places the democrat in a dilemma. He must desire more and more individualism. A society in which everybody is making and experimenting for himself will change more quickly and take to innovations more successfully than one in which everybody has to move together, which usually means at the pace of grandmother and grandfather. Yet he must also desire social peace. It is of little use to the villager for his income to increase by 10 per cent or 20 per cent if he has, as a result, to see his neighbours as rivals instead of friends.

This is another of the many problems of Asian economic development to which nobody quite knows the answer. It is, however, possible that some of the community project approaches we have already discussed may provide an answer, as if by accident.

The project reduces the gap between the naturally enterprising and the naturally unenterprising. Its new ideas are shown to everybody. Adopting them requires much less initiative than when the individual has to go and look for them by himself. Indeed the whole objective of the project is that *everybody* should adopt their ideas. It is not enough for a few daughters of advanced parents go to school. The project wants every girl to go to school. It is not enough if the most open-minded villagers adopt the Japanese method of rice-growing. The project wants to see the large increase in food-production which will come from everybody's adopting it. Innovations therefore reach a much wider layer of the village than when the villager has to find them out for himself. The vast mass of the village can move forward as a whole, instead of a few individuals jumping ahead of the rest. Status is not too much disturbed. Yet status does not remain completely static. There will be some who have not inherited or grown up to positions of leadership who will nevertheless adapt more quickly to the new life than their fellows. The Women's Institute will, after all, have a committee of women not men. There may be an untouchable matriculate, or a quite small farmer who changes over successfully from cereal-growing to vegetable-growing. These changes will, however, take time; they will not suddenly upset time-honoured relations; everybody will have long enough to be able to adjust to them, and will do so the more willingly because the old leadership positions will not be destroyed. It will still, for a long time to come, be highly respectable to be on the caste panchayat; but it will also be highly respectable to be on the village panchayat or the committee of the drama society. One may contrast the nineteenth-century situation, where the merchant-money-lender so often rose to prominence and wealth on the ruin of village and tribal society.

Next, the way the community project looks at education will help to bring about the necessary move from birth and status to individual merit and achievement. For the project, education is vocational. Here all that need be done is to emphasise the extent to which this education will be vocational, not in the narrow sense of teaching a man how to plough better or how to milk a cow better (though both may be important), but in the wide sense of making him more suited to lead successfully the life of a small peasant living in a village society of set ways. His reading is intended to give him a taste for newspapers and books, and not to be an art allowed to rust as soon as he leaves school. His history, it is hoped, will explain to him that the undesirable features of his society are an abuse, not a law of God; that the Koran does not insist on purdah, nor the Vedas on untouchability. His curriculum as a whole is being slowly changed to provide adequate room for the elementary sciences and not quite so elementary agriculture without which he cannot become an efficient farmer. Methods of teaching are at last departing from the memorising and repetition which were suitable when the main purpose of education was to give a man an ethical code by which he could act automatically, but are not so suitable when he has to learn to think for himself, to weigh one new idea against another and decide which he will accept and which he will reject.

The projects realise that there must be more years of education given in the village itself, and that it must be much more directed to village life. Middle schools are being built in villages, so that children can be educated in their own environment, without the terrible break, the disgust for the village, which comes from their having to be sent to an uncle or a hostel in the town. For what the projects are doing to have their full effect, however, the school curriculum itself will have to be more practical, as the basic schools are now trying to make it. The quickest way to get a higher standard of life is for people to learn how to get it for themselves. If clean water supplies are to wait till the Asian States can afford to provide them, they may wait for generations; if the children once learn that they will die if their water is contaminated, they will build with their bare hands, they will go without bangles for their daughters in order to buy the pipes, but their water will be clean.

If the Asian villager is to become prosperous, he must change. The Communists change him by force. The community projects are an attempt to change him by persuasion. It is a harder and a slower way, but a surer one. The answer of the countryside to force is sabotage, as it was in Russia in the early '30s; and Asian Governments in general do not have the means of pressure of the Russian Government. It is more effective in Asia for Government to accept that its function is to help people to help themselves, to teach them what to want and show them how to get it. The rest the people must, and will, do for themselves. The Asian villager is no fool. Shown a better way, he is eager enough to adopt it. It is a hard path for the official, slower than force, more exacting, but much more penetrating. It needs a missionary enthusiasm, the type of mind which finds its satsifaction in changing others, not in imposing its will upon them. If enough missionaries can be found amongst Asia's officials, the community projects will change Asia in a generation.

Chapter 19

EQUALITY

The Background of Ideas

IF Asia is to develop, it requires the talent, the effort, the innovations, the willingness to change and the capacity to lead, of all its people, women as well as men, religious minorities as well as religious majorities, untouchables as well as touchables, poor as well as rich. Asia's societies must become equal instead of hierarchic. Success must matter more than birth. Yet the advance to equality involves also great risks. The old leadership may be destroyed before new leaders arise. The rich may cease to take risks before the poor have learnt that risks must be taken. And whilst equality once achieved is a great solvent of social tension, the quarrels on the way can lead all too easily to class war. Equality may be the only path up the mountain of riches; but it is a path beset by precipices on every side.

Ever since the French Revolution the desire for equality has been Europe's major political fact. In the last sixty or seventy years it has also become the dominant political fact in Asia.

The urge to be equal did not indeed begin with the French Revolution. It was asserted in the American Revolution, in the English Civil War, and by the sixteenth-century Anabaptists. It is perhaps in the long run an inevitable political consequence of the Christian belief that all men are brothers. Since all are equal in the eyes of God, it has always required a rather gymnastic form of philosophical reasoning to prove that men should not be equal in their own, so much lesser, eyes.

Only since the French Revolution, however, have all the political consequences of this revolutionary doctrine been ruthlessly drawn. Nineteenth-century European history is above all the story of the assertion of its equality by every group which had been suppressed, whether the suppressed group was religious or linguistic, national or economic, a sex or a class. Catholics, Nonconformists and Jews became the legal equals of Anglicans in England. Languages which had been beginning to die, like Slovene and Slovak in face of German and Magyar, were revived. Nationalities which had been thought forgotten or absorbed reasserted themselves, until the Irish became the key to English politics and the Hapsburgs spent their time fending off

disintegration. The vote spread downwards from the large property owner to the small, and then to the man without any property at all. The institutions which defended the better-educated
and the wealthier, like the English House of Lords or the Prussian system of Chambers, came under steadily more severe attack
as the idea spread that every man has a right to a share in deciding his own political destiny, and that the right should no
longer be confined to those with 'a stake in the country'. Under
the influence of the Socialists from Owen to Proudhon, and still
more of the Marxists, a large section of opinion began to argue
that equality must mean not only political equality but also economic equality, or else the political equality itself would be unreal.

In country after country women began to stir and to demand
the same rights as men. Finally, the society of Europe, until 1800
based almost entirely on class, has for the last 150 years been
steadily dissolving its classes. The Communist countries have
gone to extremes, first turning their class pyramid upside down
and then creating a new class structure. But in countries like
Norway and Sweden class distinction, except perhaps for
differences in education, has almost disappeared; and for all
Western countries the model is more and more the nearly classless society of the United States.[1]

So short a summary necessarily does less than justice to the
rich complication of Europe's recent history. No more is, however, perhaps necessary in order to use European history as a
means of understanding what has been happening in Asia. Asia
awakened to modern forms of political life only in the second
half of the nineteenth century or later. 1867, the Restoration of
the Emperor, might be an appropriate date for Japan, the early
1880s, Lord Ripon's viceroyalty, for India. Probably 1911, the
Revolution against the Manchus, is the best date for China. The
exact period is always arguable. One could, for example, push
the Japanese date back to 1855, when the West first brought its
force to bear on Japan, or push it forward to the 1890s, when
Europe finally accepted Japan as a Western-style State.

Whatever particular dates are taken it is important that Asia's
modern political life begins at a time when in Europe certain
forms of equality were generally accepted as ideals, others were
still being argued about, and none were yet applied. The acceptance of the ideas of religious, national, and political equality
was widespread in the advanced countries of Europe by 1880;

[1] There are of course inequalities in the U.S., but they are inequalities
based on colour or extent of assimilation to the main American tradition
rather than on class in the European sense.

but it was still virtually impossible for a Catholic or a Jew to be a Prussian General, the Magyars showed no intention of giving any real political say to their Rumanians or Slavs, and even the English agricultural labourer did not get the vote till 1884. As for sex equality, class (or social) equality, and economic equality, they were still in 1880 the ideas of an *avant-garde*. Shaw's *Pygmalion* has no point except in a society which takes social inequality for granted, the British Labour movement did not really begin till the 1890s, and John Stuart Mill was thought slightly odd for advocating votes for women.

The Asian, as he became politically conscious, tended to accept straightaway those ideals of equality which had been generally accepted in Europe, to accept rather more slowly those which were accepted only by the European *avant garde* and to demand in all cases that Europeans should be consistent in their ideas and apply them to him as well as to themselves.

That does not mean that these ideas spread round Asia like wild-fire. They could not be expected to, for in the form in which they were to be politically important, they were European, not Asian, ideas, though for some of them Asia had equivalents. Islam is classless, Chinese doctrine gave the people the right to revolt if the government was bad, Hinduism and Buddhism are religiously completely tolerant. These equivalents have sometimes made it much easier to accept particular Western ideas; the Indian secular state gets popular acceptance because of Hindu tolerance; the Chinese Communists have been helped by the respectability of revolution in China. But what has mattered in Asian politics has mostly been not such Asian traditions, but the various forms equality took in Western politics, perhaps because Asia has never had an organised politcal life in which the ordinary citizen took part above the level of the village. Indigenous Asian conceptions have occasionally been important for the resistance against equality they have enabled privileged groups to put up. Islam justifies the Pakistani Muslim in not treating Hindus quite as equals. Caste made an overwhelmingly Brahmin leadership for long acceptable in India. They have had no importance beyond that.

Because, therefore, the Western idea of equality had to be accepted in its Western forms, its spread in Asia was very slow indeed. In order to adopt a Western idea, a man must first be able to understand it. In order to understand it he must know something of the cadre of concepts and institutions into which it fits. At the beginning, for the first people who adopt the idea, this means a very high level of education indeed. They must be able to take themselves out of their own world of ideas, and into a completely new one. That takes years, and great intellectual curiosity. Naturally it took over half a century from the British conquest of Bengal to the first great Westerniser, Ram Mohun Roy, another half century before Western ideas became commonplace even among the élite. Once, however, a Western idea does become commonplace among the élite, the process of absorbing it speeds up greatly, for the élite translates it into terms the rest of society can understand with relatively little effort and without having to understand the whole set of ideas of which the particular idea being translated forms only a part.

What the élite take over is therefore of crucial importance, for the rest of society does not go to the wellspring direct, but drinks from the élite's hands. What the élite has taken over has varied a good deal, but, with the exception of Japan, which is a rather special case, certain phenomena are common.

National equality

The idea of national equality has been accepted everywhere. There was a time when some people in Asia, like the lower classes in Europe, believed themselves inferior. That was the inevitable consequence of Europe's immense nineteenth-century bound ahead. But nobody likes considering himself inferior. Asians very soon learnt to use against Europe the European notion of the nation and its rights. This idea, more than any purely Asian reaction, has been behind the Asian nationalist movements, and it explains the passionate Asian suspicion of colonialism. It explains, too, why it is that the different layers of Asian society have normally become nationalist only when they have become Western educated, or at least susceptible to the influence of the Western educated. So deep has the idea of national equality gone that Asians do not even conduct their quarrels amongst themselves in terms of superiority and inferiority. The Japanese never thought of the Chinese, nor do the Pakistani think of the Indians, as inferiors in the way so many nineteenth-century Englishmen thought of the Irish, or so many twentieth-century Germans thought of Poles and Jews.

Religious equality

The idea of equality between religions required very little acceptance. It came naturally to the countries of Hindu or Buddhist tradition, which are most of Asia, and for a time it found some acceptance amongst Muslims too. Now, however,

Islam is reacting against an idea so alien to it, and in Pakistan especially there is an insistence on some superiority for the Muslim. The most important effect of the idea of religious equality was not, however, as between religions, but within each religion itself. Islam was already a brotherhood; all that has happened there is that the sense of the value of that brotherhood has been strengthened. In Hinduism, however, the doctrine that all men are equal before God has proved the major solvent of caste, until today caste is defended by habit, or by the vague feeling that people of other castes are 'different', or by the prejudices of grandmother, but is rarely defended philosophically, as an institution. Caste has, it is true, rather little Vedic sanction; but temple entry for untouchables, indeed the whole fierce campaign against untouchability, comes less from the feeling that caste is the result of a misinterpretation of the scriptures than from a now widespread sense that it is wrong to treat one man as religiously inferior to another.

Political equality

The third idea which was generally accepted in nineteenth-century Europe, and is equally generally accepted in non-Communist twentieth-century Asia, is that of political equality. One person, one vote, is the usual rule of independent Asia; and there have been few attempts to complicate the issue with special representation for businessmen or landowners, property-owners or university graduates. Where some section of the community is disfranchised, as with most Indians in Ceylon, it is because they are alleged not to be citizens; where representation is gerrymandered against them, as with caste Hindus in Pakistan, it is because they are suspected of being disloyal citizens. And both phenomena are rare in the extreme. Equally, where there is special representation, as for teachers in Indian upper houses, it is a gesture of respect. It does not affect the seat of power.

Asia has thus accepted whole-heartedly the three forms of equality which were generally accepted, at least in theory, in nineteenth-century Europe. Asia has also tended to accept with less question than Europe itself the three forms of equality—sex equality, social equality, and economic equality—which were the subject of fierce controversy in nineteenth century Europe. But, whereas national equality, religious equality and political equality are today in Asia on the whole facts, these three other forms of equality which require social as well as legislative changes to establish them, are still on the whole only aspirations. It is true that aspirations which are generally accepted come nearer and nearer to being facts with every decade in which they remain accepted; and this is happening in Asia. But each of these three has in general in Asia a considerable way to go.

Sex equality

Politically, sex equality is the rule. Women have the vote, and women are coming out into public life. There are women ministers, and women ambassadors, and women civil servants. Socially, it is not yet so general. In the Buddhist countries there is no difficulty. Women have always been virtually their men's equals. In Communist China, sex equality is being enforced as part of the Communist creed. In India, the Constitution lays down the equality of women, and Hindu law has been changed to prohibit polygamy, and to give women the rights of property, guardianship and divorce without which it is much harder for wives to be the equals of husbands, or daughters of sons. But it is still the exception for women to work, and a change in property rights for which the village woman has not herself clamoured may well take a generation to affect her position. In Pakistan and the countries of the Middle East, the battle against purdah and polygamy and the unilateral right to divorce of the husband goes slowly. Women do not always object to any of these three; purdah can be a protection, polygamy valued for its company; the husband's right to divorce may be used when it is the wife who wants the divorce. But all effectively prevent sex equality. No wife can be equal whose knowledge of the world depends upon her husband, or who is always afraid that too violent a disagreement may drive her husband to divorce or a second wife. On the other hand, in all the Islamic countries, the woman's property rights have always been very considerable. If she had the man's education and freedom, there would be no economic bar to her equality.

Social equality

Social equality is, on the whole, more widespread in Asia than in Europe. In general, in Asia, every position is open to anybody who acquires the qualifications, and in practice equality is limited not by anybody's prejudices, but by the limitations of the educational systems, which make it difficult for many people to acquire the qualifications. Today in most of Asia it is not very important who a man's grandfather was. In the ex-colonial countries most of the positions of power and prestige are inevitably held by new men, for until recently they were held by

foreigners; and in every country, even Japan, it was not the sons
of great houses who learnt the new techniques which give position in the modern world, but middle and lower class boys.
Samurai, not daimyo, ran Meiji Japan; the Indian Army is not
officered with the sons of princes and great landowners. Lately,
moreover, the great houses have in several countries been
further diminished in importance by land reform and by their
having supported the colonial power (in Japan the pre-war re-
gime), while in the Communist countries, China and North
Vietnam, to have had a grandfather is a sin to be expiated. The
great landowner is indeed still a force in the Islamic countries,
but there the social consequences are greatly mitigated by the
classlessness of Islam. Even caste, which to the European eye
often seems to be the class society at its most rigid, is in fact something very different, for it divides society into a series of sections
within each of which class has much less force than in Europe. It
is, for example, usually more important in deciding whether a
man is suitable to become a connection by marriage to know
whether he is a Brahmin or a Mahratta than to know whether
he is a High Court judge or a clerk.

A class structure is indeed beginning to form in Asia, based on
Western education, power and money. There are senses in which
generals, secretaries to Government and big industrialists rank
well above sergeant-majors, clerks and shopkeepers. Whereas in
Europe, however, it is customary for a man in a particular class
to have his relations in or near that class, in Asia the general's
cousins may very well be sergeants, or, more likely still, small
peasants. Given time, the situation would doubtless stabilise
itself into a class structure, as the general's sons and nephews become officers in their turn, and the village relations become increasingly remote. But the time is not being given. Equality of
opportunity is being incorporated more and more into Asian
institutions and there are not enough particularly good schools
and highly educated mothers to give one whole range of children
the advantages the children of the professional classes have in
Europe. In twenty years' time it is possible that only Communist
China with its party members and its privileged artists and technicians will be a class society.

Economic equality

Asia has, therefore, to face the demand for economic equality
—the most important form of equality from the development
point of view—without any of Europe's natural defences. Its
countries either have no aristocracy, or their aristocracies no

longer count. Asia's only approach to a Churchill or a de Gaulle was Pakistan's Liaquat Ali Khan; and he has had no successor. Asia also has no entrenched professional class, able to justify its position by its intelligence and hard work, and willing to use the hold it has on all society's main levers of power in order to defend itself. Asia's professionals are still individuals rather than a class; and these individuals are far more likely to feel guilty about being better-off than other people than to look upon themselves as the carriers of their society's civilisation entitled to a certain level of material ease as a pre-requisite for the proper fulfilment of their function.

In the ex-colonial countries there is yet another obstacle to .y real resistance to the demand for economic equality. In the European countries which governed Asia, the demand for independence for the colonies was on the whole supported by the parties of the Left and resisted by the parties of the Right. The Right's reasons were often idealistic; they believed European government was good for Asia. The Left's reasons were sometimes material; they believed the possession of colonies made it easier for their own governing classes to exploit them. With these niceties, however, the Asian seeking independence did not concern himself. One side, as he saw it, told him that he was quite capable of looking after himself, and that his backwardness was due to his being exploited by others. The other side, as he understood them, told him that, left to himself, he would descend into anarchy, and that his backwardness was due to his own ignorance, unteachability, and passion for procreation. Naturally, he did not hesitate much in choosing his side; moreover, those who did hesitate, who were not quite so sure that independence was a panacea, who fifty years ago were very important, have been discredited by the mere fact that independence has been achieved. Naturally, ex-colonial Asia is run mainly by men of the Left or semi-Left. In India and Burma, for example, to be a Socialist is quite normal even for conservatives. Even in the countries where it is not quite so necessary to be Socialist, like Pakistan or the Philippines, there is no economic conservative doctrine, only a religious one. Economic equality may in fact be resisted, but there is no theory behind the resistance; and resistance without a theory tends in the long run to be surprisingly weak.

Partly as a result of this lack of resistance, but also because of Asia's poverty and the past great inequality of its incomes, economic equality tends to mean levelling down, which is frequently bad for development, rather than levelling up, which is always good for development. In the West, levelling down through progressive taxation, death duties and the opening of all walks of life to talent, has been less important than the levelling up achieved by improving education, housing, health and above all the productivity of the poor. In the United States and Scandinavia, the most economically equal of all Western societies, the levelling has been overwhelmingly up. Levelling up, however, is a slow process. It has been going on in the West certainly since 1870, in some countries longer still.

Asia cannot wait so long. It is true that it is doing some levelling up. All its plans, all its economic development, all its new educational and health and agricultural extension schemes must result in a certain amount of levelling up. They will, however, require years to take noticeable effect.

Asian electorates demand something more spectacular. That means levelling down. Therefore, there has been widespread land reform in Japan, in India, in Burma, as well as in China, a land reform that has not merely abolished big landlords, but also what in Europe would be quite small farmers. Therefore, Japan and India and Pakistan have income taxation systems amongst the world's most severe. Therefore, Ceylon and Indonesia tax their plantations as no other enterprise is taxed anywhere to a level which leaves virtually nothing for expansion. Therefore, too, one of the major urges behind State initiative in industrialisation is to prevent too many large fortunes being built up in the private sector.

For Asia, nowadays, the ideal is the small man.

The economic consequence of all these ideas of equality are important, and so complex that it is worth giving to the consequences of each of the types of equality we have discussed separate consideration.

Chapter 20

THE ECONOMIC CONSEQUENCES OF EQUALITY

(a) National equality

THE enormous economic importance of the idea of national
equality as it affects the relations between Asian and
Western countries, is discussed in Chapter 12. It has, however, an importance within Asian countries themselves which is
less often remarked. Except for Japan, Asian countries are not
like England, completely homogeneous. They are rather like the
United Kingdom or Switzerland, federations of sub-nations.
Even in tiny Ceylon there are two major races and languages,
while Burma has Kachins, Chins, Shans and Karens as well as
Burmese. Thailand has a very large Chinese minority. And so
on. They have therefore to face an internal as well as an external
problem of equality, the more so because so much of their development is being planned by Governments, and is not the result of the spontaneous initiative of individuals.

When Governments plan, they are always torn between the
need to get the maximum profits and the need to be fair between individuals and between sections of the population. This
dilemma applies even to countries as homogeneous as England
and Scotland. The Depressed Areas or the Scottish Western
Isles have had to have special treatment in order to see that
their people did not fall too far behind those of the rest of the
country. If this is true amongst people who feel themselves one
nation, and for whom mobility is fairly easy, obviously it will be
very much truer in countries whose nationhood is always still
new, sometimes indeed largely the creation of a colonial con-
queror, and in which differences of language, habits and climate
may make mobility very difficult. A Pakistan Bengali cannot
leave his overcrowded village to settle on a new irrigation project
in Sind without changing all his ways of life; and even if he
could, the Sindhi would object to his land being used for Ben-
galis. Every plan in Asia, therefore, must pay careful attention
to the politics as well as the economics of its investments. All the
irrigation cannot be put into the sandy wastes of the Punjab or
Rajasthan, though it may there return 10 per cent or 12 per
cent; some must go to the famine areas of the Deccan, though

there it may do little more than pay its running costs, or the country will be subjected to intolerable political strains, as one group sees itself growing poorer while another grows richer.

The need for national equality might thus seem to be a straight drag on the rate of increase of the national income. On any short-run calculation, it is so. It prevents the planners from following the simple rule of maximum returns, and so leaves room for every sort of lobbying; for no other rule can compare with seeking the largest possible profit for simplicity or finality. Nevertheless, it is probable that there are also countervailing advantages, though they are too intangible to be calculated. When a backward group gets technical schools, or a famine area gets irrigation, they may give a less immediate return than when the schools go to people who already have some mechanical aptitude, or the water to bring totally new land under cultivation. But they give hope, much more hope than they can possibly give in more favoured areas. And hope is an economic necessity. Before people will work, they have to feel that their work will have a result; the apathy of famine areas is first the effect, and only afterwards the cause, of the famines. Before people will learn, they must be able to see either a job or a widening of horizons at the end of their effort; the money spent on the primary schools of a backward group may therefore be partly wasted unless they get technical schools too.

Too much care to see that each sub-nation gets its fair share of development expenditure can greatly slow down the rate of increase of the income of the nation as a whole; not enough care to see that everybody benefits from the sacrifices development plans enforce on everybody can endanger national unity. One of the most difficult tasks of Asian leaders is to steer a course between this Scylla and Charybdis.

(b) Religious equality

The effects of religious equality on economic development are relatively small. Where religious equality has taken the form of removing restrictions from oppressed minorities, it clearly releases new energies and makes available new talents; its economic effect can only be good. Where, however, the desire for religious equality takes the form of applying restrictions to those who are in advance, in order to enable a backward majority to catch up, the economic effects must in the short run be bad. Thus, in India the reservations in favour of untouchables mean, for this generation at least, that many clerks and assistant engineers will be less efficient than if they were Brahmins. Here again, however, the effect is not a simple one. In this generation there is a heavy loss. In the next generation there may be the beginnings of a gain which will get stronger with each succeeding generation, as the untouchables are stimulated into more and more education, and the education in its turn destroys their acceptance alike of a position in which other people look down on them, and of the ignorance and occasional dirty ways which seems sometimes to justify this contempt.

(c) Linguistic equality

Linguistic equality, the demand of each language for its proper place in the sun, has particularly complex effects. Unless a man can study and conduct his work or his politics in his own language, he is permanently handicapped. Moreover, when, within a nation or sub-nation, the educated habitually think in a different language from the uneducated, there arises a gap between educated and uneducated which may seriously impair that ability of the educated to persuade the uneducated to do as they themselves do without which, in any society, change and improvement will be very slow indeed. On the other hand, if the speakers of a language are few or poor, it is impossible, except at great expense and disproportionate effort, to put into that language very much of the extension of knowledge which today is going on so rapidly and in so many directions all the time; at some stage, therefore, the educated must learn to be completely at home in one of those few languages of the world whose speakers either do most of the world's research, or into which all advances in knowledge are almost automatically translated. And, having learnt one of these languages, the educated, when they contribute to knowledge themselves, have the further dilemma that if they want a market for their new knowledge, they must write about it in the foreign language; if they want primarily to benefit their own people, they must write about it in their own language.

Once upon a time the world's educated conducted their affairs in very few languages. Latin would take a man over most of Europe, Arabic, Sanskrit and Chinese over all Asia. These were, however, the tongues of the educated only; their effectiveness as *linguae francae* depended, moreover, on the fact that the educated were few. Over the last hundred and fifty years, as the attempt has been made to extend education from the scholar to the ordinary man, the use of scholarly languages which themselves took years and years to learn, has more and more fallen into desuetude. As this has happened, and as education has spread, the scholar's audience has changed. He no longer writes for the whole of his world, as St. Thomas Aquinas or Valmiki did. He now writes for his own language-group, knowing that his work will be read outside that group only by an occasional specialist or if it is of enough significance to be translated. The scholar accepts a narrowing of his range of influence in return for a very considerable deepening of it within the range which is left. Where the narrowing is very great, however, and the deepening relatively shallow where, that is, his native tongue is spoken by relatively few people, he continues to desire the wider audience; but he no longer uses the old scholarly tongues, he now uses English, or French, or, until recently, German.

Whichever course he takes, he has an unresolved dilemma, unless he is fortunate enough to have a very widely spoken language as his mother-tongue. If he writes in his own language, most of the other scholars interested in his subject cannot read him. If he writes in another language, then he helps to make scholarship an esoteric mystery and to make learning enormously more difficult to acquire for his people. In Western Europe in the past century much education was self-education. A man read up the subject in which he was interested by himself; or he went to adult classes; or he took a correspondence course or did an external degree. Without all these, there could not have been acquired the level particularly of technical education upon which the nineteenth century's sudden economic spring forward depended. This self-education becomes enormously more difficult if a foreign language has to be learnt as a preliminary, especially if the foreign language is one the student rarely has an opportunity to hear spoken.

This language dilemma has had serious consequences in Eastern Europe, especially in the relations between Slav and German. It presents in much of Asia one of the most serious difficulties the Governments have to face. In China the unity of the educated was obtained by the use of one script for a series of dialects so different from each other they were almost different languages. This script takes years to learn. It can be simplified for, say, newspaper use, but it then becomes a rather inadequate vehicle for scholarship. In all the ex-British countries, the medium of the educated has been English, in Indo-China it was French, in Indonesia Dutch. All of these for an Asian student are difficult to learn. The words, the grammatical structure, the methods of sentence construction in his own language are so totally different. For so many hundred thousands to be able to use English as well as they can do in India is an immense intellectual achievement; but it is an achievement necessarily obtained partly at the expense of other forms of attainment.

Therefore, almost everywhere there is an attempt to find a language of scholarship which can be equally the language of the common people. India is trying to make Hindi, which is already more or less understood by one-third of the population, the national language. Pakistan may have Urdu and Bengali as its national languages; nearly everybody understands one or the other. Indonesia has created Basha Indonesia which is related to the main languages of the Archipelago and simple to learn. China is trying a Roman script. None of these solutions, however, wholly meets the problem. Hindi as a national language, for example, will give an advantage to the Hindi-speakers which others already resent; and Hindi has none of the advantages of English to give it precedence over the regional languages. It does not have a literature to compare with those of Bengali or Marathi or Tamil, and so far, hardly any scientific or historical work has been done in it. As English gets pushed out, therefore, the regional languages, not Hindi, tend to take its place. The problem gets worse, not better; and the unfortunate student still has to learn English if he wants to go beyond the most elementary level in his subject, because it is in English that the advanced books and articles have been written. The Pakistani solution of two national languages does not solve the problem either. It merely adds an extra language to what was being learnt before, without as yet permitting the educated to dispense with English.

None of the solutions works properly, perhaps none of them *can* work properly. For a language to be the language of scholars, there must be enough scholars writing in it to cover most of knowledge. If there are not, another language must be learnt in order to acquire that part of knowledge which is not covered. That means in Asia that for some time to come the educated must learn a major European language, Russian perhaps in China, French in Indo-China, English elsewhere. In addition, in the big countries they will have to learn a *lingua franca;* and if the *lingua franca* is to be the language of administration and of intercourse, it will have to be learnt to a fairly high level. Finally, they will have to develop every language which is spoken by any appreciable number of their people until it becomes a possible instrument of scholarship, that is, until it has the words to represent all the concepts necessary for a man writing physics or history. This in itself is a considerable task, and it will have to be backed up by an even more considerable task of translation.

The élite may be able to do their studying in English or the *lingua franca*. The great majority will more and more want to do it in their mother-tongue. That is only possible if, first, the basic books in every subject are translated, and, second, there is an adequate translation service for the major articles. Neither of these is easy for poor countries with a limited number of scholars. The sale of the translations will always tend to be too small for the publisher to make a profit. This difficulty of making a profit is even severer for work done in the local language originally. A work on Indian history published in English has the whole English-speaking world for its market; published in Marathi it has only Maharashtra, and may not sell more than one-tenth the number of copies. With the sciences the fraction would be lower still. Very considerable State subsidies, and extensive arrangements for translation into the European languages where the market is, will be necessary if academic writing is not to find itself confined to textbooks.

The economic importance of this confused situation is great. Once people can educate themselves in their own language, it will be much easier to create good overseers and foremen and electricians, all the people indeed of whom Asian society is so screamingly short. Once, too, the educated and the ordinary man use the same language in their everyday life, the gap between the educated and the uneducated, which is today as great a feature of Asian life as it was of eighteenth-century Europe, will narrow. When it does, the leadership of the educated will become steadily more effective, as they and the uneducated (who will simultaneously be becoming less uneducated) get to know each other better. A society in which there are no officials, or works managers, or professors, who do not really understand the people under them is clearly able to change much more quickly than one in which there are severe barriers to downward communication. One can neither inspire nor easily teach those whose minds work in a different language and through different categories of thought. There is many an Asian factory where there is just enough of a common language between manager and men for the manager to be able to explain that a machine-tool has been wrongly set, but where they cannot discuss absenteeism or incentive payments face to face, because there is no language in which both managers and men know the relevant words. The linguistic problem is thus in one aspect a problem of making the leadership of the educated effective.

One of the ways in which people want to be equal, and a very natural way, is that more and more they demand that a person who talks and thinks in one lnaguage shall not by that very fact be ranked below someone who talks and thinks in another language. This happened in the nineteenth century in Europe from Ireland to the Ukraine. It is now happening in twentieth-century Asia. In itself it is a demand which will do good, inasmuch as its acceptance would enable many more people to become educated. But it cannot be simply accepted. It must be accepted in a way which permits the society to continue to have an adequate number of the highly educated, and it must leave these highly educated with their primacy. There must be enough translations into local languages, there must be a widespread enough knowledge of a world language for a Pathan or Javanese chemist or biologist to know just as much as his Western counterpart. At the same time, he must be brought sufficiently into contact with his own people, it must be made sufficiently possible both linguistically and financially for him to write for them, for the ideas he acquires to be passed on to them very much more rapidly than at present. It is a complicated task, so complicated that to solve it will require a considerable diversion of energies that in the U.S. or Western Europe can be devoted directly to development; but solved it must be, if the sense of nationhood in Asia is to become strong enough to stand the sacrifices development is going to demand.

(d) Sex equality

The only form of equality whose results are undilutedly good is sex equality, for few social phenomena do more economic damage than sex inequality. From the economic point of view, the main features of sex inequality are not its personal side, the consideration with which a man treats or does not treat his wife, or the spoiling of sons as against daughters. They are the belief that women do not need education and an inheritance system that gives women fewer rights as heirs than men.

Economically the most damaging is the belief that women's place is the home. As in so many instances in this book, it must be emphasised that this is a purely economic judgement, and that no attempt is here being made to consider whether the economic loss is compensated by other benefits. It is not our purpose to decide whether the reduction in the national income caused by purdah would be justified if it were proved that purdah reduced fornication. We would only insist that, economically, confining women to the home results in an enormous waste of labour and talent.

Among the middle classes, it results in girls of ability and education wasting their time and the money that has been spent upon them sitting at home while a husband is arranged for them. When they are married, their time is usually occupied with children; but even when the children are grown-up, or when there are not enough of them to take up the whole of their mother's time, social pressure keeps the mothers in the home and prevents their either taking jobs or, in most countries, going in for social work except on a small scale and in exceptional instances. Yet social work has been a major cause of advance in Europe, because it reduces tension, it produces an increase of governing class understanding of those they govern—one remembers the part played by Toynbee Hall in creating the men who have made the English Welfare State—and it takes the knowledge of the better-off to the relief of those too ignorant to use knowledge for their own relief. In societies where, as is usual in Asia, men of education and position have very full-time jobs indeed, the cloistering of their women is a great economic and social tragedy.

Among the peasant mass of the population, the position is usually somewhat better. The practice is for the woman to work in the fields beside her husband, and her labour is not lost. On the contrary, she is often over-worked, and there would be advantages in her paying more attention to her home and less to the land. So long, however, as Asia grows mainly cereal crops, there will inevitably be rush periods of work on the land, at transplantation time, for instance, or at harvest, and the alternatives are to let the women work or to carry a male population which would be idle most of the year. In the areas where purdah prevents the women working, agricultural efficiency goes down quite considerably; weeding is left undone, or the harvest takes so long to bring in that it is affected by weather.

Keeping women at home and keeping them uneducated run into each other, and are in part the result of the same complex of ideas. Where the underlying idea is that for a woman to go out into the world is to increase the opportunities society offers for sexual misconduct, as is especially true in purdah countries, most women will remain uneducated because of the difficulty of making arrangements for totally separate education for girls, and the expense of education at home. Where the reason for keeping them at home is the belief that women are better at the domestic tasks than at any other, the girls will be kept at home because the best place to learn to cook and to look after children is thought to be—and with Asian curricula as they are, usually in fact is—at mother's elbow.

Either way, one gets the phenomenon which has characterised all of Asia outside Japan, and which such Governments
as India and China are now trying in their different ways so
desperately to change, the phenomenon that at every level from
mere literacy upwards, the women are hopelessly behind the
men. This is more economically damaging than at first sight appears. Some of the consequences indeed are obvious. If one half
of the human race is left uneducated then the always very limited
supply of outstanding talent, whether for doctors or politicians
or stenographers, is halved straightaway. In some professions,
moreover, for which women are particularly well suited, nurses
or teachers, for example, the result is to reduce the supply by
very much more than half; most Asian primary education is
severely handicapped by having to use men, and pay the price
of men, for the teaching of the under-ten's, and in most Asian
countries nurses are in very much shorter supply than doctors,
which makes it much harder for a patient to recover than to be
diagnosed.

Some other consequences are more serious but less obvious.
Because women are secluded, they do not cease to be loved and
therefore listened to. In Asia husbands may discuss fewer subjects with their wives than in Europe; but that is largely the result of the fact that the number of subjects on which the wives
feel strongly is fewer. In Hindu and Buddhist society at least, on
any subject on which the wife does feel strongly, the marriage
of the children, for instance, it is normal for her views to be given
the greatest consideration. More important still, Asian sons as
grown men seem on the whole to be more devoted than European sons, perhaps because Asia does not have Europe's tradition of adolescent conflict and because the son is much more
likely to be living with his mother. Many a man will go so far as
to keep his wife in purdah or not eat meat purely to please his
mother.

Between mother and wife, the ordinary man is nearly as much
under petticoat influence, except perhaps in West Pakistan, as in
the U.S.A. Combined with the ignorance and seclusion of
women, this has very important results on the growth of the consumer-goods industries, particularly in making the introduction
of new products more difficult. Because women do not go out, in
a good deal of Asia the husband buys the groceries; but when he
buys, he has to consider what his wife will like or know how to
use. Because budgeting is a man's job in many areas and groups,
he not only buys but chooses, which means that the person who
uses the product and is therefore best qualified to judge its per-

formance is not the person who decides whether or not it should be bought. Yet the husband cannot change easily, in case his wife says the dinner went wrong because he bought the wrong cooking-fat. Moreover, while the husband may read a paper and go to the cinema, the wife does so much more seldom. She is therefore much less susceptible to all the usual ways of putting a new idea across to the public than the Western housewife; in some areas, like Uttar Pradesh in India, even urban newspaper readership by women is 5 per cent or lower.

This whole situation of female backwardness, female leaving of what are elsewhere women's jobs to the men, female lack of knowledge of new recipes and household hints, means that the development of mass-production consumer-goods industries is a much slower process in Asia than in the West. One cannot get at one's market to explain to them the advantages of one's product; one's consumers are tradition-bound, ridden by the most fantastic prejudices, and handicapped by the most all-embracing ignorance. They will believe that cooking-fat made from vege-table oil causes blindness and indigestion; they will buy fewer woollen goods because they do not know how to stop a sweater shrinking in the wash. Modern soap has been sold in India for seventy years; yet there are still many people who use soap-nut, which has few merits beyond its lather.

Every Asian housewife has learnt from her mother how to run a house in the traditional way. As in nineteenth-century Europe, she has family recipes and family lore. Very few Asian house-wives, moreover, are slatterns of the Western slum type, who neglect their homes. But that very fact makes change slower still. A woman who, on her own standards, runs her house well, who does not go shopping, and who cannot be got at by any of the ordinary mass media of communication, is a woman who will be very slow to try a new product. One has to rely on word-of-mouth, which is slow, or on giving out samples, which is ex-pensive. So the standard of life stays lower than it need be, be-cause the woman so often uses an inefficient product rather than an efficient one, or an expensive product rather than a cheap one. Industrial development is slowed down, too, because under these unfavourable conditions the process of education is so slow that only the most outstandingly successful of products can carry the cost. It may take years of losses to build up a mass market. Very few firms can face so dismal an immediate pro-spect. Nor does nationalisation solve anything. The State can produce on occasion very effectively. It is not good at marketing. It has too long a tradition of issuing orders to be able to persuade; it is too austere to use the tricks, from pretty girls to strip-cartoons, which are necessary if a new idea is to get a fair chance of being considered despite the resistances put up by habit and mother-in-law.

Sex inequality is damaging in yet another way. All through non-Communist Asia huge amounts are spent on jewellery and ornaments which could more usefully be used to build steel plants or dig wells. (This is, again, a pure 'maximisation of the national income' judgement; it is not suggested that women do not prefer jewellery; nor is any opinion being offered on whether the satisfaction husbands get from bridges or a larger crop is greater or less than that their wives get from necklaces and nose-rings.)

These large amounts are only partly explicable by the natural vanity of women. A North American woman is very much richer, has at least as much control over her menfolk, and is just as susceptible to female vanity; yet she spends a much smaller percentage of her income on gold and diamonds. When she wants to decorate herself, she is usually content with costume jewellery, a capital-saving innovation still almost unknown in Asia. One must look beyond female weakness for an explanation of the money spent on bullion and jewels in Asia, particularly as so much of it is bought by the men without any very powerful female volition behind the purchase.

There would appear to be two reasons. One is the anarchy of much of Asia's past. Gold and jewels are easily portable, easily hidden. This reason is probably no longer very important, though it has of late years been reinforced by the need for a hedge against inflation. The second is the position of women. In Muslim societies they are allowed property, but are often made completely dependent on their husbands by purdah. In Hindu law, until this year, they had no absolute property rights or inheritance rights at all except in stridhan; and stridhan is essentially jewellery. Therefore, a father who wishes to provide for his daughter's future inevitably gives her jewellery, which she can refuse to let her husband sell, and which will be hers whatever happens to him or to the marriage. The jewellery is also useful to put in pawn in a bad season; but that in itself is some protection for a wife; it would be a very disapproved-of Asian husband who would pledge his wife's jewellery without her permission. It is too intimately hers, she has usually physically to take it off before he can go to the money-lender with it. Few fathers believe savings certificates would be nearly as safe. Nor do the fiancés demand savings certificates, partly perhaps because they do not want to appear as if they were trying to deprive their bride of protection, partly perhaps because men everywhere like to show off their wives; in a society where conversation is not normally expected of women in men's company, and coquetry is strictly impermissible, competition is simplest in jewellery.

Simply to preach against jewellery is useless. No father can refuse to give his daughter something all other fathers have always given their daughters. To try and confiscate jewellery in order to provide foreign exchange would require totalitarian rigour and then might not succeed. The waste which jewellery represents can only be got over by providing less damaging alternatives. First the woman must be educated, so that she can contribute her ideas, and not just her glitter, to society; the woman with a degree is noticeably less inclined to spend her substance in diamonds and pearls than her uneducated sister, if only because she has so much keener an appreciation of the value of alternative ways of using her money, like sending her children to better schools. Second, the woman must be able to inherit, and must have at least some elementary capacity to manage property. She must be able to have land or houses or shares to keep her if her husband falls on evil days, or she is left a widow. She must know enough—here we come back to education—to be able to consult a banker or a solicitor about what she should do, and not to be so entirely dependent on her husband that she will put her signature to any document he may put before her, even if it is a transfer to him of all her assets. Fathers must feel sure that it will be as difficult to wheedle their daughters into cashing their savings certificates as into taking off their nose-studs. Not until that happens can the flow of the life-blood of development into the jewellery sink be stanched.

This is being realised. In India, for example, the law has just been changed to give Hindu daughters the same share as sons in intestate property, and to permit widows an absolute instead of a limited share in the property they inherit from their husbands. This means that daughters will have to be specifically disinherited if they are not to inherit. Oddly enough, these changes are being made on general principles of the emancipation of women. The economic results anticipated are bad, more fragmentation of holdings, for example, and brothers raising mortgages to buy their sisters out. All of this may happen; but it is unlikely really to have serious effects. The girls will get married; their bits of land will go to increase their husbands' holdings, the money they get if they are bought out may pay off their husbands' mortgages. But families will be reluctant to let girls have both land (or money) and jewellery; and, on the other hand, fathers looking for a bride for their sons may in time begin to realise that the son will be much better off with a bride with land, than with one with jewellery. When the new system is enforced, therefore, which is likely to take a long time, for the Indian countryside does not take kindly to such radical change, one should see gradually a shift in attitude which will greatly reduce the importance of jewellery; one may reasonably hope for a day when the marriage-broker is told the girl has two acres and a tube-well rather than that she will get $300 worth of gold and $150 worth of clothes.

(e) Class equality

Class inequality is not a major problem in Asia. People may be unequal because they are of the wrong religion, or because they are poor, or because they speak the wrong language, or because they are uneducated. The complex of birth, education, manners, and money which makes class in Europe is, however, almost unknown. Conservative Brahmin fathers do not object to their sons marrying poor Brahmin girls because they are low-class; a Brahmin is a Brahmin. Amongst Muslims the sense of Islamic brotherhood is too strong for class; nawabs have always married dancing-girls, without anybody thinking the worse of them. Even amongst the educated, what matters is not who your father was, or where you went to school, but how much education you have; the prestige of the foreign educated, or of those who have been to certain schools within the country, is almost entirely the result of the belief that their education has qualified them to earn a better living. There is virtually no sense of the importance of the right background and the done thing. Asia has very little snobbery, very little lion-hunting. People keep up with the Joneses; they do not try to catch up with the Montmorencys.

This has its economic advantages. It reduces tension. An Asian village, for instance, will not divide into the Communist classes of landless, poor peasant, middle peasant, rich peasant and landowner until it has been indoctrinated out of being Asian. Until then, family, religious and caste loyalties all cut across economic differences. In Asia people are not ashamed of poor relations, or poor relations bitter about rich ones. The class war is a Western import, and it has been an import on quota, of which in most countries, enough has come in only to infect a few industrial cities or plantation areas; and even there it is often the racial, religious or caste differences between employer and employee which really matter, not class. When the Bengali Muslim employees of a Narayanganj jute mill rioted, it was not against their employer, but against their fellow non-Bengali employees. The labour trouble on many plantations is often connected with the fact that Europeans or Chinese or Marwadis own the plantations, while quite different people work on them. In Asia, when a man goes up in the world, he does not join a generalised upper class; he stays as a leader of his own community. This makes political and social tensions much more many-sided than in Europe; there are occasions when every community pulls against every other, but it prevents the terrible economic dilemmas between right policy and pleasing the voter which come when the working class is ranged on one side and the middle class on the other.

There are, however, also economic disadvantages in Asia's lack of snobbery. In Europe and America snobbery has been one of the main causes of advance. The upper class educate their children in the humanities and the sciences; the lower class want to do the same. The upper class learns to clean its teeth and have a bath regularly; the lower class copies. The upper class experiments with refrigerators, built-in cupboards, and bicycles; in due course, when the experiment has succeeded, the lower class tries to follow. People are always acquiring new wants and trying new ways of satisfying old wants. This can be, and in Asia often is, condemned as making Western civilisation increasingly materialistic; people nowadays, it is argued, are more eager to be comfortable than to be good.

This would, however, appear to be true only in a very limited sense. There are fewer saints in the United States than in mediaeval Europe or amongst modern Hindus. There is no Western Vinoba Bhave. But there is also less need for saints. There are fewer of the destitute and the sick, and those there are are better looked after in an organised way. Moreover, while it is possible to argue that one saint compensates a society for a million poor, it is not possible to argue that Western man does not have opportunities of leading a more satisfactory life than the man who lives all his life in the narrow confines of an Asian village. These opportunities do not, perhaps, make him nicer. Certain forms of greed and exploitation become unnecessary for him, but he takes to others. They do, however, give him certain advantages. He can be healthier, for he can eat a better balanced diet and have a proper sewage system. He can have less suspicions of his neighbours, for he can travel more. He can have a wider range of interests, for he is better educated. He can be cleaner, for the means of hygiene are more easily available to him. He can avoid many sources of unhappiness; wives die less often in childbirth, husbands less often leave young widows. The potentialities of greater happiness are there, and that is all economic advance can ever offer. The connection between material possessions and either contentment or goodness is too tenuous for it to be possible to establish any definite correlation. One can only say that presumably people would be less eager to improve their condition if they did not at least think the result would be that they would be happier, and perhaps also that they would be less liable to the temptation to certain forms of sin.

If that is accepted, then Asia's lack of snobbery, however socially attractive it may be, is economically unfortunate. Economically, it is not enough to keep up with the Joneses; one must also try to catch up with the Montmorencys. Keeping up with the Joneses normally ties people to all the errors of the past, to more and more jewellery at bigger and bigger weddings. Catching up with the Montmorencys makes them willing to innovate and to change, to copy the man who has made a success of the Japanese method of rice-growing or who has built a house of brick in a village that previously knew only mud, or to copy the woman who buys an electric iron and adds salads to the food she gives her family. To introduce Europe's class snobbery or America's money snobbery to Asia would be disastrous. But to give the villager the feeling that what somebody else can do, he can do, could produce nothing but good. Once he can be freed of the inhibition that he cannot do as the teacher does because the teacher is educated, or as the official does because the official has position, or as his own village leaders of a different group do because they belong to a different group, he would change much more rapidly. It may be bad merely to imitate; it is certainly good to look at the ways of others to see if they are better, without any pre-conceived prejudice that however good they may be for the other people, they would not do for oneself.

(f) Economic equality

Of all the forms of equality which the citizen can demand the one which has the largest economic consequences is the demand for economic equality. At first blush, indeed, one is inclined to be dogmatic and say that it must be the most important demand of all. It is however, possible that this is not so, and that sex equality and snobbery (or rather the lack of it) are both more important. It may be that society can adjust itself to both economic equality and economic inequality, whereas the suppression of women or the lack of a desire to imitate successful innovations acts as a permanent drag. Economic equality has not yet gone far enough for one to predict its results with real confidence.

One can, however, already put forward some tentative conclusions.

Some Asian societies, like the Burmese, have never had a large number of really rich or really poor. One can, therefore, already venture the hypothesis that a society in which everybody is, by his own standards, tolerably well-off, will usually be a society with a minimum of tension. Every traveller has commented on the care-free cheerfulness of the Burmese and the Thai. This lack of tension is very important, for it makes it much less likely that any plan of advance will founder on sectional rivalries and cries about inequality of sacrifice.

These equal societies, would, however, also appear to be relatively unenterprising. They do not have poverty and ambition and discontent to sting them into effort; and sometimes they have not had enough rich to pay for the years of education for their children which are required to make good modern technicians; they are therefore usually somewhat lacking in the modern skills, from doctors to mine-managers. These lacks can be compensated by the State. The State can plan, and tax, and build factories, and provide scholarships for study overseas. But it would appear that the State has to do all these, or they would not get done at all. Nineteenth-century Siam owed such advance as it achieved very largely to the personal initiative of King Chulalongkorn. Burmese Plans depend almost entirely on the initiative and effort of Burmese Governments. Neither in nineteenth-century Siam nor in present-day Burma is there really a widespread popular demand for the Government to do the particular things it is doing, though in both cases there is probably a vague public desire that the Government should do something; certainly there is neither wide public discussion of priorities nor much spontaneous action by the public on its own account. One may reasonably conclude that societies which have a reasonable equality of moderate comfort are societies which are not likely to be economically very enterprising unless, like the Americans, they can regard material success as a symbol of man's triumph over his universe; and few look on it like that in Asia.

The equal societies are a minority in Asia. The main countries, Pakistan, India, China, Japan, have been countries of great economic inequality. It is, therefore, notable that all of them have made economic equality a major objective of policy in some degree.

China's Communism has destroyed the landlord and most of the richer bourgeoisie; admittedly, it has done so only in order to set up a new class structure, but the Communist cadres seem so far to be paid more in power than in material comfort, and Stakhanovism is not yet the overwhelming social phenomenon it is in Russia. For the time being, though probably only for the time being, Chinese are more equal than they were; and however unequal they may become as industrial development brings into being a privileged class of managers and bureaucrats, Communist theory will presumably continue to place before them as the ultimate ideal the rule 'from each according to his means, to each according to his needs'.

Pakistan, India and Japan all have systems of direct taxation which are among the stiffest in the world for high incomes, together with systems of indirect taxation which bear extremely heavily on such obvious signs of riches as motor-cars. One doubts whether the rich are as highly taxed even in England as in these three countries; certainly they are not anywhere else in the Western world. Moreover, against certain forms of riches all three countries have taken action of a directness hitherto confined to Eastern Europe. Japan has had a thoroughgoing land-reform, with compensation for the landlord which inflation made derisory. India has progressed far in a land-reform which is less drastic than Japan's but still drastic enough. Pakistan has abolished zemindari[1] in E. Bengal and jagirdari[1] in Sind with more or less nominal compensation. In Japan a man with twenty acres is already a big man in the countryside. In India few still have more than 30 acres of good land. Even in West Pakistan there has been a beginning; the great holdings are now measured in hundreds, not thousands, of acres. The pressure on the great landlords who control most of W. Pakistan to do likewise will then become very great. Outside parts of the Middle East, the day of the landowner, even of the relatively small landowner, in Asia is over.

Nothing so drastic has yet been done against riches in other forms. The businessman, on the whole, keeps his business, the rentier his gilt-edged. There has been some nationalisation, notably of public utilities; there have also been started a certain number of joint State-private enterprises, especially in Burma.

[1] These are special forms of landownership, whose distinguishing feature is that the Zemindar or Jagirdar was strictly an alienee of the land revenue and that his rights of actual ownership have grown by custom and usurpation.

But in general, except in China, reasonable, though not always full, compensation has been paid, and the reason for taking over has been, again except in China, a belief either that the State could run that particular section of the economy more efficiently than private enterprise, or that the section was so vital that nobody but the State should be allowed to control it. The result has not always been efficiency. The Burmese mines, oil wells and river transport might have recovered much more quickly had they been left to their original owners.

Efficiency, however, was the objective in a minority of instances. The Burmese, for instance, wanted national control of their major resources, and this they have got. Nationalisation, in fact, has on the whole had rather marginal effects. It has not produced any greater equality, only substituted senior officials for senior businessmen. It has often produced some drop of efficiency, but usually not a very big one, and often even the drop which has been produced is cancelled by the State's power to raise capital more cheaply and more easily than anyone else; the Indian internal airlines since nationalisation have provided an example of both phenomena.

Nationalisation does not in Asia have the emotional significance, as a storming of the citadels of property, which it had in Western Europe before Western Europe had done any nationalising. Asian nationalisations are often undertaken lightheartedly, with no adequate appreciation either of the shock to confidence they produce or of the complications of building-up new administrative structures. The reasons for them have hitherto, however, not normally been doctrinaire. The State always has some definite practical end in view, whether it has been getting its own nationals into key positions (e.g. Burma oil), or raising capital more cheaply (e.g. to some extent Indian steel), or simply providing better rural banking (e.g. the Imperial Bank in India). The assertions of Socialist principle with which every nationalisation is accompanied are the sauce, not the dish itself.

There is, however, one other way in addition to the direct methods of taxation and land reform, by which the Asian States are trying to get economic equality. They are creating small property-owners, and making them viable when created. Asia, as is discussed at greater length in Chapter 15, has always been an area of small property-owners, of peasants and shopkeepers and artisans, not of factory-workers, shop assistants and managing directors. Today, every government in Asia is pursuing, with more or less enthusiasm, policies which will increase the number of these small owners. Artisans are trained as cobblers and blacksmiths and motor repairers; refugees are lent money to set up small shops; in India State Finance Corporations have been set up specially to lend to the man who only wants a thousand or two. Above all, land reform creates new owners by the million. Land reform, in fact, works doubly towards equality. The big man goes. Many men who had nothing become small owners. The village loses its bottom as well as its top. The difference between a man with two acres and a man with twenty is still great, but it is different in kind as well as in degree from the difference between a man with nothing and a man with two acres.

The economic consequences of this drive towards equality may be discussed under three heads, higher direct and luxury taxation, land reform, and the preference for the small owner. The consequences and the policies run into each other, and in practice their separation is not always possible. Theoretically, however, they are distinct, and it may make for clarity if they are treated separately.

High direct and luxury taxation has certain very important economic advantages. First, it brings in revenue, and the states of Asia all have a desperate need for revenue, both for development and to provide such elementary necessities of a modern economy as education. Secondly, by reducing the real size of business incomes, it enables the State which can pay in power to pay lower salaries in money than it would otherwise have to pay, thus enabling more to be done with the same money, especially in defence. Thirdly, the squeezing of the rich makes much easier the exacting of sacrifices from the poor. If one wishes to raise a 5 per cent sales tax on food, it is a great advantage to be able to point out that one is charging 100 per cent on cosmetics; and Asia has not enough rich to be able to develop without taxing the poor. Fourthly, and perhaps most important of all, high taxation greatly mitigates the effects of that imitation of Western consumption standards which is one of the most serious consequences of Asia's contact with the West.

Standards of living are governed by what people know of, or consider possible. A mediaeval king felt no discontent because his castle was not centrally-heated; but an American steel worker would feel the most serious discontent if he had to manage with a smoky wood-fire. The advances of the last 150 years have made possible in the West a standard of comfort unknown previously. The working-man in the West takes for granted a whole series of luxuries, from bicycles to rubber mattresses, from a wireless set to main drainage, which would have been unheard of luxuries to the Emperor Napoleon. The Western working-man, moreover, lives in an economy that can afford these luxuries, an economy whose inventiveness and whose entrepreneurial effectiveness have made them possible.

Asia is still in the position of the Emperor Napoleon. It has not yet got either the inventiveness or the entrepreneurial effectiveness, though both are beginning; yet it cannot see these luxuries without wanting them. They sell themselves; people want them whatever the Joneses or the Montmorencys do. The Asian villager realises just as well as the Western working-man that one can get about more quickly on a bicycle than on a bullock cart; and if he does not yet appreciate rubber mattresses and main drainage, that is only a matter of time and good marketing. Asia therefore wants, and is more and more going to want, a whole series of things which she cannot as yet afford. This has its good side, especially when the wants are mass wants. Nothing makes people work and save and innovate like the desire to satisfy new wants; nothing produces new industry more quickly than new demands. But it also has a very serious bad side. The new wants can be satisfied only by those people who have spare money. That spare money may previously have been wasted; the economic effect of its being diverted to new expenditure is then neutral—it does not much matter whether a Maharajah's ostentation takes the form of polo-ponies or Rolls-Royces. But it may previously have been saved; and then it matters a great deal when it is diverted. To take a non-Asian example, South America has for a century been very seriously the loser by the tendency of the rich to adopt European and American standards their economies could not afford; far too much of the capital Brazil, for example, has so painfully built up by inflation has gone to build luxury flats in Rio de Janeiro. In Asia, likewise, saving was seriously cut into when men like the late Maharaja of Patiala discovered that one could have all the old luxuries and Rolls-Royces too. One reason why Japan was able to build up its industry so quickly was because it retained a very austere way of life, and borrowed from the West only a few rather cheap comforts, like frock-coats and top-hats. The businessman could plough back his profits; he did not have to divert them to impressionist paintings, Cadillacs and yachts.

High taxation is very good at producing a Japanese effect even in countries which do not have by tradition the Japanese austerity. If taxation is so high that nobody can have a yacht, and only the biggest millionaires can have a large American car, the purposes of ostentation are adequately served for the ordinary rich by a 14 h.p. car; the 14 h.p. car satisfies sufficiently well the need to get from one place to another, and it uses considerably fewer resources than a steam yacht. This saving of resources for development is particularly important when, as so often, the 'luxury' is imported. Asia normally has to import most of the amenities, and even many of the conventional necessities of Western life, like tinned salmon. If import duties can turn the conventional necessity into a luxury (as has been done, for instance, with tinned food in India), and the luxury into a millionaire's self-indulgence (as has been often done with French perfume), then the diversion of resources to satisfy these wants is greatly reduced; the saving of the individual may go down, because he will still buy a little even at a high price; but the revenue, and therefore the potential for capital expenditure of the State, goes up.

All this can be said for high taxation, and that it reduces social tension, too. On the other side, however, must be set an indictment whose seriousness is all too rarely appreciated in Asia.

First, high direct taxation reduces incentive. This is a more complicated effect than is usually thought. There is a level, though probably a relatively low level, at which taxation makes people work harder, in order to have the same real income after tax. It is also true that many of the rewards for responsibility and risk-taking are not monetary. There is the excitement of speculation, the satisfaction to be obtained from important work well done, the need many people have to see their ideas carried out, the sense of social responsibility, the thrill of power. All of these have permitted many societies to pay their generals, for example, badly and still get good generals. There are, however, many important jobs where this does not work. Much work is more necessary than satisfying. The moral force which in Europe still drives so many people to work is temporary, the result of a century when hard work was considered to have great moral value. The number of ways of spending one's leisure interestingly, from television to collecting locomotive numbers, is increasing all the time. The professional and managerial classes may soon begin to feel that it would be better to increase their leisure, as other classes do, rather than work harder to earn money which will be taken away in tax. This may happen especially quickly in Asia, which has never placed the Puritan's importance on hard work as such. That would leave as the main motives for the sort of hard work society has to have from so many of its senior officials, businessmen and professionals, either a sense of social responsibility or the desire for power. Neither is very satisfactory as a way of getting the major work of society done. The competent can nearly always be attracted by money, for money opens the way to so many other pleasures, from travel to books. The competent are, however, very often people for whom power has no very special appeal and whose sense of social responsibility is not specially highly developed. Those of them who do desire power are often of a ruthlessness that makes it highly undesirable that they should be allowed to have it, and those who do have a sense of social responsibility are often of an idealism which makes them want to change society more quickly than it wishes to change. Too many men whose motive force is the desire to do good may become a short cut to chaos. It is healthier to have a high proportion of people who enjoy their job but do not take it too seriously, whose sense of proportion is kept in balance by a healthy desire for more money and the things that money will enable them to buy, from a better education for their children to more seats at concerts.

This is particularly true of economic activity. Most businesses cannot offer the intellectual excitement of research or making foreign policy. No business offers real power. The businessman cannot make his customer buy, as a Communist planner can; he can only persuade him. And nowadays the businessmen can neither sack employees, nor endow Universities, at will. The trade unions prevent the one, high taxation the other. Moreover, though a sense of social responsibility in a businessman is valuable because it makes him treat his employees properly and prevents his cheating either his customers or the tax-collector, it can also be very dangerous. In a free market which makes its main adjustments through the price mechanism, the businessman makes his contribution to the standard of living through seeking profit. When he makes a loss, he is misusing resources. If his sense of social responsibility goes on from making him give charity to making him treat his business as a charity, the whole of economic development will be slowed down.

These difficulties arise whether the business is private or public; in fact, the risks of an improper pricing policy leading to wrong investment choices and inadequate profits is particularly severe in nationalised industries. At equal incomes, therefore, particularly in Asia, so many men of ability will be drawn off from economic activity into journalism, high policy-making, research, painting, the Church and other such exciting or power-giving functions that rapid economic development without terror will become almost impossible.

This is particularly so because business has a disadvantage no other occupation has to a comparable extent. Businessmen have to worry. They have to worry because their fundamental function is to take chances on their guesses; and, unless they have to worry whether their guesses will come out right, the guesses will be irresponsibly made. The private businessman worries over his profits, the manager over his promotion, the Communist over whether he will be accused of sabotage. But worry they all must. Their whole task is to decide in advance what the public will want, and then to provide for the public to have it. If they decide wrong, a misapplication of resources results which reduces public happiness. It is a great frustration to a man who wants to wash to find he can buy no soap because those in control of investment guessed he would want more football pools, and so built a paper factory instead of a soap factory. To prevent such frustrations there must be sanctions for those who go wrong, rewards for those who guess right. If high taxation makes monetary rewards impossible, then either one must replace them by rewards in power, which is very uncomfortable for the public, or one must remove the sanctions. If one will not pay for worry, one must reduce the worry; many countries do that, by subsidies for the inefficient or by restrictions on the efficient, especially in agriculture and against imported goods; but that is very expensive for the public; it would be much cheaper to pay for worry.

The second disadvantage of high taxation is that it reduces saving. The Indian Taxation Enquiry Commission has argued that this does not necessarily happen. If some of the money which is raised would have been spent by the private individual for consumption, and if the State uses it all for development, they contend, then saving is increased, not diminished. The first condition is normally fulfilled; the private individual rarely saves all the money which is left him by a reduction of taxation. The second condition is much more often fulfilled in Asia than in Europe. Extra money in Asia is more likely to go to development than to defence or pensions. Nevertheless, even in these very favourable conditions, it is unlikely that the economic value of the savings will be the same with high as with low taxation. People get discouraged by high taxation and cease to save at all. This is particularly true where the saving is not for one's old age, but to build up a business. There is no great point in saving to build up something that will be taken away by death duties; yet this sort of saving builds up the economy much more quickly than the buying of gilt-edged, either directly or via insurance policies and provident funds, which Asian taxation systems so encourage. Moreover, it is very doubtful whether the State on the whole uses a man's money as effectively as he would have used it himself. The State's size, its whole tradition, lead it towards the large long-term projects of relatively low return. The individual is frequently in a position to choose small projects of large return. The large return is a sign of a stronger economic need; it also provides scope for much larger saving, much greater ploughing back in the future. Therefore, even when in certain circumstances high taxation does produce larger savings in the present, the gain is likely to be outweighed by serious losses in the future.

This is particularly important when the savings which are taken away are those of business. It is fashionable for economists and planners to talk as if capital were like water, always flowing to find its own level. In fact the effective use of capital often depends on its being used by particular people in a particular business. One cannot say in the abstract this industry will return x per cent, and that industry will return $2x$ per cent. This industry will return x per cent if one firm does the investing; it may return $3x$ per cent if it is done by another firm, with more dynamic marketing, better human relations, and cost consciousness down to the lowest levels.

Now the State in Asia is frequently in a relatively unfavourable position as an investor. Its marketing is not dynamic; marketing is still a very rare skill in Asia, outside Japan it has hardly spread beyond a few foreign firms. The State's human relations are frequently good, but somewhat restricted from the business point of view by the emphasis on security, especially the almost impregnable security of management. The State's board of directors, the Cabinet, usually know nothing about the particular business and may not know much about business in general. European cabinets, however radical, usually have some members with business connections or business experience; Asian cabinet, however conservative, may quite easily have none, or one. The State has a further weakness. Much of what it is doing is either public utilities or new. Public utilities are essential. Without them development is almost impossible. But they are great capital-consumers, and their rate of direct return is usually low. It is therefore important that all public utility schemes should be rigorously scrutinised; yet under political pressure this does not always happen.

If the State gets too high a proportion of the savings of the community, therefore, there is a risk that money which might have been used to meet screaming needs elsewhere, will be used to subsidise rural electrification or to build branch railway lines which will then lose money. The screaming need may be for face-powder or children's toys; the standard of life goes up quicker when people get face-powder they want than when they get a branch line they are only going to travel on once in two years. Yet the State's bias tends to be always towards the branch line and away from the face-powder. This is seen at its worst in the Communist insistence on heavy industry. Heavy industry has no purpose except war or the production of equipment which will in due course make consumer goods. Most Asian countries are completely pacific. Yet many even of their non-Communists tend to feel not only that heavy industry gives a larger return in the long run and that it makes for less dependence on others, propositions both of which are sometimes true and sometimes not true according to circumstances, but also that heavy industry has a moral superiority, that it is in some way better and nobler than producing consumer goods, a proposition which is not true at all. Asia, therefore, needs the private entrepreneur even more than the United States does, for in Asia he has a bias to counteract. The private entrepreneur cannot fulfil this function unless he is allowed to keep the money with which to do it.

That much of what Asian states are doing is new is equally a reason against taking savings from the citizen in order to give them to the State, to invest. Successful investment requires 'know-how', the combination of skill, knowledge and experience as well as money. If 'know-how' is lacking, scarce savings can very easily be wasted. The wrong site may be chosen, with poor communications or not enough water. The wrong equipment may be chosen, too heavily mechanised in relation to the labour costs of the particular Asian country, or not really adapted to the particular circumstances of the plant being put up. It may have been designed for a different raw material—Canadian pulp, say, instead of bamboo—or may be of a delicacy which requires a higher standard of skill than the local fitters have. The product produced may not be suitable for the local market; it may be too expensive, or it may not stand up to tropical conditions. There are a thousand and one way in which money can be wasted in the process of investment. The reports of Governments and of the U.N. tend to talk in global terms, of so many millions invested in this and so many millions invested in that. They have no method of calculating how many of these millions have simply gone to pay for somebody's experience. The public therefore tends to forget that there is no reason to assume that five millions spent by X on extending an oil refinery will have the same effect on the national income as the same amount spent on new textile mills by Y or on more sulphate of ammonia by Z. It may; but it also may not. It all depends how good a guess was made when the decision was taken to extend the refinery or start the textile mill, and how well the refinery or the mill are run afterwards. Now because the State is so often doing the absolutely new in Asia, its percentage of waste must be high; it has a lot of experience to pay for. Because the private individual or firm is so often doing something he knows, his percentage of waste should be much lower; his experience has already been paid for. To transfer savings from the individual to the State is all too frequently to prevent society drawing any dividends on the money it has already invested in mistakes.

The most serious of all the effects of high taxation for equality however, in its effect on risk-taking. The big rewards come from big risks; and the big rewards, it must be remembered, come not merely to the individual who takes the risks, but to the whole of society; the reason the individual does well, after all, is that he is satisfying some want which society has hitherto been unable to satisfy so effectively or so cheaply. When Henry Ford produced the 'model T' he not only made an enormous fortune, he also made mass motoring possible. Now it is the essence of big risks that they should occasionally involve big losses. This is of course a truism, something everybody knows. But it is a truism whose embarrassing economic consequences are not always fully appreciated. Large losses will not usually be risked either by State officials or by people who are saving for their old age; for them there must be businessmen, entrepreneurs, even that most condemned breed, speculators; and for many necessary purposes these businessmen, entrepreneurs, and speculators must be rich, or the risk will be too big for them.

The unwillingness to risk large losses is probably inherent in any State system. When the money is one's own, one can run risks with it with no greater sanction against error than losing it. When the money is not one's own, there can be no such poetic justice. Rougher ways have to be thought of. In a democracy an official may face an enquiry, the loss of his promotion, even the sack, if he goes wrong; there is nothing equally startling which can be done for him if he goes right; so the odds are always weighted against the *big* risk. In a Communist State, going wrong may mean being shot; and though one does not know how the Communists promote their managers, there are few signs that it is the risk-takers who come to the top. Their preference seems to be for the target-beater, the organiser, the competent

technician. With them, too, therefore, the whole tendency must
be to do the thing which is obviously right but only slightly new
rather than the thing which just might be right but, if it were
would be a revolution. The official would not have produced a
'model T'; he would merely have reduced car prices $7\frac{1}{2}$ per cent.

The unwillingness to face loss is not confined to the State.
Those who are saving against a rainy day, and they constitute a
large proportion of all modern savers, will usually not risk their
one umbrella on a bet that may leave them with twenty um-
brellas or none. The consequences of having no umbrella are
so much more unpleasant than the advantages of having twenty
that the odds have to be almost impossibly favourable before the
risks can be taken. Insurance companies, in other words, are not
the proper people to back speculative ventures. Nor are banks.

A quite disproportionate burden of risk-taking is therefore
left to the private entrepreneur; and it is particularly disproportionate in Asia. It is true that most Asians are property-
owners, running their own little enterprises. But they are mostly
also at or near the margin of subsistence. The consequence of a
risk misjudged may be starvation. That is why so many agricultural improvements, which do not give a sure return in all
circumstances, are so difficult to introduce. Moreover, for many
risks they simply do not have the money. Most handloom
weavers cannot buy a powerloom however safe a bet they may
think it. If the big risks are to be taken, therefore, there must be
some men with enough business experience to have a judgement
to back, and a large enough fortune to have the money to back it
with. There must in fact be some rich men or firms, or the vital
functions which have been performed in Asia by people like the
Adamjees in Pakistan or the Birlas and Tatas in India will not
be performed. A society without rich men will have to institu-
tionalise its risk-taking; and nobody has yet given thought to
how that could be done.

Moreoever, it will not be enough just to keep some of the rich
men the society already has. There is not much point in their
taking risks if they have the worry of loss and the State takes
most of the gains either in super-tax or death duties. Better to
buy an annuity and live a quiet life. There must be the possibility of new men becoming rich, of those who take risks successfully being able to build up capital so that they can take bigger
risks more successfully. If a society is to develop quickly, the
successful businesses, those which are meeting the most emergent
needs at the lowest costs, must be able to grow with the greatest
speed.

A hundred years ago, when taxation was low, a man with the ability to earn 30 per cent on his money could multiply his business sixteen times in ten years. At today's Indian taxation he would only quadruple the business; and if he died in the meantime death duties might bleed the business so white that it would take years to recover. A hundred years ago a man could hope to build up a business and become a millionaire in his own lifetime. Today, except by capital gains, that is almost impossible. In the general satisfaction at not having to put up with so many new rich, it is forgotten that if the owners have not become millionaires, it is because their enterprises have stayed small instead of becoming big; and that is a loss to society as well as to themselves. When everybody can build up a future, society can draw on much more economic talent, much more shrewdness of judgement, with much more knowledge of the nature of each individual risk, than when risk-taking is institutionalised and the decisions are left to a relatively few people in Governments or the large corporations. They may be good at it, especially in the large corporations; but however good they are, the judgements of a few men cannot be altogether a substitute for the willingness to take risks of a society of entrepreneurs. If equality is to mean an equality in risk-avoidance, Asia's economic development will require many more sacrifices from the ordinary citizen than England's or America's ever did.

(g) *Political equality*

Of all the forms of equality the most uncertain in its effect upon development is political equality. It all depends upon the wishes of the electorate and the quality of their leaders. A democratic Thailand or Laos might well be completely static, where India or Ceylon are determined upon change.

It is, however, probable that democracy and development will tend to go together. When an Asian community demands to govern itself by adult suffrage, that is already twice revolutionary. It is a revolution for the peasant to wish to have a say in the wider community beyond his village, it is another for the privileged to accept that the unprivileged should have the same vote as they do, for the men to accept votes for women and the landlords votes for labourers. When the countryside has so awakened that it wants changes as profound as these, it is not possible that it will not want or at least accept other changes too. A man who wants his wife to vote is half-way to equal property rights for daughters; a landlord who lets himself be outvoted by his tenants is three-quarters of the way to land reform;

a Brahmin who lets himself be outvoted by untouchables must desire the end of untouchability.

Democracy in Asia is still too new for its results to be predictable in detail; nor need they be the same in different countries. In India democracy has produced the secular State; in Pakistan an Islamic State. The Indian State is avowedly Socialist, Ceylon had for a time a foible for private enterprise, Indonesia has confiscated all Dutch enterprises. What will happen must depend largely upon the tradition, conditions, and leadership of each individual country.

Nevertheless, some generalisations may already, very tentatively, be ventured.

First, the electorates of Asia now for the first time want their lot to be improved, realise that it can be improved, and consider that their Governments can help them to improve it. Therefore, where the centre of Asian politics has in the past been nationalism, the struggle for independence, sometimes the struggle to slough off intruding Western ways, in the future Asian politics will turn around the problems of development. The great slogan will be, not freedom, but bread. What will matter will be not the debates of principle, on how power is to be divided, or who is to vote and how—all that has been settled or will soon be settled—but by how much the national income is to increase in the next five years, how far the State is to interfere and control, whether there should be more steel first, or whether more electricity should take precedence, what the new taxes are to be and how far savings can be enforced. This would have been likely to happen in any case; it is made certain by the fact that the opposition to democracy comes from Communism, and that Communism's whole appeal for free men lies in its promise that it can make men rich .quicker. Few Asians would choose totalitarianism in preference to freedom; many might prefer totalitarianism with development to freedom without it. Even if the Governments of the free countries of Asia do not make development the star of the political stage, therefore, the opposition will.

Second, the electorates of Asia are mainly peasant. Development in any Asian country which stays free is therefore unlikely to follow either the capitalist or the Communist pattern.

It will not follow the capitalist pattern because the peasant tends to be suspicious of modern business. He feels himself helpless before the slickness of the city. He remembers how often he has been cheated by his trader and his money-lender. He has traditionally turned to the State for assistance in all the problems which are too big for him to manage alone, from famine to canal irrigation. He therefore accepts without opposition talk of Socialism or import and exchange and industrial development controls or State steelworks and electricity distribution and airlines. There can be no party of free enterprise in Asia so long as the peasant, who must be the backbone of any conservative party, likes to feel that behind his weakness stands the strength of the State, and therefore so often welcomes State interference and State initiative.

On the other hand, so long as the peasant dominates politics, there can be no pure Socialist or Communist State either. The peasant will not voluntarily accept collectivisation, and he has hitherto shown himself extremely recalcitrant to any form of co-operation which involves putting his land into the common pool; this is an Asian experience as it has been a European one. The peasant wants to become a small entrepreneur, not an employee. He will welcome co-operative credit or extension services or anything else the State may do to help him, he will not let the State put itself in his place. The State may do what it likes in modern industry; it will not be allowed to touch the small man's land. The economy will stay mixed, after a fashion whose nearest European parallel is France, where the State can run a motor-car factory and nobody minds so long as it also buys the peasant's unsaleable wine.

Third, the free Asian States will have to try to be welfare states before they have the money for it. Fortunately for them, the problem is a limited one. Peasants can manage without provident funds and sickness insurance. In the towns, however, the urban proletariats whom development is more and more creating will increasingly have to be provided with all the protections Bismarck and Beveridge have made popular. This will help development, both by increasing savings, and by providing Asia with a fixed and not too discontented working class, instead of the floating mass of unskilled casuals who were so important in nineteenth-century Europe. What will hamper development is the negative aspect of welfare, the easing of the pains of change. Rapid economic development means that many people must change their jobs, learn new skills, perhaps move their homes. People do not like these upsets to the quiet tenor of their lives. There will therefore be perpetual pressure from special groups of voters for the process to be made less painful, for the work to be brought to them instead of their going to the work, or for new methods to be prohibited if they put out of work those employed on the old methods, or for a guarantee of prices for commodities the public no longer wants but the producer is accustomed to produce. Sometimes this pressure will be resisted, especially when the Government has a coherent plan with which it will interfere; but often it will be given way to —in India already cases have arisen where goods-lorry permits have been refused to protect the bullock cart, and one remembers the American farmer—and, every time it is, development will be slowed down.

Fourth, the leadership of free Asia is likely to come from its professional classes, and especially from their lower echelons, the clerks and the teachers, the overseers and the village-level workers. The peasant takes new ideas most easily from his own educated sons and cousins. This importance of the intelligentsia reinforces the tendency to depend on the State of the peasant. The clerk or lawyer can rarely identify himself with the businessman, he frequently identifies himself with the State and its representative, the bureaucrat. He, therefore, tends to welcome controls and even nationalisations. Moreover, since his self-respect depends considerably upon the power and consideration of his State, he has a strong tendency to support autarchy and to place his emphasis in development upon the industries required for power, and thus mainly on heavy industry, rather than on those required for a high standard of living which are mainly the consumer goods industries. Most important of all, the Asian professional man, from overseer to brain surgeon, usually has a predilection for planning, which seems to him all to fit together prettily and which is run by educated men, against what appears to him to be the anarchy of the market and the appalling crudity of those who succeed in it. All of these are tendencies well enough known in Europe. They go far indeed to explain why so many European intellectuals have been on the Left. The difference which in Asia gives the Left-wing intellectual so free a run is that, because of the Asian social structure, there are so few intellectuals on the Right. Asian intellectuals are only exceptionally the sons of landowners and businessmen; and when they are, they are frequently in revolt against what they consider to be the exploitation of others involved in their fathers' way of life. There is not in Asia the mass of educated conservatives we find in countries like England and France. Inevitably, as a result, the whole politics of free Asia is Leftward oriented, with all the consequences for economic development which that entails.

Fifth, the position of business and of private enterprise in the growth of industry is further weakened by another Asian social phenomenon. The businessman is not, as he is in the West, an integral part of the community as a whole. He is usually either a European, or an Asian from elsewhere (a Chinese in Indonesia or an Indian in Ceylon, say) or a member of a close-knit small community within the country itself, a Marwari or a Bania in India, a Khoja or a Bohra or a Kutchi Memon in Pakistan, for example. As the great peasant communities rise to power—and their rise to power is the inevitable long-run result of adult suffrage, as one can already see in India—they are liable more and more to want a share of the profits and jobs of business, either through special privileges in licences and permits or through more nationalisation or through State-assisted co-operation.

Finally, it is likely that adult suffrage will more and more make the attempt to achieve economic equality a central theme of politics. The history of the last hundred years elsewhere suggests that those who hold equal shares in power do not see why they should not also hold at least more equal shares in wealth. In India, indeed, the movement towards equality has already proceeded far, and it is visibly gathering way elsewhere.

It is still too early to be sure what the economic consequences of political equality will be, but probably the result will eventually be everywhere a mixed economy of the type which is growing up in India. The features of this economy are a mass of small owners, peasants and handicraftsmen, who are protected and assisted and pushed into change and co-operation by the State; a State which controls and often runs all the commanding heights of the economy, and which interferes infinitely in the workings of private trade and industry; a private industrial sector whose dynamism is perpetually clogged by returns and applications for permits; and a taxation system one of whose first objectives is equality. It is a curate's egg method of development, good strictly in parts; but it begins to seem that it is the inevitable result of adult suffrage in societies as heavily peasant as are all Asia's except Malaya.

Chapter 21

POPULATION CONTROL

NO nostrum is more popular among amateurs of Asian development than to suggest Asians should stop having babies. If the population would stop increasing so rapidly, it is argued, then Asia's savings, small though they are, would be enough to provide for some increase in the standard of life for the existing population; Asia's trouble, it is said, is that every sacrifice is swallowed up by more babies, more people to provide for. And the amateur shudders melodramatically as he thinks of what is going to happen as modern medicine goes on reducing death rates while birth rates stay as high as ever.

This has truth, but it is not, as the amateur thinks, either an eternal or a specially Asian truth. Rather is it a temporary truth, true now because Asia is peasant, has so little spare land, and has embarked on a capital-consuming process of change; and, true or not, practical difficulties prevent its providing an immediate answer.

For many centuries, Asian populations did not increase. The population of India in 1800 may have been no higher than 2000 years before. Yet India had got no richer in the interval. Until the late '50s most Asian populations—the notable exception is Ceylon—were increasing no faster than that of the United States, and slower than that of Canada; yet the United States and Canada are not poor. Birth rates are no higher than those of Britain or Germany were for some time after the beginning of their Industrial Revolutions; yet Britain and Germany got rich quick enough, faster than France whose population was increasing much more slowly. Obviously population increase by itself accounts for nothing.

Whether or not an increase of population reduces or increases the chances of development depends indeed upon a whole complex of factors.

Under certain circumstances it may help development. An increasing population may induce an atmosphere of buoyancy. The entrepreneur is always optimistic, always willing to take risks in the confidence that the growth of his custom will justify them; this is true in the United States and was true in nineteenth-century England. Again, an increase may be necessary in order to give a population of adequate size to carry the overheads of development; without a certain density of population neither railways nor schools are possible. Finally, every new baby is a new brain and a new pair of hands. It takes from the community, but it also gives. Fewer babies mean fewer grown-ups to keep the old people. A community with a low birth rate may have fewer crèches or baby napkins for its adults to pay for; but it needs relatively more crutches and old-age homes.

All these advantages are, however, conditional upon society's being able to provide occupation for its babies as they grow up. Asia's difficulty is that so many of its people are peasants, living on land which does not expand. The new adults all too often merely split the old work over more hands. So long as there was free land in Asia, population increases offered no problem; the new generation simply cleared some more jungle; that is still happening in parts of South-East Asia. The density of population in Asia's rice-growing river-deltas is due primarily not to some past population explosion, but to the very heavy demands rice-growing makes on labour; there will still have to be a family on every two and a half acres even in areas where there are thousands of acres of bamboo thicket available for the cutting down and embanking.

Today Asia is both trying to find new forms of occupation, in industry and by intensive farming, and to give its people a higher standard of life than is possible from old-fashioned rice-cultivation. To do so, as we have already seen, requires capital in enormous quantities. The strain would be greatly eased if Asia did not at one and the same time have to find the capital to change the life of its existing people and to provide for the new ones. Asia has to build schools for the existing children, provide fertiliser for the existing farmers; if it has also to build schools for a lot of extra children or reclaim land for new farmers, the burden increases to creaking-point.

Very little of Asia, moreover, needs an increasing population for the purposes which it has served in the West over the last century. If Asia can begin really to change, as we have tried to show it needs to change, the entrepreneur will have cause for optimism without an increase in the population figures. The builder does not have to calculate how many new households there are going to be; there are plenty of existing households without houses. Nor does most of Asia require populations of greater density to make its social overheads pay; its need is for populations of greater spending power. The railways have enough people on their routes; what they need is more people who can pay the fare more often. Finally, Asia's percentage of the aged is at present very low. It could carry an increase without much loss. What these peasant societies with their rules of equal division of the inheritance among children cannot carry is the further splitting-up of the land which will come from more children.

In short, although the rate of increase in population in Asia is not in itself excessive, and although, once Asia's economy has become industrial and dynamic, an increase may be very useful, at the present moment, when Asia's population is heavily peasant and at the beginning of a difficult and expensive process of change, it would ease Asia's problems if there were not every year so many new millions for whom occupations must be found.

Modern population control, however, is another Western institution which cannot just be turned on in Asia like a tap.

Before the nineteenth century, Asia, like the rest of the world, had its own methods of population control. There were famines, and war, and epidemics. These, however, are not only methods nobody except the well fed without imagination can advocate; they are also methods which create as many economic difficulties as they solve. War destroys capital; famine engenders unproductive debt; epidemics may come at harvest-time. Nor is Asia's other traditional method, self-control, more helpful. Few today are willing to become monks and nuns; and, were more willing, a large diversion of resources would be required to endow the monasteries and nunneries. Mahatma Gandhi used to advocate self-control within marriage; but few have been willing to follow him; indeed, were many people to pursue brahmacharya, there might be a large need for psychiatrists and mental hospitals long before more than a quite small dent was made in the birth rate. Finally, Asian values require marriage for those who do not retire from the world; the spinster daughters, the middle-aged bachelors, the West tolerates so cheerfully appear incomplete, people who have missed everything that matters in life, to the Asian mind.

Population control in Asia, therefore, in the short run at least, means birth control. Except amongst Catholics, this does not come up against a direct religious prohibition. It does, however, face two other difficulties, one practical, the other emotional.

The practical difficulty is itself many-pronged. The village home often gives the married couple little privacy. The rhythm method is very complicated for the illiterate. The ordinary contraceptive, in a poor society, often appears at the time more expensive than a baby. Sterilisation, to which a few have taken, is an extreme measure. Probably the best method is something cheap and traditional, like the cotton dipped in oil which is being tried in Bihar. It is not guaranteed effective, but, after all, the people who are using it are married. They do not need to be certain they will not have a baby. All they want is to cut down from six or seven to three or four.

The emotional difficulty is simpler. People in Asia like children. On the whole, they neither find them a nuisance nor prefer television sets. No woman establishes herself with her husband or with her husband's family until she has a son. Children are a social necessity. Society despises or pities the barren and the childless. Children are a religious necessity too. A Hindu, for example, must have a son to perform the proper ceremonies after his death. Children are an insurance; it is children, not endowment policies, to whom parents turn in old age for support. All of these needs could perhaps be satisfied by two children or three. But Asia, except for Japan, is accustomed to high infantile death rates. Therefore, people always have more to make sure. The desired number is four or five rather than the Western two or three.

Nevertheless, various pilot investigations which have been made in India suggest that both the villager and the townsman would take fairly freely to a suitable method of control, first in order to space births and to reduce the strain on often anaemic mothers of repeated pregnancies; second, to keep the total size of the family down to about four. This second motive becomes more important as public health improves, or as one goes up the social scale, so that people no longer feel that they must have spare children to make up for the ones who die.

Contraception is a possibility, provided it is cheap, and easy, and its advantages are explained to the people. At present it may be a subconsciously felt need; outside the professional middle classes it is rarely an actively felt one. It will take time, and money, and research, and propaganda before the masses of Asia begin to plan their families. The first Indian Five-Year plan made a small provision for family planning. For the third plan the provision is nearly £14 million, and the effect on middle class birth rates is already visible. But it may be another 20 years before there is any great drop in village birth rates. There have been indeed some signs that the Indian birth rate has decreased in the last generation. In Japan the birth rate has decreased sharply over the last thirty years.

The precedents both of the West and of Japan[1] suggest that

[1] Whose birth-rate is now down below 20 per 1000.

as Asia urbanises and industrialises and becomes educated, its birth rate will drop enough to catch up with the drop in death rates and perhaps more. In between, however, there is likely to be a generation when rates of increase are going up because fewer people are dying faster than they are going down because fewer are being born. In the long run, population control may ease Asia's problem; but for the next decade, perhaps for the next generation, Asia will have to carry the burden of its babies.

CONCLUSION

THE qualities required for economic development are not the highest of which man is capable; for both the individual and the nation there are more important ends in life than becoming rich. It is still pleasanter and more proper to die for one's country than to save for it; and loving our neighbour, not making money, is the way to salvation.

Economic progress is, in short, only doubtfully also moral progress. Riches subject man to nearly as many temptations as poverty. Economic development is only good in so far as it is achieved without an increase in envy, uncharitableness and exploitation. The sweating of labour in the first half of the nineteenth century in England permitted some very necessary accumulation, the enclosures of the second half of the eighteenth century saved England from starvation in the Napoleonic Wars; but they were not good for the souls of the sweaters and enclosers.

Economic development, therefore, would appear at first sight something over which no one could get excited; and so it was, on the whole, in ancient India or mediaeval Europe. But today it has become mixed up with a whole series of moral considerations to which it is somewhat doubtfully relevant. Those who love their country now believe that to be great she must be powerful; and to be powerful she must first be rich. Those who love their neighbour now regard the salvation of his body as more important than the salvation of his soul; there is much rejoicing over a 5 per cent increase in the national income, little over new endowment for temples. Those who love God often feel that He is better worshipped by high taxes than by prayer.

Economic progress is, therefore, sought today, in Asia as elsewhere, for reasons which are not economic. That provides a drive profounder than any known before, for the sacrifices men will make for religion are far greater than those they will make for riches. But it also has its dangers. Because the qualities and the policies required for development are so often religiously uninspiring, the resources needed for economic progress are perpetually being diverted to satisfy some non-economic principle, often with only the dimmest idea of the economic sacrifice involved. High cost industries are built up, because they are thought to contribute to national power. Amenities for labour more expensive than productivity justifies are enforced, so that labourers shall have a better life. High incomes are taxed almost out of existence to increase equality. Location of industry is interfered with so that every part of the country shall have its 'fair' share of development. Such large farmers as know about agriculture have their holdings cut down so that more of the landless can enjoy the pleasures of ownership. And so on. The criteria applied in judging economic problems mostly have nothing to do with economics; and the result is naturally that, though there may be more equality, or greater regional fairness, or possibly, fewer revolutions, there is also less development.

That does not necessarily mean that these non-economic criteria are wrong. Economic and non-economic standards of value are not better or worse than each other, they are different. Which should be applied in any particular case is for a man's conscience rather than his reason to decide. It is an irrelevance to tell those who believe cows to be sacred that they would be better off if useless cattle were killed. All that can properly be said is that sometimes those who apply non-economic criteria are not altogether aware of their economic cost. Those who shout for equality now might do so less loudly if they knew it would make their children poorer. Those who build high cost factories to make their country more powerful today might be less enthusiastic if they realised how much weaker the waste of resources will make their country in the long run. Any major decision, national or personal, should in the end be guided by men's beliefs, and not their interests; but before the decision is made the facts should be understood.

The requirements which have to be fulfilled for Asia to get rich are clear. Getting rich must be a major objective, for which people are prepared to sacrifice old habits as well as present consumption. They must save instead of hoarding, or spending on festivals or ceremonies. They must invest productively instead of buying jewellery and brocades. They must admire innovations, and inventions, and successful entrepreneurs rather than writers of commentaries and men who conform to perfection to the methods of their ancestors. Business must become as respectable as administration. The State must take the initiative in change, it must develop public utilities, put through social reform, make available extension services and widen the scope of co-operation; but, because it has so much it ought to do, it must refrain from doing what can be done by others. It must restrain itself from unnecessary nationalisations and meddling controls. There must be politicians who can lead their people to change, and bureaucrats who can make actual the politicians' dreams. There must be equality for women and the traditionally oppressed, so that society may draw upon the initiative of all, but economic equality must not be excessive, so that some will have the leisure and the money to study or take risks. Education must be reformed to bring forward an adequate supply of the technically trained and economically adaptable. Above all, in deciding between alternative possibilities of action, the most profitable should be chosen, not that which will be most advantageous to a special interest, or will benefit the most backward, or the best behaved, or the largest number. If wealth is the aim, wealth must be the criterion, not power, or autarchy or even fairness.

The needs of development cannot be absolute. There must be occasions when defence or justice will override them with propriety. But for that there is a price. The poor will remain poorer for longer.

GLOSSARY

Banias: Hindu traders, usually moneylenders.

Basha Indonesia: National language of Indonesia.

Bhagavad Gita: Sacred book which contains the basic approach to Hinduism.

Bhakra-Nangal: Major multi-purpose scheme in the Punjab.

Bharat Natyam: South Indian dancing, originally religious.

Bhoodan: Gift of land movement.

Bhora: Muslim sect.

Birlas: Leading Indian industrialists.

Chins: Burmese tribe.

Coke of Holkham: English eighteenth-century improving landlord.

Daimyo: Japanese feudal nobles.

Damodar Valley Corporation: Corporation running large multi-purpose schemes on the Damodar river in Bihar and Bengal.

Gal Oya: Multi-purpose scheme in East Ceylon.

Harijan: Untouchable.

Jagirdari: Feudal landholding.

Kans: Deep-rooted weed.

Karens: Burmese minority people.

Khoja: Muslim sect.

Krishnamachari T.T.: Minister for Commerce and Industry, Government of India.

Kutchi: Man from Kutch in Western India.

Liaquat Ali Khan: Pakistan's first Prime Minister.

Mahabharata: The greatest Hindu epic.

Manu: The codifier of Hindu Law.

Marwari: Trader from Rajasthan.

Meiji: The epoch after 1867 in Japan.

Memon: Muslims, originally weavers, now often traders.

Morarji Desai: Chief Minister of Bombay.

Owen: Early-nineteenth-century socialist.

Ram Mohan Roy: Early-nineteenth-century Hindu social reformer.

Samurai: Japanese warrior.

Shans: Burmese tribe.

Stridhan: Hindu lady's separated property, usually jewellery.

U Nu: Until recently Burmese Prime Minister.

Vedas: Hindu sacred books, mostly about ritual.

Vinoba Bhave: Saint, leader of land gift movement, and disciple of Mahatma Gandhi.

INDEX